Whiz Mob

WHIZ MOB

*A Correlation of
the Technical Argot of Pickpockets
with Their Behavior Pattern*

by **DAVID W. MAURER**

THE UNIVERSITY OF LOUISVILLE

COLLEGE & UNIVERSITY PRESS · *Publishers*

NEW HAVEN, CONN.

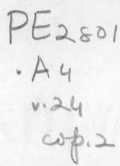

MANUFACTURED IN THE UNITED STATES OF AMERICA BY
UNITED PRINTING SERVICES, INC.
NEW HAVEN, CONN.

ACKNOWLEDGMENTS

Several people have helped in the preparation of this book, and I wish to extend to them my thanks and warm acknowledgments for their assistance. My wife, Barbara Maurer, not only has handled most of the typing and proof-reading connected with this project, but has brought to it her very sound counsel based on long experience in this field. She also assisted in the early stages of the field-work and interviewing.

Lindsay Almand, my graduate assistant at the University of Louisville, has done much of the excerpting of pertinent materials, outlining, and transcription. JoAnn Shipley of Louisville, Kentucky, generously volunteered her skilled stenographic assistance in the transfer of interview materials to typescript. Mr. Robert O'Hara, now of the University of Minnesota, and Mr. Stuart Flexner, now of New York City, did some work on the early version of the glossarial materials on which this study is based. Mr. O. E. Bissmeyer, now a graduate student at Indiana University, assisted with sound-recording. Mr. Everett DeBaun, now of New York City, was especially helpful in the early phases of the study by assisting in field-work and verification, the recording of illustrative materials, and the analysis of raw data.

To Professor Thomas Pyles of the University of Florida, Secretary of the American Dialect Society, I am indebted for his patience and his editorial counsel.

To the American Dialect Society, I am particularly indebted for having originally published this material in their November, 1955, issue of the *Publication of the American Dialect Society,* No. 24.

The thieves and pickpockets, who must remain anonymous, should receive credit for cooperating in the collection of raw materials, both linguistic and sociological, upon which this book is based.

The Research Committee of the Arts College of the University of Louisville very kindly provided a modest research grant to help defray the costs of sound-recording, transcription, and clerical assistance in connection with this project.

D. W. M.

CONTENTS

Introduction

INTRODUCTION

This book is an experiment in what might be called the social structure of language. It will attempt to bring together some elements of language and selected aspects of the social structure of a single criminal subculture. There may be some value in thus correlating elements which in nature occur as a single complex, but which are conventionally separated artificially when they are studied.

The resulting picture is inevitably somewhat broad, despite several limitations on the elements selected. First, the language discussed is limited to argot, and the lexical and semantic elements used will be largely differentiae which separate argot from nonargot American usage. (I define argot as specialized language used by organized, professional groups operating outside the law; these groups normally constitute criminal subcultures, and the language is usually secret or semisecret.) Second, the argot selected reflects either directly or indirectly the technology of one minor category of thieves. Last, only those elements in the behavior pattern connected with making a living by theft from the person are discussed. In short, all aspects of both language and behavior which are similar to or identical with those commonly found in the dominant culture are excluded.

Even with these limitations, the problem bulks too large to permit excursions into side-issues which are in many instances important. For instance, what are the geographical divisions in thieves' usage and how do we explain them? On the surface it appears that we have an East Coast, Midwest, and West Coast usage-pattern, but this is only a convenient generalization to be used until someone does the painstaking work necessary to establish more scientific conclusions.

What about morphemics? Syntax? Juncture, especially in reference to changes in lexical meaning and semantics? Stress and intonation patterns? For example, it seems to me that there may be certain patterns of intonation and stress which differentiate the speech of the pickpocket from that of the dominant culture and, at the same time, from some other criminal subcultures. To what extent are these patterns indigenous to the argot? These are problems in microlinguistics which are outside the scope of this general study.

4

There is also the provocative question of the relationship between stress and intonation patterns of certain criminal groups and those occurring in the speech of identifiable psychopaths, psychoneurotics, and paranoids within the dominant or legitimate culture. The answers to these questions require the attention of experienced investigators who have the time and the facilities to concentrate on controlled data taken from the speech of carefully selected informants. They will yield, I think, to the techniques of descriptive linguistics plus the interpretative skills of clinical psychiatry.

The whole problem of *offices* among criminals, and especially among pickpockets, has seldom been recognized by criminologists, and *offices* are only mentioned in this study. Some are verbal, some articulate without being verbal, some visual, some tactile, some kinesic, etc. What place do these phenomena have in communication, and what relation do they bear to language as such? In certain criminal subcultures they may be more important than language strictly defined.

How does argot generate within the various subcultures, escape into the dominant culture, and come to bear heavily upon the language of the legitimate culture? This movement is an observable historical fact, not only in English but in other languages, but no one has analysed it with a view to detailed explanation. Also, after it happens, it is very difficult to work backward and put the pieces together. We have a good contemporary example of this movement of argot in the sudden appearance of the speech of the Harlem brothels, black-and-tan joints, and tea-pads in our middle-class homes. This comes in, obviously, via the teen-agers who almost compulsively identify with this semicriminal subculture and insist on calling themselves *cool cats*. But no one has examined this phenomenon scientifically.

On the other hand, we have in the past five years seen the mass-invasion of a criminal subculture by teen-agers from the dominant culture, with havoc resulting in the established argot. This has taken place in the subculture of the criminal narcotic addict; in fact, it is still going on. Within the range of my observation, it is without precedent.

But these are more than linguistic problems. They are social as well. The time is past when they can be considered academic, for the identification of juveniles with various criminal subcultures—

imperfectly understood through the romanticization of crime in the movies, on television, and in the comic books—is creating a problem which urgently demands the attention of the legislators, law-enforcement specialists, and the judiciary.

With respect to source-materials, the reader will notice that there are very few references to other works in this general area. The reason for this is that most of the books published about thievery contain, along with some material which is sound, some which is also obsolete, inadequate, superficial, and at times romantic or misleading. As this book progressed, it became increasingly clear that the introduction of material from other authors would not only require verification in the field, but would involve lengthy explanations and qualifications in the text as well. I have therefore preferred to work directly from informants whom I consider reliable, and to present both the argot and the behavior pattern of the pickpocket as it has come to me from original sources. Naturally, neither the linguistic nor the social data is complete.

Likewise, historical material has been largely omitted, for any major attempt to explain either the subculture of thieves, or the history of the argot, would extend this study inordinately. Therefore, while I have occasionally commented on both social and linguistic history, these remarks are intended to be illustrative rather than definitive. With regard to both argot terms and behavior pattern, I have worked within the memory of living informants, with the emphasis on the last decade.

Specialists in the several fields across which this book cuts will observe immediately that I have used relatively little specialized technical terminology. I have deliberately made this choice since I am not a specialist in these fields, and since I am writing this book for those educated people who have a serious interest in language and social structure. At times, also, I have taken the liberty of using technical terms in senses which may be a bit unorthodox, though I always attempt to define my terms either parenthetically or in context. For instance, I have no precedent for the use of the term *subculture* to designate parasitic criminal groups with a way of living which differs from that of the dominant culture. However, I have decided after careful consideration that *subculture* says almost exactly what I mean.

A word about the quotations used. These are intended primarily to illustrate the argot terms cited in the text. Sometimes, however, quotations contain subject matter which bears upon the social structure or the behavior pattern; sometimes they simply show the word in use, without reference to the social structure, or with an oblique reference to it. When it has seemed necessary to edit them to protect the identity of an informant and to delete extraneous material, I have done so. The quoted statements represent the opinions and observations of informants who were speaking; they may or may not be true; many of them will probably provoke high controversy amongst the brethren. While I have refrained from using any statements which I suspected of being false or erroneous, I have not hesitated to quote statements which may be controversial. In fact, if one restricted himself to statements on which all thieves could agree, he could never say anything, for thieves as a group are highly individualistic, temperamental, and contentious.

This brings us to the problem of generalizations, which must be made in a study of this kind, even at the risk of making slight and inadvertent misstatements. While it is impossible to make a generalization about thieves with which all thieves (even in one group) would agree, it is necessary to make these generalizations in order to render the data usable. The only alternative would be to take the statement of one informant as basic, then append endless exceptions or minority reports. Or, perhaps, to present the data in raw form and let the reader make what sense he can from it. Therefore, I have assumed the responsibility for making those generalizations necessary to delineate the behavior pattern and to establish argot usage.

Perhaps I should state that, although I have worked for many years with criminal argots and the groups which use them, I have never had any actual experience on the *rackets*. To a certain extent this is a handicap, for much of the argot of thievery involves delicate kinesthetic, tactile, and emotional reactions which are difficult to grasp vicariously. On the other hand, actual experience might restrict my thinking in that I would, like every thief, tend to generalize on the basis of my own experience and reject other observations as spurious. Hence, it is perhaps sound to observe professionals operating and to try to interpret what they have to say about what they do as well as how they feel about doing it.

Last, I should say that none of the people in this book are fictional; their names have been altered, however, and certain acts have been attributed to pickpockets who did not perform them, or who are already dead. This has been done to protect the identity of informants, as well as persons to whom they may refer in the course of giving information. Names and places mean nothing, for this is not an exposé, but a serious attempt to correlate language and behavior in one criminal subculture.

CHAPTER I

THE NATURE OF PROFESSIONAL CRIME

Despite the growing importance of professional crime in the modern world, the dominant culture has made painfully slow progress in dealing with it. Perhaps one reason for this lag is the fact that we insist on "dealing" with crime without first understanding it. Society has, from the earliest historic times, attempted to outlaw the criminal, to protect legitimate citizens from the depredations of criminals, to deport criminals into desolate areas (such as Australia and frontier America) where they could not prey upon the wealthy in their home society, to rehabilitate criminals both morally and socially, and to reduce their influence in politics and business. These efforts have been directed at both professional and nonprofessional criminals, for society makes little distinction. While none of these efforts has ever succeeded, society continues to struggle for at least a measure of control over a phenomenon which seems to thrive upon every device which is intended for its eradication. Within our own generation we are principally disturbed by the ever-mounting cost of crime—as of 1951 Barnes and Teeter estimate the annual cost in the United States at 28 billions of dollars—and by the mounting tide of juveniles identifying with the criminal subculture, for as of 1955 well over one half of the crimes against property in the United States were committed by youths under twenty-five.

That this failure to check crime in contemporary society has grave implications, we would be the last to deny. However, this is not the place to advocate measures designed to correct man's social blunders which have been cumulative during the past several millennia. In fact, the key to man's failure to control crime may well be his tendency to explain it (according to the fashion of the times) by various rationalizations which are chiefly significant in that they reveal with great clarity the changing attitudes of so-called legitimate society, but leave practically untouched the nature of professional crime itself.

At this point perhaps we should distinguish briefly between the professional and the amateur criminal, a distinction which will be elaborated upon later in the book. The professional works at crime as a business; he makes his living by it; he is recognized and accepted by other professionals in his class as a professional; he knows and uses the argot or semisecret language of the profession; he subscribes to the code of behavior long established for professionals in his group; he has status and is known within a considerable circle of other professionals; he adopts certain attitudes toward other criminals, the law, the *sucker*, society in general; he feels no shame or guilt for his acts against the dominant culture, and seldom if ever "reforms." *He is, in short, a member of the parasitic subculture.*

The nonprofessional criminal, on the other hand, might commit criminal acts, such as theft, for instance, repeatedly without being caught; or, as is more often the case, he may steal once or twice and get caught. He may serve time in prison for his acts. But he does not know the language or the techniques of the professional; he does not have the contacts necessary to operate with some security under the law; his attitudes, ethics, morals, and behavior pattern are still basically those of the dominant culture, except insofar as he has violated the code of the dominant culture, and, even worse, has been caught at it. He is an amateur or "occasional" criminal, but *he is still a member of the dominant culture* and identifies with it. He feels shame, guilt, and severe loss of status for having become involved in a crime; a professional feels none of these, as long as his act is directed at a member of the dominant culture who is accepted by his profession as a proper victim. This study is concerned only with the professional thief, and particularly with the professional pickpocket.

It would appear that much can be gained from going a little beyond current psychiatric and sociological concepts of professional crime to the point where we recognize it as a cluster of subcultures, some of them, like the culture of pickpockets which we are about to comment upon, very ancient. It is helpful if we visualize the dominant culture as bounded by a large circle, with these subcultures, projected as very small circles, clustering about the rim of the large one.

Thus some of these small circles will be largely within the dominant culture, some encysted wholly within it, some only slightly within it, and others barely touching the periphery so that for all practical purposes they are outside it. We might then think of the position of these circles as indicative of the degree to which the criminal cultures are absorbed and accepted by the dominant culture, if we bear in mind that this degree will vary substantially with geography as well as with social structure.

For example, the subculture of the professional stick-up men would be partly within but mostly without the dominant culture; the subculture of the professional gambler is largely within the bounds of the dominant culture, and in some places—like Nevada— could be entirely within it. The big-time *confidence men* are flexible and are equally at home in their own subculture or in the dominant culture—in fact they are able to simulate behavior within the dominant culture to a high degree of perfection. On the other hand, a criminal subculture like that of the Gypsies touches the dominant culture so slightly that for all practical purposes it is completely outside. While this sort of image is mechanical and oversimplified, it may, like the diagrams of antibodies which no one has ever seen, enable us to handle abstract concepts, the referents for which are not yet isolated.

Even though these subcultures intermingle at many points with the dominant culture, and in some instances—like that of the moonshiner in the agricultural South—are almost indistinguishable from it, they all have in common one factor which differentiates them from the dominant culture. They are parasitic. But all nevertheless retain their identities as subcultures, with a behavior pattern which is well defined, with mores which are often enforced more rigorously than those of the dominant culture, with technology which enables the subculture to live parasitically—and often quite prosperously—at the expense of the dominant culture, and with a language which adequately reflects not only the behavior pattern of the subgroup, but the attitudes toward the dominant group as well.

It is with this language, called argot, and especially with the lexical and semantic aspects of it, that we are primarily concerned in this study. In addition, however, we are concerned with projecting the theory of the subculture and with correlating the argot with the behavior pattern of one highly specialized group of thieves, in a study of what might be called the social structure of language.

The recognition of these subcultures, together with their systematic exploration, would seem to constitute a challenge to those who wish to go beyond the armchair approach to the problem of crime and all its peripheral implications, both theoretical and practical. There is more than enough work for all—the social anthropologist, the sociologist, the linguist, the criminologist, the psychiatrist, and the law-enforcement specialist. In addition, these subcultures offer an almost unlimited—and to date practically virgin—field for serious fiction-writers, who appear to be missing the boat insofar as they might record the operations of the most colossal "underworld"—which is only a romantic name for this cluster of subcultures—that human civilization has ever witnessed; the currently popular Crime-Does-Not-Pay radio, television, and magazine features may be dismissed as thoroughly phony; they bear the same relation to organized crime that the wooden cigar-store Indian bears to primitive anthropology. They fool no one, not even their sponsors.

Actually, we know little about crime as a way of life; in fact, we have more data on the behavior pattern of almost any obscure primitive tribe than we have on these problem areas within our own culture. Perhaps an examination of these subcultures has been neglected because of the aura of secrecy which has traditionally surrounded them; perhaps the fact that underworld areas have not been traditionally considered "respectable" for academic research has discouraged some investigators; perhaps the strong pressures built up by the liaison between law-enforcement agencies and professional criminals have made it difficult for researchers to work; perhaps a reluctance on the part of the general public to accept cold facts in preference to romantic mishmash has discouraged incisive fact-finding; perhaps the general corruption of government, especially the enforcement arms of government, has led to a tacit acceptance of professional crime as a part of the system—as long as it is organized, politically protected, and commercially successful. At any rate, we need more light thrown into these areas, not so much to reform society as to understand it.

A study of the argot as correlated with the behavior pattern seems to have some value in that language is the most obvious key to any particular subculture, to the psychology of the professional, and perhaps eventually to the nature of crime itself; at least, it makes possible a view of crime not too heavily tinged with traditional legalistic, psychoanalytical, and moralistic shibboleths. Second, it should clarify the underlying semantics of argot-formation, and suggest reasons why argot makes a constant contribution to the living standard language in the form of slang.

Last, it may illustrate how the behavior pattern is reënforced through language, and how the techniques are transmitted by means of the argot. This study, then, will concentrate on the technical argot of one small criminal subculture, that of pickpockets, and its relation to the pattern of professional operations.

It is important to note that, despite the many changing attitudes which society has adopted toward crime, the basic nature of crime itself has changed little, if any, during historic times.

Thus we see, if we survey the past, all kinds of motives ascribed to crime, and a wide variety of contradictory causes advanced by the learned of each age. In early tribal days crime was often regarded as an individual matter, with each man privileged to achieve personal vengeance if he could do so. This attitude still persists in some isolated areas of Western civilization. With the rise of larger organized groups, this personalized causation of crime was codified, as in the Code of Hammurabi, and appropriate compensations for those injured or robbed were prescribed by law. With the advent of Christianity, crime was explained by demon-possession, and this theory continues to influence our handling of criminals to this day, though it appears under the guise of many sectarian, humanitarian, and even scientific approaches. And so through the centuries, with men like Jeremy Bentham, Beccaria, Isaac Ray, Lombroso, and Freud bringing some aspects of science to the problem.

In modern times we are to some extent guided by the work of such investigators as Hooton (who painstakingly correlates physical measurement with the types of criminals found in prisons, but inadvertently omits those outside, and thus perhaps presents a meticulous cross-section of criminal washouts) or the approach of Rorschach (who believes that the interpretation given ink-blots by criminals reveals their unconscious motivations). However, in order to keep our perspective, we should remember that these highly technical approaches tell us a little (a very little) about the criminal, a good deal about the investigator and his methods, and almost nothing about crime. This is so because, through the ages, legitimate society has persisted in viewing each act as a separate crime, each individual as an isolated and distinct offender, motivated by warped, misguided, demoniac, or immoral motives; the approach of some modern psychiatrists to crime illustrates the epitome of this view, and we of the twentieth century will be remembered for our belief in the causative influence of personality-frustration, the impact of environment on the individual, and the inability of the criminally-inclined to "adjust" to normal society because of unconscious conflicts.

We may rest assured that the coming generations will have their own theories about crime and the criminal. We can only hope that they will throw more light upon the nature of crime itself, and less perhaps on the inadequacies of the society trying to control it. As we look back through the centuries of preoccupation with crime, we cannot escape this observation: *crime itself is the only constant factor*. While the theories of causation and punishment shift over a wide range, the basic nature of professional crime remains the same. If we examine the multifarious rackets practiced by the legions of professional criminals in the United States today, we are hard put to it to discover a single new type of crime. Each has its prototype in some culture going back to the beginning of recorded history. Every principle of thievery known today was chronicled by Petronius as he surveyed the Roman underworld; the principle of every confidence game operated in our own times is to be found recorded in the great mass of picaresque literature which flooded Europe during the 16th and 17th centuries; these principles were already ancient and timeless, it should be noted, by the time they were written down. Techniques change, but the principles remain the same.

Within the present generation there has been a tardy recognition of the social aspects of crime. In the works of Edwin Sutherland, the Drs. Glueck, Frank Tannenbaum, Barnes and Teeter, and others, we see the beginnings of a concept that professional crime is primarily a social phenomenon and only secondarily an individual event. This discovery that the criminal cannot be studied intelligently separate from his social matrix may have profound influence upon our thinking about the problem within the next generation, although the theories based on the conflict of free-will with predestination (we like to call it determinism today), as well as those predicated on deep individual maladjustment, die hard.

As a brief illustration of how tenaciously Freudian or pseudo-Freudian explanations for crime influence contemporary thinking, I find in the 1954 publication of the Isaac Ray Lectures, delivered at Yale by Dr. Gregory Zilboorg, the following passage in which he comments on a diary by Barrington, the famous 18th century thief, who notes that pickpockets in London like to go to work on the crowd the moment the victims swing at a public hanging:

> If we recall the intimate relationships between murder and suicide in our psychic economy, we may understand a little better the pickpockets who plied their trade while within the sight of the strangled criminal swinging from the gallows. After all, they had vicariously participated in the act of execution and also, therefore, had vicariously paid for their past crimes. This automatically brought them into a state of combined vicarious expiation and challenge against those righteous possessors of full pockets which they proceeded to pick with a complete sense of doing what they wanted to do, no matter what. This was their revenge for their own vicarious execution.[1]

Now Dr. Zilboorg is an eminent psychiatrist and perhaps as well qualified as any to write on the psychology of the criminal act. But if he had even a rudimentary understanding of how pickpockets live and work, he would never have made the statement just quoted. He does not know that the timing of theft from the person can be easily explained on the basis of a very sound mechanical principle of misdirection which is as old as organized thievery. "You can't steal a man's money as long as he has his mind on it," is the way a thief phrases it, and it matters little what takes his mind off his money, so long as the thief knows exactly when the victim's shift in interest occurs, or better still when the thief controls it. An automobile accident, a fire, a public hanging, touching the back of the victim's neck with a lighted cigarette, all serve equally well for given thieves under certain circumstances which we will discuss more fully later on.

Lacking an understanding of this principle, Dr. Zilboorg contrives a labored Freudian explanation which, because of its plausibility to the uninitiate, will undoubtedly find its way into the growing mass of misinformation about crime. Barrington explains this timing of the act of theft by saying "Everybody's eyes were on one person, and all were looking up." This very sound explanation Zilboorg brushes aside almost contemptuously: "Barrington may have been the greatest pickpocket in the history of man," he says, "but he knew nothing about the psychology of pickpockets. His explanation is too facile, too obvious, and too untrue."

[1] Gregory Zilboorg, *The Psychology of the Criminal Act and Punishment* (New York: Harcourt, Brace and Co., 1954), pp. 65–66.

To the contrary, Barrington understood exactly why thieves moved in on the crowds at the moment of execution, but I suggest that Dr. Zilboorg is confused when he interprets Barrington's statement as attempting to explain "the psychology of pickpockets." Barrington is commenting on the *psychology of the crowd*, and that psychology is just as sound today as it was in the 18th century. Let anyone who wishes to do so verify this by taking a *whiz mob* into a hotel room or other private place and inviting them to take his wallet without his feeling it. *This cannot be done, regardless of the skill of the thieves, so long as the victim is thinking about his wallet.*

But let the victim walk casually about the room, talking and smoking and handling objects naturally until the thieves can apply misdirection (verbal, kinesic, tactile) to take his mind off his wallet—if only for a few seconds—and he will be astonished to find that he has been robbed without feeling the slightest disturbance. What, one is impelled to ask, has this to do with "vicariously paying for their past crimes" or "vicariously participating in an act of execution" or "vicarious expiation" (of what, Dr. Zilboorg does not say)?

Again, I suggest that perhaps we should go a little beyond the armchair rationalizations of modern psychology and look to the behavior pattern for some cues. Several points arise in this connection. First, the members of the criminal subcultures do not, as we would like to believe, suffer acute feelings of guilt as a result of robbing members of the dominant culture. That is their way of life; they are parasitic on the dominant culture, and have been for many centuries. They have no more feeling of guilt than does a fox who takes hens from a farmer. During the course of many years I have interviewed many professional criminals; I have yet to find a professional who develops severe guilt feelings in connection with any specific routine act of theft from a so-called *sucker*, or member of the dominant culture, though many learn in prison how to simulate such feelings in order to influence the parole board.

Second, because the thief is a member of a parasitic subculture, it is about as reasonable to attempt to bring him into the dominant culture via psychiatry based on conflicts thought 'to exist on a widespread basis in the dominant culture as it would be to transfer an old-time Sioux Indian from his culture to ours by the same method. I venture to suggest that any psychiatrist who tried to give the participants in the Custer massacre insight into their "guilt" feelings in connection with this event would have had rough going indeed. Those Sioux who exterminated Custer's force were behaving as they were expected to in their culture; they enjoyed every bit of it, and derived status from it which they carried to their dying days.

Third, the professional criminal *does* develop conflicts of varying kinds and degrees, but these are largely with his own subculture. Most of these cannot be explained—or treated—in terms of the behavior pattern of the dominant culture. That is, he may experience severe guilt complexes because he has violated certain codes within his own group; we see these complexes very clearly sometimes in the case of stool pigeons who have turned informer and have betrayed their own kind to the law; if their transgression is serious enough, they may develop a kind of apathy and await death with striking indifference. Ernest Hemingway, incidentally, has treated this conflict very incisively in his short story "The Killers."

Fourth, professional criminals do develop conflicts because of their ostracism from the dominant culture. They sometimes wish they were not professional thieves, or stick-up men, or burglars. They regret that their children often cannot participate fully in the life of the dominant culture. They feel the stigma that a criminal record leaves upon them. In their old age they *pack the racket in* because they cannot any longer face up to the handicap of operating a criminal *racket* against the superior forces which a dominant culture musters against them. I have never known a well-established professional criminal to "reform", although many leave the subculture temporarily or permanently for a fling at life in the dominant culture on whatever level they may be able to establish themselves—usually in some form of semilegitimate business. They do not, however, change their basic values and attitudes; they only conform insofar as they think necessary to the superficial behavior pattern of the dominant culture. They like to be "accepted" by the dominant culture. Sometimes we see professionals who become quite prosperous (either within the law or without) going to inordinate lengths to gain some small degree of status in the dominant culture, as, for instance, Al Capone, who established his mother in a soup kitchen open to all the hungry in Chicago during the great depression of the thirties.

Last, the occasional criminal or amateur criminal—who is first of all a member of the dominant culture and a criminal only because he has violated the laws thereof—may suffer unconscious maladjustments with his culture pattern which manifest themselves in criminal behavior. For this type of thief, psychotherapy based upon known conflicts with the dominant culture may prove quite effective in some cases. Thus an employee who steals habitually and compulsively from his boss may be a sick man; the housewife who experiences an uncontrollable urge to steal merchandise (for which she often has no need) from a store may be suffering from maladjustments within her own culture, probably within her own home. Both are very different phenomena from the professional pickpocket, who steals from a culture not his own with great skill, complete detachment, and a conscience as clear as that of any other craftsman.

This dichotomy between the dominant culture and the sub-culture, together with a certain amount of overlap which makes for humor tinged with an afterthought of tragedy, is shown in this brief excerpt from an interview. The informant is discussing a man whom he and I both knew in former years, but who has been gathered very recently to his fathers via the electric chair, not for the murder mentioned in this discussion, but for killing another policeman who interfered with a later bank robbery in Florida.

He killed a policeman out there, you know. In jail. It was a getaway. They broke jail out there, but he's a bad little guy, you don't need to worry about that. He's been bad all of his life. And I guess he's spent more than half his life in penitentiaries.

When we was at Leavenworth he was working in the dining room, and I was working in the laundry. But I want to tell you something, he is the most peaceable sort of guy. And one of the nicest sort of guys you'd ever want to meet. You'd be tickled to death to entertain him right in your home. Very peaceful when he ain't on the heist. Very peaceful, very courteous, very nice and everything. He's one of the very few heavy gees who was like that in Leavenworth. A lot of them, when they saw you would only say "Hi ya" in a very rough voice.

And he would always say, "Good morning, Jack. How are you this morning?"

And I'd say "Good morning, Benny, how are you this morning?"

Well if he felt good, he'd say so; if he felt bad, he'd say so. He was always so courteous about everything. Seems like he got such a . . . well, he didn't have such a good education, but it seems like he was brought up right anyway. His mother and father must have taught him how to treat people.

CHAPTER II

THE PICKPOCKET AND LEGITIMATE SOCIETY

The entire underworld may be said to constitute a subcultural adjunct to the dominant or legitimate culture. The following statement shows this division between dominant and subculture clearly. It was made during a discussion of whether or not making narcotics legal would take them off the contraband market, with the result that some addicts would no longer need to go on the *rackets* to make the big money now necessary to buy drugs.

> I believe I've lived with him long enough to know that, well I don't give a damn if morphine was selling for a penny a gram. This guy would still be a thief, because he is a thief, he thinks like a thief, he's got a criminal mind, and he will always be a thief. The same way with me . . . try as I may I try to think like the rest of our organized society wants me to think—like they say I'm supposed to think. I don't know whether I'm supposed to or not, but I don't think like other people do and irregardless of how much or how little dope would cost me, that would not change my criminal intent or my criminal activities one iota.

Each specialized group within this large cluster of criminal subcultures (which is a much more accurate descriptive phrase than the more romantic "underworld") has cultural ties of three types: first, each specialized group (say *confidence men*) has a strong internal structure which enables us to classify it as a differential subculture. Second, each group has observable ties with all other criminal subcultures (despite some internecine warfare or professional competition) and thence with the major divisions of the underworld; thus, a *confidence man* would identify immediately with the *confidence rackets*, perhaps qualifying himself as a *big con man* or a *short con man*, but certainly identifying himself further with the *grift* as a way of living; these common elements tend to be obscured in some instances and emphasized or intensified in others.

No criminal subculture that I have studied exists separate and distinct from the dominant culture; in fact, because of the parasitic nature of crime, all criminal subcultures tend, to a greater or lesser degree, to simulate the outward aspects of the dominant culture for protective reasons; thus, *confidence men* may simulate the behavior pattern of the successful tycoon so effectively that the rate of mortality among real tycoons whom they fleece is impressively high. Likewise, the language of each criminal sub-culture—which I have called *argot*, though this term is used by only the more sophisticated of the brethren—is characteristic of both the specialized *racket* and the major underworld division; at the same time it has much in common with the spoken and written language of the dominant culture.

While I have on tape some argots which might at first appear to be non-English, these can be readily related to English when the key is known; all argots spoken in America are obviously patterned on English, though their specialized morpheme structure usually renders them partially or totally unintelligible to those who speak only the language of the dominant culture. Meta-linguistically they conform, in general, to the pattern of spoken American English, though to date only the gross aspects of criminal argots have been studied and published; further analysis will undoubtedly reveal much more precise information on all aspects of argots in relation to the pattern of the language of the dominant culture. In this study, the emphasis will necessarily fall not upon morphological and syntactic differentiae, but upon the lexical elements in relation to behavior.

When we attempt to state how the subculture of the pickpocket differs from the dominant culture, our problem is immediately complicated; first, because we have no full and adequate description of the dominant culture; and second, because those treatises which have been written on the dominant culture are often so frag-mentary and often so detailed that they are useless for com-parative purposes. Also, no one seems ever to have described a criminal subculture fully and completely. However, Dr. George Trager has recently evolved a system of stating cultural indices which appears to me to be sufficiently clear and, at the same time, sufficiently inclusive to make it useful as a device for suggesting a comparison of the subculture of the pickpocket with the dominant or legitimate culture.

Trager develops ten indices to culture. He uses these in his very cogent treatise on the relation of language and culture, now in preparation for the *Encyclopaedia Britannica*.[1] They have great inclusive-exclusive merit and permit us to manipulate the elements of culture—and hence of subculture—within a limited framework.

[1] *Encyclopaedia Britannica*, 1955 Edition. (Cited from manuscript.)

They are therefore most useful, though it should be understood
that they only assist us to grasp the problem; they are not in
themselves answers, but rather provocative signposts suggesting
further analysis. Furthermore, they can be summarized here only
in a very brief form which hardly does justice to the original.

If we take up Trager's indices one by one, and in a most general
fashion, we begin to see the contours of the pickpocket's subculture, albeit in a somewhat oversimplified form. Subsequent
treatment of the argot will develop these contours in more detail.

1. **Interaction.** The pickpocket manifests at least three major
levels of interaction with people, the first with members of the
fraternity or profession, the second with members of the underworld, including other *rackets*, and the third with members of the
dominant culture. Within the fraternity itself there are several
levels of interaction based on caste, on professional competence,
and on personal status as determined by integrity and conformance
to the group mores. The relations with other types of criminals
are somewhat unstable and unpredictable largely because the
pickpocket's status differs with various groups, and because his
racket does not have a very high underworld rating.

The interaction of the pickpocket with legitimate culture is of
a predatory nature. His interaction with environment likewise
may be classified on three similar levels. Of major interest to us
here, however, is the fact that his language is a natural outgrowth
of interaction; each underworld pickpocket (there are a few who
cannot be so classified) knows the argot of his specialty, the general
argot of the *grift*, and the spoken (if not the written version) of
the language of a certain class in the dominant culture. We will
also have a peripheral interest in several other aspects of communication, including signs and *offices* some of which might be
considered phases of kinesics and tactilism.

2. **Association.** Impelled by the cohesive forces which bind all
criminal groups together, the pickpocket organizes primarily
within the underworld. The basic organization, the mob, is very
tight and controlled by tradition; the organization of the *fix*
varies with localities, being tight in some areas and loose or
casual in others. There is also the very loose organization of the
entire *grift*, which is handled through hangouts, through the
activities of bondsmen or professional *fixers*, and through individual
intercommunication. Among pickpockets there is nothing like the

effective, nation-wide syndication of crime, together with a ruthless system of underworld government enjoying, ironically enough, appropriate protection from the law, which we have had in recent years in some of the big-time *rackets*. However, the pickpocket may, by association, utilize fringe areas of this large organization, or be used by it, or both. As a pickpocket becomes an established professional, he tends to drop associations he may have had in the dominant culture. Exceptions may be his family ties, fraternal orders under some circumstances, church membership, and the loose social associations which develop in the hangouts. He sometimes maintains from childhood a few other associations with the dominant culture.

3. **Subsistence.** The pickpocket works for a living like everyone else, although his theories of economics and distribution of wealth may be at variance with those held by the dominant culture. The technology of thievery from the person is complex and varied—so much so that no one in either the dominant culture or the criminal subculture knows all about it. It is an ancient craft, world-wide in practice, and subject to constant revision and improvement. The language which is used by pickpockets in articulating the technical aspects of this craft constitutes the entirety of the lexical material in this study; it would be more accurate to say that this study discusses only a portion of this technical argot as it is used currently by the professional groups contacted by the writer. Argot is especially important in the criminal subculture, since it is the earmark of the professional and essential for discussing professional techniques.

On the other hand, few pickpockets have any knowledge of or aptitude for making a living in the dominant culture by legitimate means; most have worked only in their youth, or in prison, or for brief periods when they could not ply their chosen craft. Of those who save up enough money to open a business (usually a tavern, cigar store, amusement business, etc.), few succeed. This is not to say that they are as a class lacking in either industry or ingenuity, for many mobs observe a rigorous working schedule, tending the crowds at certain hours as diligently as any grocer catering to his trade. They simply do not do the kind of work commonly pursued by the legitimate society. They are not productive; they do not serve any of the needs of the dominant culture.

4. **Bisexuality.** Although the subculture of pickpockets does not

appear to emphasize the factor of bisexuality as heavily as does the dominant culture, the pattern of the dominant culture with special reference to the lower middle class seems to be followed rather generally. This is especially true of *local* pickpockets, who live permanently in one community and maintain a home; here the man steals a living while the woman keeps house and raises the children. Among the *road mobs* this division of labor often breaks down, especially where the woman is herself a professional, for women are accepted on an equal professional footing with men and have great independence. A certain class of male pickpockets tend to become pimps in hard times, using their women as wage-earners, but men of this type (sometimes ostracized by other thieves) are almost certain to cling closely to the lower middle-class mores of the dominant culture and take the earnings of their women without question, the women accepting this situation as natural.

5. **Territoriality.** The haunts of the pickpocket are in the great urban centers, in the arteries of travel, and in crowds wherever they collect. He follows the spatial pattern of the dominant culture, but only in certain respects. In large cities the pickpocket may be a permanent local inhabitant; in other places where crowds congregate, he is strictly transient. He cannot live in any community where he is known by people who will see him regularly; even *local* pickpockets who live in large cities make it a rule to prey largely upon transients, and traveling pickpockets strictly refrain from appearing on the street with *local* pickpockets, even though they might have strong personal or professional ties. Pickpockets must always have a sufficient number of strangers present to appear inconspicuous, and this means that they cannot *work* rural or small town areas except under special circumstances when large out-of-town crowds are present, as for example at circuses, fairs, or conventions.

Pickpockets follow the eddies of humanity like sharks playing in a school of herring. Geographically, American pickpockets may follow these human eddies to Europe or Canada or Mexico or South America, but they always ply the urban centers and the well-traveled routes; socially, they tend to live in lower middle-class residential areas, though some *road mobs* travel strictly first-class. The *hangouts*, which are usually bars, bookmakers' establishments, restaurants, or even barber shops, are of a kind; a classic example, which flourished for two generations, was Hinky Dink Kenna's Workingman's Saloon in Chicago. Damon Runyon described very accurately some of the *hangouts* around Broadway and 50th street in New York of the 1920's. Sutherland's *Professional Thief* (pseudonym, Chic Conwell) describes some both in Chicago and in New York in the vicinity of Broadway and 47th Street in the 1930's. Today there are some active ones (largely eating places) between 45th and 46th Streets on 6th Avenue, and on 33rd Street near 7th Avenue. These are only examples, for their number is legion.

Today's pickpockets are more cautious and do not socialize so freely as in former years. Some of the most successful ones go rarely to the *hangouts*. To sum it up, pickpockets live and work everywhere that people live and work in the dominant culture except where the crowds are thin; even in jails and prisons they will be greatly outnumbered by members of the dominant culture. As a result of numerous state habitual-criminal statutes, an increasing number of pickpockets are residing rather indefinitely behind bars, a situation which results not only in the elimination of many of the *local* pickpockets from circulation, but keeps many *road mobs* from entering territory covered by such laws.

6. **Temporality.** In the main, the pickpocket accepts the concepts of time which are used by the dominant culture, although his attitudes toward time, its use, its projection into the past and future, etc. may differ considerably from those held by the dominant culture. For instance, the pickpocket lives very intensely in the present. The past and the future are alike unimportant in his thinking, though he may derive much pleasure from reminiscing over past experiences, and likewise daydream grandly about his prosperity in the future. He can block out with ease any unpleasant past experiences, as well as any concern for his ultimate fate. Also, speed is so dominant a factor in his work that he operates constantly under pressure, while, at the same time, he must maintain an outward appearance of casual unconcern. His argot is full of words which reflect this concern with the speed-image in his work, and, apparently derivative therefrom via the frustration route, violence-images which are out of all proportion to the actual force, speed, and movement which a given act requires. The term *whiz* is revealing in this respect.

7. **Education.** The "typical" pickpocket is usually subject to three phases of education: preschool, in which the influence of his

parents and their associates form strong and early impressions; school, during which he is subject to formal indoctrination with subject matter and the attitudes of the dominant culture (most pickpockets have little schooling, many cannot read and write); professional education, during the early phases of which a pickpocket is *turned out* (coached and used as a partner) by an older and experienced professional, after which he is on his own. I have been unable to verify the various journalistic reports of "schools" for pickpockets where such fantastic audio-visual devices as dressed man-sized dummies with bells attached to their pockets are used to train young recruits. During both the first and third phases of this education, the pickpocket learns informally not only the attitudes, the mores, and the wisdom of the *grift*, but some techniques—if his parents or their friends are thieves; in the third phase he learns, by observation and participation enhanced by coaching, the techniques of his craft, as well as the argot of his profession.

This is the picture of the typical or classic pickpocket. However, basic to all this development is the possession by the individual of an interesting psychological complex (as yet practically unrecognized and undefined by the criminologists and criminal psychologists) called *grift know* or *grift sense*. Without it, no individual can become a good pickpocket, regardless of how much coaching he receives from experts. With it, an individual readily becomes a pickpocket (even without coaching) and with some help he responds to suggestion from older professionals with great success. It appears to be partly inherent, partly learned from experience and other *grifters*. This phenomenon reminds one of the behavior of bird dogs bred to point, and merits serious investigation by specialists in criminal psychology. I have knowledge of individuals well endowed with *grift sense* who have departed from their entire family pattern (which followed that of the dominant culture in a most conventional manner) and who have sought out the "profession" of pickpocket without early training and without exposure to the underworld until after they had become professionals; in Chapter VII we will see the unusual case of a skilled female pickpocket who had never had any contact with the underworld and maintained all her normal connections with the dominant culture, including marriage to a man who did not suspect her occupation. She was entirely self-taught.

8. **Recreation or Play.** Although the entire range of recreation

of the dominant culture is available to the pickpocket, his choice of recreation seems to follow the pattern of other *grifters*: the racetrack, the night club, the bar, the gambling house, and the ladies. He may often include narcotics, which are for him an escape from the tensions of living; today he uses the needle, but that is recent; twenty-five years ago he gathered with his friends for sessions of opium smoking, now a luxury beyond his means. There is a secondary type of exposure to the recreational or cultural aspects of legitimate society in that the pickpocket works in crowds, and this may take him into all sorts of places he might not frequent by choice—baseball games, football games, movies, public lectures, etc. A few may acquire a liking for these events *per se*, but most of them seem to regard them only as adjuncts to their work.

9. **Defense.** This activity occupies an increasing proportion of the energy and resources of the dominant culture, but few pickpockets ever participate in legitimate defense in either civilian or military capacity. However, their subculture is organized to a certain extent for defense against the threat of the law of the dominant culture; this includes principally a well-developed information system (sometimes popularly called "the grapevine"), various security devices for the detection and exclusion of non-criminals from the criminal subculture, the raising of considerable funds to be used in emergencies, and very good connections with the politico-criminal liaison, popularly called the *fix*, which extends like a network across the country, with headquarters in all sizable cities. So strong is this last defense device that a known pickpocket has at his disposal, once he is arrested, forces which are never available to the legitimate citizen. The *fix* is always set up primarily to protect the members of the criminal subculture, and only in a secondary way to protect legitimate society. In some communities, the criminal subculture has been known to dominate both the police and the courts for considerable periods of time. The police, and, to a degree, the courts may sometimes become instruments by which the amateur, occasional, or nonprofessional transgressors are made to pay the price for the operations of the professional criminal. While there are many exceptions to this police-criminal liaison—for it can operate with only a few dishonest policemen strategically placed—extending in several directions and operating on several different levels, that is the predominant pattern.

10. **The Exploitation of Resources.** The dominant culture concentrates on the development of the products of nature, raw materials, industrial processes, the advantages of trade and business, etc. for its material prosperity. The criminal subculture, on the other hand, is parasitic and contributes nothing to the wealth of legitimate society; in fact, the cost, simply in dollars and cents, of maintaining the criminal subculture is staggering. The pickpocket, as a relatively minor member of a criminal group, is entirely parasitic, and preys directly and personally upon members of the dominant culture, and sometimes, though rarely, upon the members of other illegitimate subcultures as well. Therefore, the economics of the pickpocket only reflect those of the dominant culture; in good times, the pickpocket eats well; in hard times, he goes hungry. He can be no more prosperous than the dominant culture upon which he depends directly for resources, and to this extent he likes to see the dominant culture in a state of perpetual prosperity.

The value of these indices to culture in connection with this study is principally that they enable us to partition all culture into a small number of basic elements which can be easily understood and manipulated. At the same time, each of these elements is capable of almost indefinite subpartition—together with consequent classification and subclassification of the resulting subelements. In other words, we can discuss the elements of culture on a gross level without having to break them down; or, we can break them down as far as is necessary or desirable; or, we can leave some in the gross form and break others down to any desired degree. Thus the indices give us a flexible device for handling certain elements of culture on any level without having to attempt a breakdown of the entire culture pattern in order to isolate the elements we wish to discuss.

While this book is not organized around Trager's ten indices, they have been used from time to time to enable us to abstract from the behavior pattern of pickpockets certain elements which we need to discuss, and to eliminate others which might be interesting in themselves, but which do not apply directly to the problem at hand. For instance, once we decide which of the indices are wholly encompassed, that subject matter can be treated fully, as are the data on technology and making a living, which is basically what Trager means by Index No. 3 (*Subsistence*). On the other hand, such an index as *Territoriality* can be treated quite briefly, by isolating and analyzing those elements of territoriality peculiar to the pickpocket culture.

Furthermore, these ten indices enable the reader to visualize the subculture of pickpockets and the dominant legitimate culture in the same terms, except where they differ enough to attract attention. This is most helpful, since it is not easy to project the behavior pattern of a criminal group in terms of itself alone. With the dominant culture always in the background, it is perhaps easier for the reader to draw upon principles and factors with which he is familiar, and to use these known elements as keys to the less familiar elements in the subculture.

CHAPTER III

THE PLACE OF THE PICKPOCKET IN
THE UNDERWORLD

Classification of Criminals

The general public tends to lump all criminals together in a sort of romantic hodgepodge; the movies, fictioneers, and television programs do little to clarify the nature of the modern underworld. The law classifies crime mainly into three classes: crimes against the person, crimes against property, and crimes against the state, although there are many degrees of criminality within these categories.

In recent years, the courts, desperate under an avalanche of juvenile crime, some amateur and some professional, have taken steps, all of them well meant, to separate the beginners at crime from the old-timers, and the devices for doing this in various states are many. As a result, in some states, a juvenile may have a history of arrests, convictions, and sentences served in correctional institutions which surpasses the records of some professionals who have operated for many years. Yet these juveniles may not legally have a "criminal record"—all because they are under twenty-one. It is quite possible for them to enter the professional levels of crime as experienced and capable operators, but without a record as such. They obviously pass the age of twenty-one with considerable reluctance.

We have thus established a new classification of criminals—the adult and the juvenile. Criminologists generally follow the classification of the courts, with some exceptions. Criminal psychiatrists and psychologists look to motive and to personality disturbances as a basis for classification, and hence we have the psychopath, the psychoneurotic, the paranoid, etc.

However, if we are going to classify, say, physicians, or farmers, or craftsmen, we go first of all to those groups for a classification. As a result, we see that there are internists, urologists, orthopedic surgeons, etc., or truck farmers, ranchers, cotton farmers, fruit growers, etc. And if we go to the criminals themselves, we find that they have a classification which makes a good deal of sense. First, they divide all crime into amateur and professional. The amateurs they eliminate immediately—though roughly eighty percent of the inmates of our prisons and reformatories are amateur or "occasional" criminals. The amateur repeats his venture a few times and is caught—in the case of murder and robbery, he is often caught the first time out; the professional repeats indefinitely with relatively little trouble, so long as the *fix* holds, and so long as he does not cross the lines of rival operators or the politicians who protect them.

It is reasonable to estimate that perhaps ninety-five per cent of all our crime is committed by professionals, who are represented by a small minority temporarily in our prisons, while the amateurs, representing a heavy majority of convicts, account for only about five per cent of the crime. Amateur adult criminals are looked upon by the underworld only as another variety of *sucker*; only after they have been exposed to the postgraduate curriculum of prison life do a few of them make possible recruits for the ranks of the professionals, not bred to the subculture, but indoctrinated to it by the state itself.

Therefore, if we look at the classification accepted by the professionals, we see first that amateurs are not accepted as criminals at all. The remaining professionals are divided into four groups. The first constitutes the *heavy rackets*, comprising those criminals who use violence or the threat of violence in order to operate—for example, bank robbers, safe crackers, racketeers, extortionists.

The second is the *grift*, which includes all the infinity of rackets which utilize the skilled hand or the sharp wit, or both—for example the *big con*, the *short con*, professional gamblers, thieves of all kinds, burglars of certain kinds, *circus grifters*, *carnival grifters*, almost without end, for there are literally hundreds of rackets within this category.

Third, there are the *lone wolves*, who are professionals, but who operate predominantly alone, without the support of a mob, and sometimes without the protection of the *fix*—for example, jewel thieves of some types, swindlers, expert forgers. Some of these operators are complex personalities, gifted with exceptional intellects. Little is known about them because they are not easy to study; they seldom come into conflict with the law. Just recently one was unmasked in New York City where he practiced medicine —without a degree; he was trapped when his colleagues planned a dinner to honor him at a large hotel; he committed suicide when he realized that he would be identified as a swindler.

Last, there are those who might be called the quasi criminals, the label being mine, since the underworld does not offer a term covering all the rackets which are, nevertheless, recognized as belonging to the same category. This group includes prostitutes, underworld narcotic addicts (those who do not affiliate themselves with one of the other branches of crime), criminal homosexuals, blackmailers, pimps, etc.

This classification seems to me to make sense, and, although it does not follow the precedents set by the academic and legal experts on crime, I shall use it consistently in this study, for it effectively encompasses the multitude of *rackets* which comprise the contemporary underworld.

The lines between these four major categories are not always sharp, but they are quite recognizable, and difficult to cross because the various criminal groups not only attract and develop a different type of operator, but have a different subcultural matrix. However, some individuals do cross major subcultural lines, and within each of the four major groups there may be considerable extension of a single operator's activities; for example, a pickpocket might also (sometimes) be a professional card cheater or a dealer in a gambling house. It would, however, be unheard of for a pickpocket to be a professional bank stick-up man on the side.

Some professionals stick to one group all their lives, never deviating from one *racket*, and sometimes becoming spectacularly proficient at it. Others stay with one *racket* simply because they are not sufficiently progressive to learn anything else; they grind away desperately from day to day, threatened always by extinction if conditions change so that their old formula does not work. There are, of course, numerous differences in status within the subcultural groups. A *big con man* would not by preference associate with pimps and a bank robber would be likely to distrust a *carnival grifter* on principle. Some professionals in one category refuse to recognize professionals in another category as professionals; as an interesting case in point, I once asked an international *confidence man* if his wife had ever been on the *rackets*. "Oh, no," he said, "she is a business woman, strictly legitimate." "What business is she in?" I asked. "Oh, she has a string of houses," he answered without a trace of irony.

There are always exceptions to these concepts of status attached to certain *rackets*, and the fact that a man is on a certain *racket* is in itself no index to his status in the criminal subculture. For example, pickpockets are not commonly associated with big-time crime, but some individual pickpockets have excellent connections reaching into the upper areas of other subcultures, their status apparently deriving not so much from economic success as from (strange as it may sound) character, reliability, and reputation for integrity. Arnold Rothstein, for instance, had as close associates for some years half a dozen pickpockets. And no one would rate Arnold Rothstein as a small-timer.

The four major divisions named above differ somewhat in their mores, their operating technology, and their argot, though they also have some things in common. Even within each major group there are noticeable differences between those operating in different *rackets*, as for instance, *flat jointers* opposed to *smack players*, or professional *card dealers* as opposed to *touts*, though all of them belong to the same major class, the *grift*. In a series of previous publications, I have demonstrated the differences in argot among many criminal subcultures, both within the same major classification, and among various major categories.

Pickpockets belong in the second category, the *grift*, and constitute a subdivision of thieves, of which there are many varieties; within the pickpocket subculture there are several types, while at the same time there are several peripheral *rackets* which are related to pickpockets, but are not accepted by them.

Status Factors

Although there are individual exceptions, pickpockets as a class do not have very high status on the *grift*. They are not respected by the law as some of the big-time criminals are, and they are not glamorized in film and fiction. The public tends to regard theft from the person, however cleverly executed, as comical; it is a trick, like one performed by a magician. The pickpocket, when he is used in fiction, tends to be a kind of clown operating on a near-slapstick level. This formula-treatment is misleading, since there are among pickpockets individuals who rise well above the popular concept and who have not only cultivated a good deal of wisdom in regard to life, but who have a stable code of living within their own subculture.

On the other hand, Mr. Danny Campion, who has spent much

of his life catching pickpockets in New York City, tells me that he does not agree with those who would classify the pickpockets as in the lower brackets of the underworld, and he particularly mentioned Sutherland[1] in connection with this generalization. However, Campion was talking about solid *class cannons* and not about the riffraff of Harlem who call themselves pickpockets. I would agree with him personally, but always with the reservation that we exclude the majority of bums and include only the minority of better-class operators.

It is significant that some other types of criminals fear pickpockets and do not like to associate with them. This is not a physical fear, for pickpockets as a class are almost universally nonviolent; it is a fear of betrayal based on the belief that pickpockets tend to operate as stool pigeons for the police and for various detective agencies. This is particularly true of small-time operators who can be permitted by the police to work in certain places at certain times with the understanding that they do not rob local people; in return, these thieves keep the detectives who protect them informed of any underworld movements which may involve bigger operators or out-of-town operators.

In the course of working with scientific police-training programs, I have observed that the great majority of detectives still depend heavily on stool pigeons; in fact, most urban detectives would be helpless without them, though their use is kept quiet, their identities are protected by the courts, and the public is unaware of their importance in police work. The small-time pickpocket is a natural victim to be exploited by the police; the immunity granted thieves of this type is usually limited, however, for detectives can use a thief as a stool pigeon only as long as he is not suspected of informing; once he is known, his usefulness ends, and the very detectives who protected him are often instrumental in sending him off to prison—where he may continue his informing activities in a fresh environment. His chances of getting killed in either location are good. "Set a thief to catch a thief" is an ancient maxim which still holds so true that some private detective agencies hire former pickpockets to operate on their staffs. Says one *grifter*: "I'd say that better than fifty per cent of Pinkertons are

[1] Edwin Sutherland, *The Professional Thief* (University of Chicago Press, 1937).

ex-cons.[2] Well, you know that Dago Foley killed one of them here. You know that. He killed a guy named Graham. He was an ex-pickpocket and he was working for Pinkerton."

On the other hand, it would be inaccurate to leave the impression that all pickpockets are stool pigeons, or potential informers. This is by no means true. There are among the upper echelons of pickpockets men (and women) who have steadfastly resisted strong pressures to turn informer. For pickpockets who turn informer, the underworld has its own types of vengeance; killings and beatings are common; some individuals are marked for life by being cut on the face with a knife. Possibly the most effective long-range means of controlling informers is the age-old process of ostracism, for once an informer is known, he finds it increasingly difficult to work with or to associate with his kind, and thus is ruined economically.

The stigma under which pickpockets as a class operate (at least among their betters on the *grift* and among the upper brackets of the *heavy rackets*) is intensified by other characteristics sufficiently common among pickpockets that they are sometimes, perhaps inaccurately, attributed to all pickpockets. First, the incidence of narcotic addiction is very high among thieves, and highest of all among pickpockets and shoplifters. It has been conservatively estimated at 60–75 per cent. Aside from the natural revulsion which nonaddicts feel toward addicts, there is a stability factor involved here; addicts as a class are said to be less reliable, less resistant to police pressures, and more likely to talk when faced with the terrible abstinence syndrome in jail. Therefore, nonaddicts distrust addicts, and this division carries over in the form of internal divisions among pickpockets themselves; nonaddicts do not like to work with addicts and vice versa, though it is done; the tendency is for addicted pickpockets to work together, and nonaddicts likewise.

Of course, a part of this preference stems from the fact that all addicts have certain common problems—the maintaining of connections whereby they can get regular supplies of drugs; the need for avoiding federal narcotics agents as well as other types

[2] I happen to know that this estimated percentage of ex-convicts hired by Pinkerton is much too high; a former head of the organization tells me that nowadays they are hiring mostly ex-FBI men, ex-Secret Service men, and officers who formerly worked for the City of New York or the Parole Board.

of enforcement officers; the absolute and irrevocable necessity to stop work at regular intervals (roughly four or five hours) and find a private place to take drugs by needle; the risk of transporting drugs, and equipment for taking them, on their persons or in their luggage; and the disruption of normal sex life which usually accompanies drug addiction, with addicts having little if any need for sex, while nonaddicts pursue the normal course. In short, the subculture of the drug addict cuts across the various ancient subcultures of thieves. The problems of the narcotic addict, both in the dominant culture and in the criminal subculture, were recently analysed by the present writer, and more details may be found in this study.[3]

The sex life of the pickpocket has certain characteristics which tend to differentiate him from the higher brackets of the *grift*. I have examined this topic in some detail in a study of the *confidence men*.[4] First, the pickpocket, like all *grifters*, leans toward the common-law arrangements with women, in preference to the more binding ties of holy and legal wedlock. However, he picks his women, generally, from the ranks of shoplifters, female thieves, and prostitutes. Also, unlike many if not most other types of underworld operator, he tends to take his woman on the road with him, teaching her what she needs to know to work with him, unless, as sometimes happens, she is already expert herself. Pickpockets who do not work on the road tend to follow the same pattern with their women on a local basis. Thus the girls, unlike the kept women of many other types of criminals, come into very close contact with the nature of the racket by which their men make a living; they understand it technically and are constantly exposed to it socially. Often they contribute as much as, if not more than, the men to the economic stability of the couple or to the mob, as the case may be. Therefore, it is natural for the woman to feel a greater sense of economic responsibility than do the women of other operators on higher levels.

Also, the spending habits of pickpockets are such that savings, investments, insurance, and other aspects of security, which are important on higher levels of the *grift*, are neglected. Possibly all

[3] D. W. Maurer and Victor H. Vogel, *Narcotics and Narcotic Addiction* (Springfield, Ill.: Charles C. Thomas, 1954).

[4] D. W. Maurer, *The Big Con* (Indianapolis, Ind.: Bobbs-Merrill, 1940). Reprinted by Pocket Books (New York, 1949).

of these circumstances contribute to the tendency of some pick-pockets to turn pimp in times of stress and to live off the wages of their women. This is by no means universally true, but it happens with sufficient frequency to give the professional a reputation for falling back on what the old-timers call the *odds* to make the ends meet, if and when evil days come upon the racket itself. It should be noted, however, that this practice is largely confined to the rank and file of pickpockets, among whom are many from the dregs of the underworld; among so-called *class cannons* it is practically nonexistent.

Pickpockets as a group compensate for these many inadequacies or perhaps handicaps (according to the point of view) by a number of defense-mechanisms.

It is important to remember that the pickpocket never gets into the higher brackets of income which distinguish many other operators. He is restricted in each act of theft to the amount the victim has in his wallet; unless this is a *jug touch* or *set up* (where the thief sees the victim put a large amount in his wallet, or has it reported to him by an accomplice) the same amount of work, skill, and risk goes into each theft, even though the wallet may contain little or nothing. He has no way of knowing how much he has stolen until he *turns over* the wallet. There is a pickpocket saw (humorously used by old-time faro bankers when they draw a *gun turn* or double five) which says: "Two fives together, what the mark has in his leather," and this condition seems to prevail with distressing regularity.

We just made a thousand-mile trip and knocked up exactly $22 over and above expenses. I guarantee you there wouldn't be nobody . . . there ain't no copper that knows anything about the whiz that's going to believe it, that people go and steal every goddamn day without having more than $22 in a thousand miles. But that actually happened. There just wasn't no money. I just never seen no money below this line [refers on a road map to Tennessee, Arkansas, Texas]. Whenever they're at an auction, they have a lot of those . . . I don't know what they call them exactly, but down in that oil country down there, they have them sales and get-togethers where they sell the oil leases. We was dressed just like all the rest of them hoosiers . . . had overalls on and hip boots, and everything, flying right around with the rest of them.

A sucker would say, "I offer number 8."

Some other guy would say, "Well, I offer 9."

" 'I'll give 10.'

" 'Sold for 10.'

He'd mean ten thousand, see, and all he'd do, he'd hold up his finger, see. ou get into his poke, and he ain't got a quarter, not a fine quarter. He'd just hold up his finger for 10 grand. Next day he goes to the bank and writes a check for the 10 grand.

If we look for a moment at the economics of a *three handed mob*, the reasons why pickpockets do not count as big-time crime becomes obvious. Let us assume that they are the average *road mob*, not the best and not in the lower brackets; they just work hard to make a living. For each day they work, they must pay an average of no less than $100 per day for police protection in the various cities where they work for a day or two, then travel on. Based on a five-day week, at minimal prices, this is $500; it may cost twice that much or more. If they travel by car, as many do, their expenses will average no less than $20 per person, or $420 per week at a very conservative estimate, for thieves like to live well. If we allow $30 per week per man for maintenance and replacement of clothes (pickpockets must maintain a first-class *front*) and other incidentals, we get another $90. This adds up to $1010. Then, if the mob uses drugs (and chances are very good that all the members have a habit) another $500 or more per week must be available, usually in advance, for they like to buy their drugs in quantities and to be assured of at least a week's *rations* at all times. This adds up to over $1500 per week which must be *knocked up*—just to meet operating expenses. Recreation, such as gambling, horse races, night clubs, and other cultural pursuits dear to the hearts of pickpockets, will cost extra and heavily. All this is counted as *nut* (though individuals usually pay their own hotel bills and gambling costs) and anything they make over and above this they consider income. In order to clear $100 per week per man, the minimum for which any average pickpocket (not a *class cannon*) would consider working, this mob would have to gross around $1800 per week. We have made no provision for emergencies such as serious illness, the need to replenish or build up *fall dough*, the immediate, and sometimes large, cash demands forced by sudden and unexpected trouble with the law, the constant requests of others who are in trouble and need help. Indeed it keeps three average pickpockets *hustling* to steal from $1800 to $2000 per week and remain free on the streets.

With the relatively few *class mobs*, it is different. These operators are highly skilled and have the know-how to produce at a maximum of efficiency. They plan their itinerary effectively, they *fix* in advance and along well established channels, they have little if any trouble with victims because of their methods of operation, and they work constantly with great diligence.

You can take a three handed mob—a broad and two guys—and get three scores in a week and average $15,000 a year without any trouble—without any trouble at all . . . say three scores a week and a three handed mob, and knock up $45,000 a year. That is, if they know their business. I'm talking about strictly class mobs. I'm not talking about makeshifts and pickups and this and that. I'm talking about knowing what you're going after. I'm talking about those jug touches.

Considering the risks and the labor involved, an annual income of $15,000 per man, or $45,000 for the mob, cannot by any standards be considered a big-time income; also, it should be noted that few pickpockets achieve and maintain this level. If pickpockets reached the $50,000 and $100,000 incomes made by some *con men* and operators on the *heavy rackets*, their underworld status would be quite different.

Most cannon mobs go out to make about ten thousand dollars a year, apiece. That is over and above the nut and everything. You can't figure on those big ones. You get a lot of two dollar pokes . . . you've got to keep going. Eventually that $40 poke will drop in, and then a $67 one, a $100 one, and then that darb with $850. But you got to take them as they come.

Last, pickpockets as a class are regarded as ignorant and lacking in the type of intelligence which makes big-time criminals, though these faults are certainly not universal; some pickpockets are capable and intelligent by any standards. However, the great number of illiterates and operators with cunning but low intelligence gives the *racket* a bad name. Some of the best operators I know or know about cannot read and write; most of them who can read never go beyond the tabloids and the racing form sheet. Literacy, however, is no requisite for either ability or status. One internationally known pickpocket, so popular that when he killed a Pinkerton detective more than a hundred thieves from all over the world poured in to testify successfully in his defense, never learned to read and could hardly count money. He was Dago Foley, who was known as The Duke because of his meticulous dress, his good manners, and his magnanimous way with his colleagues. He has now, alas, been gathered to his fathers.

On the whole, pickpockets are distinguished for neither their gracious manners nor their summary fashion in dealing with policemen. In fact, if thieves have any group tendency whatever so far as manners are concerned, that tendency is toward brusqueness rather than friendliness. They do have a definite and well-recognized group tendency toward nonviolence; especially do they shy away from violence in robbing a victim. This is thought by some members of other criminal subcultures to indicate a lack of personal courage on the part of pickpockets. I am inclined to doubt this generalization, since many pickpockets will engage in personal combat, sometimes deadly, over women, the division of spoils, points of honor, or any of the other issues which men commonly fight over.

It is notable, however, that they definitely avoid violence in their professional work (*lush workers, mary ellen workers*, etc. are looked down on by pickpockets because, even though the *rackets* are related, the pickpocket likes to make his theft without even the marginal type of violence used in these other rackets) and as one goes up the scale among pickpockets, avoidance of violence gives way to a deference to finesse which among the top practitioners reaches almost incredible degrees of refinement. There are, for instance, among pickpockets those crude operators who use a razor blade to cut the pocket which holds the purse or the topcoat which covers the pocket; even this type of violence is looked down upon by the better mobs, who pride themselves in the fact that they do not have to cut anything. "It gives the racket a bad name. You can roll it up like a window shade, so what good does it do you to cut it?"

Compensations

While all these things—a class reputation as stool pigeons, a reluctance to employ violence, a relatively low income as the spoils of modern crime are counted, a suggestion that pimping sometimes supplements professional incomes, a high percentage of illiteracy in the broad sense of that word, and so on—have a tendency to depress the profession, there are generous compensations.

One of these is the expansion of the ego. While this syndrome is by no means restricted to pickpockets, but is commonly found throughout the underworld, it is perhaps more noticeable in the pickpocket because of the relatively lowly nature of his calling.

Every pickpocket has to believe that he is good, or he could never face the prospect of the next day's work; he must believe this even if he is the most bumbling of operators. Those who are really good elevate their talents considerably in their own estimation and like to claim a place with *class cannons*. The real *class cannons*, who are indeed few in number, and who have in a sense "arrived" both status-wise and economically, are notably free from this inflation of the ego, and discuss their exploits, when they discuss them at all, with reserve and modesty. This type of pickpocket, it should be noted, is passing from the scene; most *class cannons* now operating are old-timers. "The only youngsters I see breaking in on the whiz are jigs, and they are coining a bebop lingo that is something."

Other compensations are the development of a high degree of professional organization in the narrow sense of division of labor and specialization within the *racket* itself. Also, there is what is known as *grift sense*, a sort of sixth sense by which a pickpocket senses the man he can beat, the timing of his operations, etc. Every pickpocket has some *grift sense*; most believe they have more than they have; the top-notchers have it to a very high and a very sensitive degree. Then there is the handling of the *fix*. Pickpockets are universally known to the police (with the exception of a very few lone wolves who do not *fix*, or do so obscurely) and they do business with the police on a well-established basis. Some have excellent connections with *fixers* of considerable influence, and in some communities where there is a close affinity between organized crime and organized politics, the pickpocket may attain considerable underworld status. This is all very much on the quiet, however; it is a far cry from the balmy days in the early 1900's when pickpockets had sanctuary and, for practical purposes, immunity, in most large American cities.

There is one area, however, where the pickpocket has no peers, and this is the deep source of his professional pride—manual dexterity. If a pickpocket knows where his victim carries money, he can take it. The good ones can take it from almost any place of concealment on the person; the real experts, who use misdirection like professional magicians, can perform spectacular acts of theft; there literally is no place where money can be carried safely if they are determined to take it—from shoes, from money belts, from secret pockets, from inside pockets where it is pinned down, sewed in, or connected to the person with a chain. Some of these techniques will be examined in detail later on. For the present, suffice it to say that good pickpockets have raised the business of stealing from a victim's person to a high art in which timing, bodily contact, the psychology of misdirection, *grift sense*, the use of concealment both personal and extrapersonal, the rhythm of movement, speed, and an impressively delicate dexterity are all blended into a single, almost instantaneous, and practically invisible act of theft.

This act is carried out while the victim is walking down the street, ascending in an elevator, leaving a bank, or boarding a train—in fact, while he is engaged in any normal routine activity. While the theft itself may be considered difficult, especially where the victim is carrying a large amount of money which weighs heavily upon his sense of responsibility, the amazing aspects are the ways in which the theft is concealed from other onlookers and the speed with which it is executed. Ten seconds is a long time for the consummation of this act—too long for the really good ones. It must be accomplished in a flash of movement which eludes the eye and which, within the very narrow limits of manual movement, is usually complex beyond the understanding of the layman. For instance, when an expert *reefs a kick*, he takes many tiny pleats in the lining of the victim's pocket with incredible speed—the only visible effect of which is that the victim's bankroll seems to rise of itself and emerge into the thief's hand.

The pickpocket, then, is a well established operator on the *grift*. While he does not rate among the big-timers of modern crime, his place in the criminal subculture is secure. His income may not be so high as that of other professionals, but he develops compensations for this limitation, and, within the narrow margins of his own specialty, he has no peers. He has raised the act of theft from the person to a high art. He works diligently and steadily·at his craft. He is always represented in prisons, and his face appears more frequently, perhaps, than any other type of criminal in "rogue's galleries" and police files. His connections with the *fix* are reflected in the small number of his convictions in relation to the very large number of his arrests. Among the better class of pickpockets, the conventions of the subculture are rather rigorously observed, and a man's reputation depends more upon his character than it does upon his income.

CHAPTER IV

USAGE LEVELS OF THE PICKPOCKET

Nonargot Usage

Although there are always exceptions, American pickpockets generally speak a rather low-grade American English. It might be said that the general speech of pickpockets follows the pattern of the lower middle class, although this must be recognized as over-simplification. Certainly it does not conform to the patterns of educated people, nor does it manifest the skillful amateurism with which many uneducated persons use the language—persons who, though lacking formal education, read and think and employ language with some natural grace and feeling. However, if the pickpocket's speech smacks of the lower middle class, it has an almost inevitable urban flavor; seldom does a pickpocket speak in a way which identifies him as decidedly rural. This is natural since pickpockets live and work almost exclusively in cities, and most of them seem to have an urban origin.

In respect to geographical dialects, the pickpocket speaks the dialect of his part of the country much the same as everyone else in that locality. Those who are *locals* (operate exclusively and more or less permanently in one city) conform closely to the local pattern of speech; those who travel on the road may lose their local dialect, or modify it to some extent, although their regional derivation is usually obvious from their speech. In the argot itself there is a recognized East Coast, Midwest, and West Coast pattern, the differentiation being largely based on different lexical items common to one area but not to the others; there are also a few argot terms which are identical lexically but which differ in pronunciation from one of these roughly defined belts to another. *Road mobs* are perhaps more sensitive to regional dialects, since they are always outsiders in any community they visit and do not like to have their speech call attention to them. However, even the smartest *road mobs* have nothing like the sensitivity to dialects that some other operators—for example *confidence men*—develop and often make practical use of. It must be remembered that the pickpocket seldom needs to talk very much to strangers in situations where his speech would attract attention. Unlike the *confidence man*, who may spend days in close association with his victim, the pickpocket never has a word of conversation with his victim—unless he is caught or suspected, and then the situation has usually gone beyond the subtleties of linguistic usage. It is a well recognized fact that pickpockets do not like to talk to *suckers* and do not encourage conversation with them. Comments one *con man* in this connection: "Guns are the most suspicious grifters on the road. They think everyone is wrong but themselves." Says another: "Cannons will not talk to marks, nor will they give up their kisser to any mark on the street. . . ." My transcriptions show several instances of pickpockets talking to *suckers*, but only during or after the *sucker* has been *rumbled* and is accusing the pickpocket of trying to rob him or actually robbing him. One *class cannon* of my acquaintance has trouble *filling in* with good mobs because he has a tendency to argue with the *sucker* too much.

Most successful pickpockets are careful to avoid argot in their general conversation and rigorously eliminate it when they are being observed by anyone not on the *rackets*. However, their general speech is usually heavily loaded with slang, much of it only recently delivered from its argot sources. They like the lingo of sports (especially baseball, racing, and boxing) and the smart cracks of the more sensational newspaper columnists and radio entertainers. Some, notably among the lower levels, think, speak, and live in the argot, and are unable to avoid it even if they so desire; without it they would be inarticulate, and it is doubtful that they have any real awareness of language outside the argot levels. To pickpockets of this class, standard English is virtually a foreign language.

On the other hand, a few of the more intelligent professionals— often in the upper brackets of the profession, though not necessarily so—read something besides the tabloids, and develop a real interest in the literary language as they understand it. Again, let me emphasize that these men are rare among pickpockets, most of whom, even after deleting all the argot phraseology they can identify, still speak what they conceive to be legitimate English with patterns of stress, intonation, and juncture which strongly suggest the argot to anyone already familiar with it, these patterns being natural and totally out of their awareness.

Following is a sample of the speech of an unusually intelligent professional, taken from a lengthy transcribed account of how a certain mob got narcotics from a legitimate physician who did not suspect that he was supplying addicts. The speaker has very little education, but reads omnivorously and has an unusually high degree of linguistic awareness for a pickpocket.

First you had a phone call. It was just a matter of form then to get a narcotics prescription for at least 50 tablets. But in this particular instance we never did see the doctor. Talked to him on the telephone and told him my brother-in-law was visiting me and he had tuberculosis. That he was hospitalized, but was out of the hospital at this time, and was visiting home. Owing to the fact that we had an estate to settle, his presence in the city was required for a short time.

I told him, "My brother-in-law is allergic to certain of the medicines used in the treatment of pulmonary tuberculosis and under no circumstances should there be any substitutions other than those advised by his doctor."

And he says, "What drugs does he have to have?" And so I told him I had a letter there from his doctor that described what care he should get and how his dishes were to be boiled, and all that. "Here are the drugs he needs," I told him. "100 capsules of calcium lactate. 50 5-milligram capsules of Vitamin K, Menadino. And 50 one-quarter grain tablets of morphine hydrochloride, or one-sixteenth grain tablets of dilaudid."

So he said, "You just bring me the letter down and give it to my nurse, and I'll write out the prescriptions."

But as it turned out, I never did see the nurse. My partner's wife took the list into the nurse, and the nurse made out the prescriptions. Then she took them into the doctor and he signed them, and she paid the doctor one dollar per prescription. Each time she would go back, she would take this letter with her and the nurse would write out the prescription and the doctor would sign them.

Some pickpockets do not speak any English, or only a smattering of English. An even larger number speak broken English, or English with a heavy foreign accent. There are immigrants, some of them old-timers from Russia, Poland, Slovakia, Greece, or Germany. Other more recent immigrants, many of whom speak almost no English, come from Cuba, Puerto Rico, and Mexico. Most of these Latins congregate on the East Coast, notably in New York City, and within the district of Harlem. While some of the Jewish and Slavic or Germanic professionals are quite expert—albeit illiterate in the language of their land of adoption—the Latins do not rank so high, with few if any of them achieving the rank of *class cannons*—a rating which reflects professional and ethical preeminence, but not necessarily social polish or intellectual superiority. A few of the most respected professionals cannot read or write.

There are also the all-Negro mobs, operating chiefly in large Eastern cities and most of all in New York. Most of these Negroes are native Americans of the zoot-suit variety, but some are immigrants from the Bahamas and other Caribbean areas. I have observed that they speak an argot somewhat different from the native white pickpockets and that its lexical content suggests that it derives from the thieves' argot of London around 1800, perhaps coming in via the West Indies. No attempt will be made in this study to present material on either immigrant or Negro groups and their usage (either argot or nonargot) although some terminology, especially from the Negroes, is known and used (with reservations) by native white pickpockets. These terms will be indicated in the section dealing with the lexical details. The argot of the all-Negro mobs is deserving of separate and meticulous study.

While this book is restricted to the technical argot of the pickpocket—the argot spoken in connection with the practice of his craft—it is perhaps important to include here one or two examples of his general speech. Here is one in which two men are discussing an experience in Philadelphia. They are both *class cannons*.

X: Now, I come out of that hotel. I just got tired setting up there. After the coppers left, and I cleaned and moved everything, then I'm clean as a whistle . . . just as free and easy as you are now, see? Now I'm gonna get coffee, so I take a walk, and soon as I hit the street, I got a tail . . . . I never had no meet with the guy . . . . He was supposed to call me. I never had no meet with him here . . . two blocks from my walkup . . . .

Question: They knew him?

X: Yes, they knew both of us. This man, he's a big man, he could put the finger on me and have me killed before I get out of town, and I'm dead, without my coffee, I guess. And I'm paid for. No investigations . . . just another hoodlum. And I don't want that to happen . . . . There's a man, I'm not exaggerating a bit, he's got four or five thousand dollars a day take. You know he's a big man . . . .

Y: Tell him how he beat that rap in Buffalo.

X: Yeah. I told him that before. There was twenty-three indictments, and he beat every one of them . . . the judge throwed every one of them out of court. They was just as worthless as the paper they was written on . . . . He's making a thousand dollars while I'm making a buck. He's got thirty, forty, fifty people working for him. He's got this money rolling in like popcorn. So I took him outside and I said, "Act natural if you possibly can. Nobody can hear us, but they're looking at us. We are completely surrounded by the United States Government." I said, "They've got three squad cars here, and they're full of dicks. They've been up to my hotel

and shook down my hotel, and I must've had a angel on my shoulder . . . ."
He got excited right away when I told him, I said, "We're surrounded. We
ain't got a chance. They're back of you, in front of you, on the side of you,
and everywhere else. When we first started out, there was only two. Now
God knows how many agents we got around here, I don't!"

Following is an account of an experience of a different kind, a
fall in which the tool was arrested, but the stalls escaped. The
speaker, a very good operator, is about the same type as those
just quoted.

So everything is free to the full membership, you know, everything is
free. You could go and eat; everything is free on the house. You had to put
down a dime, and you got ten numbers, or something. Every turn of the
wheel you pay way-station fare. Oh, man, there were marks in there—out of
west hell, from all over the country. So every time they turn the wheel,
we'd step in there and get four or five pokes and step out. So one time this
God damn thing. I had two stalls with me, and they let a woman see my
duke. I had this stiff, and I get this stiff up too high, and this broad behind
me sees my duke and she screams, "Ah-h-h-h; he's in that man's pocket."
And Fossatti, he's standing in the back, and he ain't seen the whiz yet.
So I got this guy's okus, and I can't get it back either. It was one of them
positions, you know, and a lot of times when you got a guy's okus you're in a
position where you can put it back. But this is one of them places where I
couldn't put it back in the pocket it came out of. And I didn't have any
other available pockets. So I am stuck. I had it in my hand and I am stuck
with it . . . see? So I took off and they run me all over the park. Finally run
me down. Oh, I got rid of the poke, and finally some punk kid found it out
there. I didn't get caught with the poke.
So the broad said, "Yeah, that's the man. That's him."
"Yeah," I said, "I was with her, I sure was. I couldn't help it."
So this Fossatti says, "You're with who? What do you mean?"
"Well, I didn't know she was a married woman. If I had, I wouldn't have
been out here with her." I had to have some kind of an alibi.
"So," he says, "I want to hear that story. You got that man's pocketbook
and now you say you were with her. I didn't see you with no woman."
I said, "Well, I'm sure glad that you didn't see me with her. That's proof
that I am in the clear." I told Fossatti that when I told her to get away
from me, she said that was her husband. Then she told me that was her
husband and I told her to get away. So they didn't find no poke when they
searched me. They didn't find no poke.
So Fossatti said, "What did you do with that wallet? The guy just
lost a wallet."
And I said, "Man, I don't know nothing about that pocketbook. If you
lost your pocketbook, someone else got it, I didn't get it."

Pickpockets do not write much, so that it is difficult to generalize about their written usage. A favorite method of communica-

tion, for instance is to cut or tear out a newspaper clipping, put it into an envelope, and mail it to the person who might be interested. Sometimes there are words or comments written on the margin. I am the recipient of hundreds of such clippings, as well as many postcards and letters. Many of these brief comments, regardless of their grammar, are masterpieces of concentrated communication, as for instance a postcard which reads: "Never round on an office. It might be fur."

However, most of my communications concern the technical phases of the *racket* which will be taken up later on in detail. While pickpockets may correspond on a nontechnical basis with each other, I see very little of their written usage on this level. Furthermore, most of my correspondence is, by natural selection, with those operators who are the most articulate and at the same time expert technically. Here is a note from such a man who writes mostly about nontechnical matters:

Enclosed find a couple hundred words of Blah, Blah, Blah. Thought you might get a chuckle out of it. I did. Rec'd your Xmas card and thanks for remembering us. Well, Doc, I have a few more months of this paper its up July 10th of this year. Thought I was in for some trouble a wk or so ago. Did you see when they knocked off some big connections in Chicago. Well I was doing a little business with one of them. Had borrowed some dough from him from time to time the last was $1400.00 and I had paid it back except $400.00, and that I sent in from St. Cloud. Anyway, the Feds got the letter where I sent him $400.00 in Post Office money orders. Of course they surmise it was for junk and it was not—it was borrowed to square a beef. Anyway I haven't heard anything about it and if they were going to do anything about it they would have nailed me by now for I have been available. Even visited this party went to his fathers "wake" all the boys were there. What a collection they could have made for that night Ha!

I still do not have a car or I would have dropped in on you, without an invite but alas and alackaday the Chino is on my back and it takes all I can get to keep him and the home fires burning. Have my Sis and Bro-in-law & their brood with us till spring. He had an operation & sold his place going to buy another in Illinois & move in March or April. I seldom stay at home, just run in and out. Let me hear from you.

Here is one which suggests Runyon in its delicate and sometimes elegant understatement:

I find your most welcome letter on my return here as of today. My partner is here with me and we will be glad to collaborate with you on the glossary and we promise to do our best with what little knowledge we have to offer on this subject. Being in the East this past winter while he was in Florida we did not get the opportunity to go to the Derby; but we do look forward to having the pleasure of seeing you again in the not too distant future, and we re-call with much pleasure the splendid visit we had the last time we met.

I also recall that you were correcting some galley-proofs of a new book of your own. Would you be so good as to inform me where I may be able to secure a copy?

If I remember correctly, this book was on a medical and psychological subject.

Returning to the "lingo" in question. I might add that most all of the "professions" have a "lingo" that are somewhat co-related. It is always interesting to note how some of these words came about and even though these expressions are used by experienced "professionals" very few can explain their origin. Should you desire this information I should be glad to impart my knowledge in this category. So send on your papers and we will go to work on them.

George left here some two months ago to visit his mother. He did intend coming back to Buffalo at least for the purpose of working for reasons of being inconvenient in more ways than one.

I do hope this finds you in the best of circumstances. Best regards.

In order to keep our perspective, let us see how a professional on the *heavy rackets* expresses himself in writing. In these letters he is, conveniently, discussing the argot of pickpockets. This man is not the average *heavy man* by any means; he had the same standing in his racket that the pickpockets quoted above have in theirs—he was at the top. The first letter is in answer to a letter I wrote him enclosing an outline of material I proposed to present in a paper for the Modern Language Association. I asked him what he would say about the argot of pickpockets if he were invited to speak for the same organization. He replied:

I think that my version of the talk, remembering that it is being given before a body of linguists, would run (chopped to the bone) somewhat as follows:

The subject of the present investigation is the professional pickpocket. This group has been chosen for the study for three reasons. The first is that the profession, an ancient one, has a literature, meager though it is, extending nearly four centuries into the past—a condition necessary to valid etymological work, Second, the profession, while reflecting to a meaningful degree the social changes which have taken place during the past few hundred years, has at no stage undergone so radical a transformation as to throw the overall picture out of focus. Third, first-hand sources of information, not commonly present, are in this field, open to the investigator. The details of the work will but bore you. Suffice it to say that the history of the pocketpicking profession has been carefully looked into, the pickpocket's social background, past and present, has been studied, and particular care has been devoted to his present-day professional attitudes and language in all their respects. Turning aside for a moment from all linguistics, it may be noted that insights valuable to the sociologists, the criminologists, and the psychiatrist have grown out of the work, as it were incidentally.

If I were doing it, I think I would now list the insights, linguistic and otherwise, turned up during the course of your investigations somewhat as you summarize them at the end. Then I would take each separately and illustrate it with an example or two clearly and thoroughly explained— insight into the makeup of the grift etc. would come clearly enough in the course of these explanations. For instance: Some terms of the pickpocket's vocabulary reflect environmental factors in a very basic and direct way. So intimate is the relationship, in fact, that content sometimes follows background fluctuations with the utmost fidelity.

Catholic, as the pickpocket uses it, is a fascinating term, though used now only by old-timers, and rarely at that. As it appears in the pickpocket's vocabulary the word is applied by one old-timer to another by way of indicating that the person spoken of is of the profession and particularly that he is skilled and dependable. "What about his guy The Midge is fillin' in?" one of the mob say, "He don't look so good to me." And the reply may run: "Don't worry about the guy; he's a *catholic*."

The term probably evolved out of social conflicts engendered by the great influx of European labor during the latter half of the last century. The tide of peasant immigration aroused resentments of which the American Protestant Association and the political party called the Know-Nothings were one expression. These animosities and the counter-resentments which they of course produced inevitably were reflected in the speech-habits of the group involved . . . .

Today, *catholic* apparently survives only in this argot offshoot. As used by the pickpocket, the term reflects conflicts within our society at large, together with an implication of the prejudices and counter-prejudices; it shows the ever-present consciousness of group-solidarity and the importance of status among professional criminals; it illustrates language waxing and waning in emotional content in accord with fluctuations in the culture matrix.

Or again: The verbs beat, clip, clout, nail, which are applied by the pickpocket to the victim *as* victim, indicate the force and depth of the cannon's feeling of animosity towards the sucker and suggest, in terms of the Freudian psychology, a possible anti-paternal orientation, etc. For historical angle, take them from Michigan Bankroll back [through *mish*] to commission step by step, etc. Of course, all this is very easy to suggest and very difficult to accomplish in the little time left not to mention the little time they give you to speak. It is just a suggestion.

The second letter deals specifically with the possible derivation of two pickpocket words from Old Norse forms, and shows a high level of both literacy and intelligence. This man, it should be recalled, is not a pickpocket but a *heavy man*, and is commenting on an argot not his own. He is, needless to say, an exceptional *heavy man*. However, his comments give some indication of the intellectual range which separates topnotch pickpockets from topnotch *heavy operators*.

I have been looking over your suggestions on those couple notes on the cannon glossary and will cut them up briefly while waiting to hear from you again.

I think you are partly wrong about *bang*, and *bing*. I doubt that there are the two roots, and it seems to me that *banga* is more plausible a source than *bingr*.

The meaning of harvest does sound reasonable in the case of *to bing a hanger*; however, I don't know of a single other usage of *bing* that would support the supposition. The ancient cant had *bing* in the meaning of *to go*: 'Bing a *waste*—get you hence,'

Again Dekker, 1612:

> "*Bing* out good morts, and tour, and tour,
> Bing out good morts and tour;
> For all your duds are *binged* a waste;
> The bene cove hath the hour."

Then there is later usage:

> "On, where will be the culls of the *bing*,
> A hundred stretches hence?"

The meaning here is obscure, but I take of the *bing* to mean *on the grift* or *on the town*. Perhaps this usage derives from *bingo*, which was hard liquor (whence perhaps *binge*). . . . The *bingo boys* were the bottle bums of an earlier day. Then our own (the heavy man's) cant has *bing*, a prison *slough-up* or dungeon, and *bing*, a jolt of junk, as well as the one we are concerned with. Does it not appear to you that if *binge* and *bing* were related, intermediate forms would be bound to show up somewhere along the line? Do you know of any such forms? I am now pretty well grounded in the British cant all along the line—that is, up to 1850 or so—and I know of none.

Bang, on the other hand, is something else again. The language, standard as well as slang, is shot through with obviously related terms which may quite well trace to *banga*, or *bangan*. We have the *bangs* girls used to wear, and in the slang *bangtail; bang*, a blow as with a hammer, and in the slang *bang*, a blow as with the fist, *bang*, a jolt, as of liquor, *bang* a thrill (jolt, kick: "I sure got a bang out of that."), *banging*, a beating, *banged*, arrested (knocked down), etc., etc. We also have the obviously related *bang*, as in to *bang a box*, for the process is simply that of banging or hammering off the knob, and I do not think there can be much doubt that we have another relative in *bang*, as in to *bang a souper* or a *hanger*.

You must think of the technique in order to get a clear sight on the relationship. Remember that the watch is *cut off* (actually broken off) from the chain. One does not *bang a poke*, as would quite likely be the case if, as you suggest, the source were *binge*. A watch is *banged*, not because it is *harvested,* stolen, but because it is *broken off* from the chain. Now when we come to *banging a hanger* or a satchel it is true that nothing is cut or broken off, but think once more of the technique of *banging* a watch—the ring is taken between the thumb and the fore- or middle-finger and twisted deftly from the stem. Until quite recently women's handbags almost invariably were fastened with knob clasps. Now, think of the process of opening one. It is exactly that of *banging* a watch—the same fingers are used, there is the same deft twisting motion. It is true that a hanger is also said to be *binged,* but *bing* in many other instances is simply a variant of *bang* and I think that that is its status here.

A *bing* then is a minor sort of a *bang.* This is also its status in the pickpocket's vocabulary in a sense, for it takes nothing like the skill to *bing* a handbag as it did (the practise is no longer fashionable) to *bang* a *prop* or *souper.* The reason I suggested looking for a Dutch or German word is that I do not reject the possibility nonetheless that *bing* may possibly represent a naturalization from one of these languages. It may be a sort of collateral relative of *bang,* but I think there can be no doubt at all that it is a relative.

I see I haven't space to go into *bucket,* but will defend that derivation at another time.

So much for the nonargot usage of pickpockets, spoken and written. It has been described in some detail both as a point of departure for treating the several argot levels, and because many persons wonder how a thief talks when he is not using argot. In fact, there is a widespread popular misconception that criminals speak argot all the time (that's how you can tell they're criminals) and that no criminal could possibly use or understand standard English—misconceptions akin to the belief among many tourists that all American Indians should be addressed in some form of synthetic pidgin-English because Indians talk that way in the movies and the comic strips. Pickpockets, it should be noted, are perhaps less language-conscious than most professionals, and are more likely than others to use argot either consciously or unconsciously in the presence of noncriminals; even among pickpockets this infiltration of argot usage into general speech is peripheral and minimal.

In fact, as one goes up the scale, it becomes obvious that there is an increasing tendency to screen out all argot and slang in the presence of outsiders; among the *confidence men,* for instance, there are many operators with a command of standard English which will admit them to any society anywhere; at the same time they are able to use the technical vocabularies of various legitimate industries or professions convincingly, and may use effectively two or more regional dialects. These men also have a rich and colorful argot which is used strictly among themselves. I have never encountered a pickpocket with anything approaching this range of usage.

Argot Usage

The argot of the thieving professions is very old, with reference to that of the pickpockets (in English) appearing in print in the 16th Century, although it must be much older than that. While in this study we are not concerned with historical aspects—which incidentally suggest much provocative philological work—I mention the fact that the argot of the pickpockets is an historical continuum in order to emphasize its recognized function in the subculture. It is not simply what the sociologist might identify as an overt and current verbal deviation. It is the vehicle of the content of the subculture, and especially the technology.

If we return for a moment to Trager's indices of culture which we discussed with reference to the pickpocket in Chapter II, we will find it a convenient device for limiting and describing the aspects of culture which will be treated in connection with the notes on argot to follow. Index No. 1, *Interaction*, will be treated more or less continuously throughout, since language is basic to interaction. No. 2, *Association*, will be of importance only insofar as mob organization is concerned. No. 3, *Subsistence*, will be treated in some detail, since the technical argot of the pickpocket functions largely in this cultural area. Index No. 4, *Bisexuality*, will receive little mention, except as women participate in the actual business of theft, and insofar as there is a division of labor on the basis of sex. Likewise, items No. 6, *Temporality*, and No. 5, *Territoriality*, have little to do with actual technology, except insofar as the working areas are defined and the concepts of time and space are reflected in the argot. No. 7, *Education*, includes the argot connected with the induction of professionals. No. 8, *Recreation and Play*, is a cultural aspect which will be almost entirely omitted. No. 9, *Defense*, will be discussed only insofar as the argot reflects the parasitic dependence of the pickpocket on the dominant culture and insofar as this dependence involves the technology of theft.

In other words, the great body of argot terminology to be

handled in this study reflects the cultural activities included in Index No. 3, with some excursions, as indicated, into other indices. This restriction is necessary, since the totality of argot reflecting activities in all ten phases of the subculture would bulk too large for any single study. We are, then, limiting the argot to be discussed to the technical aspects of professional operation, though we are well aware that the argot is used to express many other phases of life–activities within the entire subculture, and is particularly pertinent when it is used to express those aspects of behavior which deviate substantially from the dominant culture.

This technical argot is used only by professionals for the discussion of the business of theft and its immediately related activities. Ordinarily it is spoken only in the presence of professionals, persons accepted by the underworld, or persons engaged in some other *racket*. It is richly expressive not only of the technology, but of the attitudes, motivations, and relationships inherent in the professional behavior pattern. The thief lives, thinks, and works in terms of the argot. Criminal activity—behavior on the level of the subculture—is the only reality. The dominant culture is not respected or even recognized as a dominant culture by many; it is actually seen by professionals as a somewhat foreign area in which one can conveniently work and make a good living. Since the pickpocket has little empathy with the dominant culture—and in fact little real understanding of it—it is not strange that he regards it with suspicion and even hostility and that he restricts the use of argot, and especially technical argot, to discussions with his own kind.

In passing, we should note that the pickpocket differs from most, though not all, other criminals in that he sometimes uses some of the technical argot in the presence of the victim and during the actual act of theft. When the tool locates the victim's bankroll or wallet he may name that location to the stalls in argot. That is, he may say in an undertone *"Left bridge,"* or *"Right bridge,"* or *"Kiss the dog,"* or whatever instructions may be necessary to inform the stalls, so that they can put the victim into position for the tool to work. The tool may likewise communicate with the stalls during the theft, giving them instructions such as *"Raust,"* or *"Come through,"* or *"Stick,"* or *"Stick and split me out"* or *"Turn him in for a pit,"* etc. All tools give the stalls an *office* or signal when they take the wallet. This may be a chirp, a cluck, etc; some tools and stalls work together so closely and so long that they do not need this *office*, but sense that *it's off* from the body movement of the tool. Usually some verbal signal is given. This communication takes place very rapidly and unobtrusively, for good tools can take a *score* within five to ten seconds —if it takes longer, the really good ones don't want it.

It seems incredible that the victim does not register this dialogue centered so personally upon him, but I do not know of any court cases where the victim either caught the pickpockets in the act or became suspicious as they rifled his pockets, in which the victim reported having heard any of this interchange; this failure to register what he must hear is indicative of the dichotomy which divides the dominant culture from the subculture.

All in all, the pickpocket's technical argot is highly specialized not only because it reflects work which is highly specialized, but also because that work lies outside the law. The argot grows out of the techniques and attitudes of the professional toward the victim, toward the law, toward other professionals, toward others who live by a *racket*, and toward legitimate society. Although its vocabulary occasionally overlaps the technical argot of some other specialized types of thief, it also resembles in some respects the general argot of the *grift*. This general overlapping with the other argots of the *grift* is natural, since thieves of all kinds identify themselves with the *grift*. There is, however, notably less in common with the argots of the *heavy rackets*, the vocabulary used in common lying largely in that body of general underworld argot used to some extent by all *rackets*. As soon as one goes into the specialized aspect of the *heavy rackets*, words and idioms common to pickpockets appear to occur infrequently; the same is true for words and phrases common to the *heavy rackets* and their incidence among pickpockets. I have also observed that there are perhaps significant differences in intonation and stress patterns occurring between speakers from the *heavy rackets* and those from the *grift*, though these aspects will not be treated in this study.

Short samples of the technical argot are sufficient here for comparison with other types of usage cited earlier. Quotations will appear in abundance throughout the following chapters, which deal in great detail with the technical argot and its relation to the professional behavior pattern.

The first sample is taken from the correspondence in which a pickpocket gives a slightly burlesqued account of what happened to him in police court:

Judge: Now you just tell the Court in your own way what you were doing.
Me: Well, Judge, your honor, I was out gandering around for a soft mark and made a tip that was going to cop a short. I eased myself into the tip and just topped a leather in Mr. Bates' left prat when I blowed I was getting a jacket from these two honest bulls. So I kick the okus back in his kick and I'm clean. Just then this flat-foot nails me, so here I am on a bum rap. All I crave is justice, and I hope she ain't blind.
Judge: You seem to be honest. You're discharged.

The second is taken from an interview and shows the spoken technical argot used seriously.

Yeah . . . I was forcing it up, high up under his chin, like this. That insider was tight, very tight . . . . After I unsloughed his vest I could tell . . . . his leather, Doc, I'm not lying, it was that thick. But I couldn't come with it. This bates, he was tall, lots taller than I am and that is bad when you're taking it from the front. And I felt him try to go for his kick, as far as he could . . . . Them broads had him right in the frame, but there was no doubt in my mind I rumbled him. And when I rumble one like that, a pit score or an insider, I let him go. There is too many okuses in too many other pockets. Well, I must've fooled around just a second too long, so he felt to me like he tried to make a grab for my mitt, like I said. The broads split me clean, or we'd've been in for it. He just thought he felt something, but he couldn't get ahold of nothing.

You never did meet this new broad did you? Well, she's quite a gal. On the cannon or on the boost, or what have you. My broad and her works all right together. So when this bates tumbles, I say I better blow because there is just a chance he seen my kisser. He might beef, you know, and then the fuzz . . . . So after we split, them broads hit them department stores hard for a couple of hours on the boost. What with the knockup my broad already had, knocked up before the tumble, I mean, they show up over here with that four C's junk-money. Now we can cool off and lay dead for a week or two, or maybe they can work the stores two-handed. If it ain't too hot.

CHAPTER V

THE ACT OF THEFT

The Mob and the Mark

Theft from the person is a highly specialized act which has pre-occupied a certain class of thieves throughout the ages. While these thieves have never distinguished themselves by spectacular acts, they have built a prosperous illicit profession (perhaps second only to prostitution in venerability) which has survived a multiplicity of social changes and innumerable efforts to stamp it out. As has been suggested earlier, thievery is more than an illegal act; when practiced professionally and consistently, it becomes a way of life, a parasitic subculture.

In order to observe this act of theft more closely—along with the argot which translates it from a complex of body movement into symbolic articulation—it will be necessary to break it down into the several stages through which all thefts from the person must theoretically pass, individual exceptions to the contrary notwithstanding. The act is usually perpetrated against a representative of the dominant culture, and within range of the hazards which attend such an act. It must be shown happening within the considerable variety of situations under which professionals are known to work. In short, we must observe various types of pickpockets at work and consider some of the variations in their pattern of activity.

This chapter is almost totally concerned with Trager's Cultural Index No. 3, Subsistence, as indicated in Chapter II. Furthermore, this index in the pickpocket's subculture is strictly limited to theft from the person. While a few pickpockets develop other types of lucrative operation, the pickpocket's subsistence comes almost exclusively from the act of theft. Probably this is why theft from the person occupies so much of the pickpocket's thinking and conversation, and why it looms so large in the factors which characterize this subculture; since there is little or no diversity of occupation, the tendency is to refine, insofar as possible, on this one source of subsistence, the result being that the entire subculture becomes what we might call craft-directed. Shop talk dominates; in fact, few pickpockets see much point in discussing anything else; hence every act of theft is hashed and rehashed by all concerned.

In order to avoid confusing the reader, the act of theft from the person will be presented three times in the course of this discussion. First, immediately following, it will be described in a paragraph or two so that the reader may get a quick review of what the act is. Second, in the section on *mob work*, it will be expanded and treated in some detail in order to illustrate how the mob achieves the act. Last, in the sections on *The Tool* and *The Stall* it is described in very intimate detail. This last treatment is the heart of the chapter and would hardly be comprehensible to the lay reader without the preparatory descriptions referred to.

First, however, let us oversimplify the act of theft and describe it in terms which can be well understood by persons not familiar with the profession. Initially, of course, the thief must want to steal someone's pocketbook. He must have anticipated a great variety of disasters, both legal and nonlegal, which may befall him during or after this act of theft. He must have taken what seem to him adequate precautions against these disasters, or at least be prepared to meet them offhand as they arise, if and when they do. We are right if we presume that most of these disasters will stem either from the victim who is being robbed, or from the law, which is supposed to prevent this very sort of thing. We will assume that this particular thief is sufficiently astute and skillful to avoid detection except by the most exceptional victim—and we will not let him operate on this type of victim at this time. Let us take it for granted that he has cleared with the law to the tune of a hundred dollars a day for the privilege of working unimpeded, except under certain circumstances which will be described later on. Unless this pickpocket is exceptional, he will have one or more partners; we will give him only one in this instance, just to keep the action as simple as possible. The thief will not think of these elements as we have stated them, but will image them in terms of his rich and vivid argot.

When this pair appear on the streets, their first concern is to find a potential victim. Unless they are very primitive in their methods, they will want to have some assurance that they are robbing someone who has enough money to make the theft worthwhile. Professionals become quite adept at selecting such victims by sight, then following up their selection with a rapid and deft manual exploration of the person to ascertain where the money or wallet may be carried. They are right a high percentage of the time. This act is performed by the tool, whose action of *fanning* the victim is covered or *shaded* by his stall. Once the loot is located, the stall rapidly and unobtrusively maneuvers the victim (called a mark) into position so that the tool can work. The stall, working from signals given by the tool, or simply so familiar with the tool's technique that he automatically functions in a variety of situations, then holds the victim in position with his body, using his upper arms, his back, his elbows, or his legs to block any movement the mark may make, and to keep the mark's hands clear of the pocket to be picked; this is called *framing the mark*, or *putting up for the mark*, who is held, unawares of course, in position for the few seconds necessary for a good tool to take his money. "You have to wait till they frame for him." "Well, you can't frame with a single-handed gun." "The idea is the frame, the way a man is framed for. If he walks out natural to get in a train or a bus or a taxicab— he has to be going somewhere, in other words, he has to be moving. But then it's up to the stall to maneuver that man, to put that man in a position so that he can be worked on, so that you can handle the mark in the proper way, and when you handle the mark, naturally I mean clip him."

When the theft is complete, the tool signals the stall, who takes the wallet, and they move on to another spot and locate another victim. The stall usually carries the wallets until they call a halt, when the wallets are thoroughly searched, the money divided, and the wallets disposed of. This last step may vary with different types of mob.

The act described above in an oversimplified form is basic to all theft from the person by professional pickpockets. The entire profession is built around it, although it may be extended, expanded, or varied in a score of different ways. Some pickpockets work by themselves, without a partner or other support; some work *two handed*, *three handed*, or even *four handed*. In Europe some mobs may work as many as eight or ten *strong*. "Everybody's a tool over there. Everybody's a hook, except them four guys on the points of the compass. They are eight or ten strong over there." But all professional pickpockets, however expert or however clumsy, operate on the basis of the situation just outlined.

From here on, this study will be concerned with the technical

argot and its use in connection with the act of theft in all its ramifications, but especially as it concerns *mob work*, or the teamwork
of specialists following a sharp division of labor.

The reader should be reminded that the pickpocket is strictly
nonviolent; that he is set apart from the *heavy rackets* in that he
does not use violence to take money, but lets a victim—even a
well-heeled one—go rather than excite his suspicions, or call attention to the fact that thievery is being committed; and that this
psychology is diametrically opposed to the behavior of professionals on the *heavy rackets*, who do not hesitate to use any amount
of force necessary—even unto the shooting of the victim—to take
his valuables. The act of theft from the person by stealth is essentially what is referred to as a *sneak job*, which implies the successful
robbery without the victim's knowledge. The pickpocket differs
from other operators on the *grift* in that he steals directly from
the person, and in that he cannot capitalize on the cupidity of the
victim, as do those who use the numerous *short con* and *big con*
rackets.

The pickpocket uses psychology in his work, but it is rather the
psychology of bodily contact, of tactilism, of strategy in maneuvering his victim into position, of misdirection which distracts the
victim's attention so as to take his mind off his money. The pickpocket likes to perform successive acts of thievery in the same
locality without attracting attention; he then likes to move on to a
new locality before his victims discover their losses and call upon
the law. He moves softly and melts into any crowd with great
skill. If he is really good, he dresses so unobtrusively that he is
difficult to observe and remember; but at the same time his
clothes are of good quality, and, once singled out, it is difficult
for the average person—and even the law—to imagine that a man
of such substantial appearance could be guilty of trying to steal a
pocketbook.

It will also be noted that *the argot hardly reflects this gentle art,
but rather evokes images of violence and aggression far beyond those
elements actually involved.*

Mob Work

When a mob is active professionally, they are *working* and the
same verb is applied in a secondary sense to stealing in certain
localities or from certain people, as *working a tip, working a get on,*

working right spots, etc. "On this occasion there happened to be quite a little tip in there. So we root right in and work it." For purposes of illustration, we will use a *road mob* which is *working* racetrack crowds in various cities. The terms *hustle* and *grift* are also used in some senses as the equivalents of *work*. Let us expand the simple *two handed mob* just briefly described and say that this mob is *hustling three handed*. This means that they have two stalls and one tool. One of the stalls is the *steer* for the mob.

Pickpockets over the centuries have established a sharp division of labor. The tool selects the mark to be robbed, and actually takes the *score*. "The first five scores was cold." The stalls work within a short radius of the tool as he prospects about in the crowd for marks. It is their responsibility to watch the tool closely at all times and to follow his cues. They must close in rapidly, unobtrusively, and almost automatically to *make the frame*. They often sight the mark as soon as the tool does; if not, they can tell from the direction of his movement where the *chump* is; when the *hook* ("A hook is a britch tool who actually hooks his finger onto the poke instead of pinching the poke") steps in behind a man, they know definitely that this is the mark. The tool makes the decision in selecting the victim; the stalls work under his guidance somewhat like bird dogs working with a hunter. And like bird dogs, they must know a great deal about the habits of the game as well as the habits of the hunter. They close in smoothly, without appearing to do so. "The frame seems natural to the sucker, but it really isn't. A smart dick will notice that." The exception to this is, of course, the rare tool who works entirely by himself; he will be considered separately later on. Normally the tool has the constant support of one or more stalls.

When the tool sees a potential victim, he falls in behind him to *locate*, that is to *fan* the *chump* to see whether or not he has a fat wallet or a roll of money worth taking, and if so where he carries it. "I went up to this guy and fan him, and he's got on a pair of jeans underneath those overalls." Around racetracks, where our theoretical mob is working, much of the *locating* is done by sight, for people there are notoriously careless about handling money. However this information is gathered, it is communicated by sign, signal, or actual argot terms, such as for instance, *left bridge impression*, which means that the man has a good bankroll in his left-hand side pants pocket. Some stalls work so closely with their tools that they do not need to receive specific manual signals or to say anything; they read the tool's body-stance and attitude so automatically that they know as soon as he does what the situation is. Rarely stalls *locate* for the tool, but usually not in *organized mobs*. Routinely they depend on the tool to *locate* as he makes bodily contact with the victim.

Usually, as the tool makes the first contact with the mark, he *locates* immediately and communicates with the stalls so that they may put the mark into position for whatever type of *score* the situation demands. That is, he may say to the stalls, who have closed in as soon as they see from his movements that he is making contact and is *locating* with a mark, such a phrase as *turn him in for a pit* or *pit*, meaning that the mark is carrying his wallet in his inside coat pocket and that the tool wants the stalls to maneuver the mark so that he is in position for the tool to take this type of *score*, which in this instance will probably be taken from the side. "So I said 'pit' to Mickey. And of course he came through." Good stalls read the body movements of their tool just as readily as he reads theirs, and automatically sense the type of *score* that is to be taken. "When the tool says, 'Turn John in for a pit,' the sucker wouldn't associate that with himself at all. After hustling for a number of years, they won't need many words. A clever cannon talks as little as possible." "Sometimes in a police line-up, the sucker will say, 'Have him say something' and those few words might make a lot of difference."

Pickpockets operate cautiously and so unobtrusively that only a trained observer can tell that they are *working* in a crowd, or anywhere else for that matter, for, contrary to general belief, they do not necessarily work in crowds at all. They are, however, very aggressive, within the limits which mark their profession; they study the victim rapidly but with great care; they size him up from several angles; they project any of several possible approaches to him, thinking in terms of bodily movement; they are (unconsciously) highly sensitive to his rhythms of stride, his size and weight, the problems presented by his clothes or by the *location* previously mentioned, and the presence of onlookers who might see the *touch* come off from certain angles; they register firearms, knives, or other weapons on his person; they note the fabric of his clothes, his necktie, his stance and build, the very complexion of the back of his neck, which some tools retain with photographic clarity.

It is important to sense immediately and with great precision not only whom to rob and how, but even more important whom not to rob and why. It is better to refrain from picking the pockets of FBI men, for instance, though some would do it; and it is also good to avoid *rumbling* marks who have just previously been taken. The nature of the mark will be discussed in detail in a later chapter.

In order to clarify the phase of the act of theft now being discussed, suffice it to say that within a matter of seconds after a mark is spotted and his money *located*, the mob has closed in and the stalls are preparing him for the safest and most effective type of kill that this particular mob is capable of executing. This continuum of spotting a victim and closing in on him, with the tool in a position to *work*, or actually *working*, is known as *playing for a mark*, or *playing*, or *making a play*. "I spotted the guy. At Columbia I want to make a play for him, see." The presence of marks who are worth robbing with the consequent natural action of *mob work* is known as *play*. When the mob is working smoothly and profitably together, they say that they are *digging in, rooting in* or *batting away*. "And they never seen anybody like us. And we're rooting in and they don't savvy."

To summarize, then, we have the situation for an act of theft from the person when one or more stalls puts a victim into a position so that the tool can rob him. The act of the tool is the climax and takes place within a very few seconds. Let us see how this division of labor works out.

The Stall

Although it might at first appear that the most difficult part of the act of theft is the removal of the wallet from the victim's pocket (and indeed this is a key act), a good stall makes it much easier than it could otherwise be. Men who have done both seem to agree that stalling is more demanding than *hooking*, or playing the part of the tool. "I learned both. I learned to stall and I learned to hook too, and I broke in many a stall. A lot of stalls won't break in, you see, because they're thieves and they won't be told. That's the reason they are thieves. They don't want people to tell them what to do. So if you can't tell a man what to do, then he can't stall."

The stall's work is diverse and intuitive, compared to the tool's. He must have a fine eye for marks which the tool wants to *fan* and be able to cover much ground when necessary in a crowd without attracting attention. While he may use his entire body, including his hands and feet, to maneuver and hold a mark, he uses his back as much or more than any other part of his body. He refers to his back as his *hump*, and speaks of its use in stalling as *throwing a hump* or *putting his hump up* (for someone). "So Frenchy said, 'Come on, Conk, and put your hump up for me.'" "I throwed a hump at him in the doorway." "I put my back up for him." The same phrase may be used with the "someone" indicating the victim rather than the tool, as "Slim, why don't you put your hump up for that mark in the white hat?" It also occurs as *to put up for*. "We put up for him at the get on."

This focus on the back is functional, since much of the time the stall works with his back to the victim, expertly using his body to control him. However, a good stall uses the upper part of his back also, including his shoulders, and especially his elbows. "The buttocks are seldom, if ever, used by a male stall. Broads plant their kiester against the mark, but just for an instant. The upper part of the back and the elbows is used to keep the mark in position."

When a stall is *working* in front of the mark, he is called the *front man* and said to be *fronting the mark*. "Yeah, Al got that score, but I was fronting for him." This is seldom a permanent position from which he operates, since a mob is a versatile group, and the stalls should be able to work in any position desired by the tool. Either stall should be able to work in this position, but one may be more effective than the other. "The tool might have a preference in some instances, because one stall has more moxie, so he'll say, 'Louie, you front this mark.'" Usually it works out so that whichever stall gets into the front position is, for the time being, *front man*. In fact, the stalls may change positions several times if they have to give the tool more than one *slant* at the mark. This term also occurs as a verb with the meaning varying according to who is the subject. If a stall says, "I was fronting the mark," it means that he was in position as described above. But if the tool says, "I'll front the mark," or "I'll be front man," it means that the tool wants to take the *score* from the front (not a very safe practice, which will be discussed further under *The Tool*), and the stalls immediately fall to a position beside and behind the mark, to hold him in the proper position. The stall who then works directly behind the mark is called a *backstop*, especially in the Chicago area. "John O'Keefe lost more backstops on the dip than Sherman lost men marching to the sea." "Old Windy Dick could take it out of your eyes. Always singlehanded. Didn't need no backstops for him."

Stalls must also be expert at maneuvering a mark about in a crowd so as to get him into a good position for the tool, or to hold him in a given position until the tool gets to him. This is called *pratting in* or *pratting out*, as the case may be. "That String Kid was a bang-up tool. He could nail them as fast as two stalls could prat them in." This is called *pratting* because of the way in which the hips are used to move a man one way or another—though, of course, all parts of the body are used in order to keep the action from attracting attention. For instance, suppose a tool has spotted two *fat* marks in a *tip* boarding a train. One is just about to go up the steps, but the other one is far back in the crowd. So the tool may say, "Prat that big mark out and we'll beat him." The stalls then get in front of the big mark indicated and rapidly *prat him out of the tip*, that is, work him backward so that he cannot board the train until the tool has robbed him; the stalls then *prat him back into the tip*, so that he will get on the train immediately and be gone before he *blows*. "Some mobs put a stall on the mark's tail to see if he blows before he gets on the rattler." Meanwhile, if the second mark the tool selected has not already moved up into the *tip*, the tool will get the stalls to *prat him in* so that he can be robbed unobtrusively just before he boards. Or the stalls might simply *prat* the first mark *out* in order to delay his progress until the second mark could be *beaten*; then the tool could step in behind the first mark. *Pratting out* may also refer to moving a man out of the way so that the tool can get at the mark. "This John just stood there and I like to broke a leg trying to prat him out."

This type of *action* by stalls is not easy to describe because there is so little to see; if any of their moves attract attention either from the mark or from anyone else in the crowd, they are not *bang up* stalls. "Good stalls are few and far between. There ain't any good ones turning out any more. Stalls are at a premium." Every move they make must be slight enough and natural enough to be inconspicuous, but at the same time definitely calculated to move the mark in the direction and into the position desired. When they work in pairs, their movements are beautifully synchronized, and they get results with incredible swiftness. They use their bodies with the surety and timing of professional dancers, at the same time disguising each move as a natural one.

When the stall is a woman, the technique may be the same; she uses her back and elbows like a man. She also knows, however, how to use her buttocks in a very different and much more effective way. The male stall must never attract the attention of the mark as he maneuvers him in or out; the woman, on the other hand, may be skilled in doing just the opposite. She uses her buttocks against the genitals of the victim in such a way that he is startled, flattered, and perhaps confused or embarrassed. This is usually done just as the tool is ready to *get his duke down*, or rob the victim, and must be perfectly timed. "She knew exactly how long to put her prat against a mark and then take it away. It was just enough to lead him on, to give him an idea that there might be some chance for a make, and then take her prat away from the mark because it's liable to be in the way at any time. She uses her back and elbows just the same as a male stall, but even more so than a man, because a woman can get away with more in a crowd at any time."

Of course, this sexual approach is extremely brief and no opportunity is given the victim to follow through, even should he so desire; many of the more alert marks are said to seize the girl's buttocks in both hands, throwing all caution to the winds, and counting on the closeness of the crowd to conceal their movements; as they clutch at elusive sex appeal, they become completely vulnerable to the tool who works from behind or from the side, as conditions demand. The girl remains in contact with the victim only for a matter of seconds, then eludes his ardor by swiftly *pratting out* other persons who block her way and *pratting in* persons who may block the path of her recent admirer. The girls used as stalls of this sort are sharp, attractive girls, very well dressed and in no way resembling prostitutes. Their effect on upper middle-class men is immediate and disastrous.

Stalls of both sexes also perform other coöperative services for the tool. At the command *"come through"* they know how to reverse position, or turn to the right or left, holding the victim in position and blocking his hands from possible access to the pocket being picked by the tool. "The stall comes through so as to put the mark into position for the wire. You [the stall] come through when there is a little squeeze in the crack at the top of the kick and the poke is tight there. It's to distract the mark's attention for just a split second. The wire is careful not to let the mark bump into him when you [the stall] come through."

The stall *comes through* on the side where the *score* is *coming off*; that is, he will reverse position from immediately in front of or to the side of a mark and double back toward the tool. The contact between the stall and the mark is slight, not enough to attract much attention but strong enough to make the mark conscious that someone wants to pass him going the other way. The stalls usually *come through* for *left* or *right britch* or *pit scores*.

They may be required to *raust* a victim, that is, by bodily contact or specific movement cause him to respond to what the professional magician calls "misdirection" and take his hands off his money or move into a more favorable position. "The office 'raust and come through' means that you [the stall] actually bump the mark as you come back. But there isn't much bumping done by a class mob. Root-and-toot mobs—maybe yes. It's the business of the whiz to be as inconspicuous as possible, for anything that attracts attention may be recalled later on." Some tools like to use a very gentle *raust* when taking a *pit score* (*insider*) from the side. The less *rausting* the better, however, if the mark is not to be *rumbled*. "Say, 'Raust . . . come through . . . raust.' That would mean in order to raust him, you know how to raust a mark? Just take his hat like that." [Informant pushes my hat forward over my eyes with a gentle touch from the back.] "Now that is a raust. Well, then, the first thing he does is he takes both his hands. Did you ever see a man straighten his hat with one hand? He'll come up with both hands and straighten his hat and [the informant chirps the office for '*it's off*'] that's all she wrote."

The stall may be required to *stick* the victim (hold him firmly) for the tool. "Jigs, they work a lot different from us. I mean, you stick one for me and I'll stick one for you." "I was sticking this mark down for Bradley and I got my own mitt down on another mark in front of me." The latter quotation shows a very unorthodox act on the part of the stall, who was also trying to act as a tool, a diversity which is never practiced in well-organized mobs. "The tool is the only member of the mob who steals. The stall isn't even allowed to fan a man unless it's an accident. That sort of thing will really get him hurt." Or he may receive an *office* or an argot communication from the tool like "*stick and split me out*," which means to hold the victim firmly until the theft is complete, then move in instantaneously between the victim and the tool so that there is no chance for the victim to catch or see the tool, even if he becomes aware of the theft. This act of *splitting the tool out* is not habitually used by smooth operators, but in the event of an emergency every stall must be prepared to *split out* the tool for the protection of the mob. Stalls also *shade the duke* for their tools; that is, they cover the hand of the tool with a coat, a newspaper, or their own bodies so that his actions in *fanning* or *locating* are not visible to onlookers. "I shaded her duke with my raincoat, my tog." Coats used for this purpose are carried over the arm, and are called *togs*; sometimes the stall wears the coat and expertly spreads the front of it to complete the *shade*; newspapers carried for this purpose are called *stiffs* or *sheets* or, by old-timers, *blutes*.

In mobs which have more than one stall, whichever one covers the tool's hand and takes his position on the side of the victim where the money is located is called a *duke man*. He also usually takes the *score* from the tool as soon as the theft is complete, so that the tool will not have it in his possession in the event of trouble. A *duke man* is not a specialist; he simply happens to be in that position at the tool's direction.

In *road mobs*, such as the one we are using for this example, the stall also is the *steer* or *steer man* for the mob; that is, he plans the itinerary so as to catch various races at conveniently related locations, and attempts to work in any other fairs, athletic games, or celebrations which might make the trip more profitable. "A good steer man has to know all the doin's and the right spots." He often also has an encyclopedic knowledge of how the fix operates in each community, what territory is worked by which other pickpocket mobs, what the best transportation is between cities, and a good deal more besides. "A good stall can always get filled in, especially if he reads the papers and can steer."

A stall who does this specialized work is also called a *folder man* (because he handles the *folders* or time-tables), a *finder* (because he "finds" the best places and times to work) or an *advance man* (because he plans the work in advance for the mob). "Ninety percent of the racket is having a perfect folder man." Of course so-called *local mobs* do not need and do not use a specialized *steer*, but *road mobs* would be handicapped without one.

While we are speaking of stalls, a concept commonly misunderstood by the public—and often by the police apparently—should be mentioned. This is the concept of *jostling*. It is commonly believed that a stall *jostles* the victim, that is shoulders into him roughly, elbows him, throws him off balance, etc. "Now if that man is jostled, if you knock into the mark, or brush into him roughly, you're liable to knock the tool off balance." (Detective showing use of this term): "It was rough work, so about that time the Kid threw him the jostle." (*Class cannon* commenting on the illustration): "Whoever told you that wasn't no pickpocket. That's a dick's term." Another *cannon* comments: "When you're working in a guy's britch, your hand . . . it's a suspended animation. You're in his kick, and yet you're not in his . . . you understand what I mean? And if you, if your stall knocks into that man, he's liable to cause your hand to hit him, and that's all of it. So that's a dick's term strictly, that 'jostle'."

This concept is so firmly established, however, that the police use it all the time and in some states like New York there are laws designed to enable officers to arrest pickpockets even though they are not caught stealing, or to arrest the stall even though he has stolen nothing. These statutes refer to *jostling* and the participation of the stall is commonly referred to as *jostling*. Actually, except amongst mobs who operate so crudely that we could hardly call them pickpockets, the victim is never *jostled*, nor is he conscious of the stall's work at any time. Skilled pickpockets do not use the concept or the term to refer to their own work. "I want my mark to behave and step along like a little gentleman. I don't want nobody stomping on his toes or bumping into him, or knocking him around or jostling him. That will wake a sucker up." Rough stalls (with *hit and run* mobs) sometimes push the mark around if they think they can get away with it. "If they grab a sucker and shove him on the train, that would be a snatch score. Good mobs don't do this. It's only in New York."

The work of the stalls is called *framing* or *framing for the mark*; the situation at the moment when the tool takes the *score* is called the *frame*. This concept applies even if there is only one stall, but of course is not present technically, at least, when a pickpocket is working singlehanded—a situation which will be discussed in detail later on. When a *four handed mob* are working, they use a *double duke frame*—that is, one stall on the right, one on the left, and one in front. The tool *works* behind. Should the tool want to *front the mark*, he changes places with a stall who goes to the rear.

The Tool

The tool, as we have shown in the early portion of this chapter, does the actual stealing. He is also called a *hook, wire, mechanic,* etc. Old-timers or Britishers may call him the *claw.* There are also various kinds of tools, such as *careful tools,* ("Some careful tools reef every score." "Little Midge was a careful tool. He didn't take so many scores, but he'd go for weeks without a rumble."), *cautious tools, rough tools* (those who work without finesse; those who are not too careful about *rumbling* the victim), *wild tools* (those who will try anything), *buggy tools* (those who are unpredictable), and *hungry tools* (those who are *on the hustle* day and night because they are *money hungry*).

While the division of labor between stalls and tools is sharp, and is usually observed in so-called *organized mobs,* some professionals can work equally well in either position, or can *fill in* as stalls, even though they are properly tools, and vice versa. It is important during the act of theft that each mob member observe the division of labor agreed upon by that particular mob in advance, for a stall who suddenly decided to turn tool and take an *easy score* might well jeopardize the safety of the entire mob. However, among *makeshift* or *pickup* mobs, and often among Negro or Latin-American pickpockets, there is a very loose mob-organization. "Among Jigs, it's 'You put your back up for me, and I'll put my back up for you. If you get caught, you're in jail.'"

The tool may be so versatile that he can take money or wallets from any pocket, provided he can get into position and depend upon his stalls. "If I can get that hook in, it don't make no difference whether it's a left britch, right britch, or left prat, right prat." Some, however, are not so versatile, or have definite limitations regarding certain types of *work.* For instance, many tools cannot go in successfully under overcoats; these are called *summertime tools* or *summer cannons.* They are often glad to get work as stalls in the winter if they do not go to a warmer climate. Others specialize in hip pocket work and are called *prat diggers.* "There's a lot of guns I know specialize strictly in prat pokes." Sometimes these tools who specialize in the hip pocket are really superior at taking *prat scores*; others are just not very good tools. "Some tools have something in one line. Some like prat kicks, others like insiders and coat pits, and some play for britch kicks." Most American tools like to work from behind the victim, or from the side; part of this is tradition, part of it the dislike which they have for *giving up their kisser*, or allowing the victim to see their faces.

I like to take a top britch from the side, if the mark doesn't look at me. If a man looks at me, that's the end of it. Anytime a guy points me out in a line-up and says, "There—that's the guy that stole my pocketbook," he's telling a damn lie, because if he even so much as wrinkles them little muscles on the back of his neck, and acts like he's going to look around, I let him go, because there's a lot of people in this world, there's a lot of pockets, and a lot of pants. There's always another guy right behind him, you know what I mean. It ain't worth while jeopardizing your liberty, the most valuable thing in the world to a thief. There ain't no use in jeopardizing that unnecessarily and that's what you do any time you let a sucker look at you.

Some Americans, however, are *front workers* or *front men*; that is, they can and do *work* facing the victim. "A jug score is easy for a front worker, because it's usually a pit or an insider." Most of the European tools, especially the old-timers, are *front workers*, probably because of the custom, generally more prevalent in Europe than in America, of cutting men's side pants pockets with the opening parallel to and just below the waistband, instead of with the opening following the line of the outside trouser seam, which runs at right angles to the waistband. Thus a European tool will *take* this type of pocket, called a *top britch* or *top bridge*, while facing the victim, and he *takes* it exactly as an American tool would *take* a hip pocket when standing behind the victim. Trousers cut with *top britches*, while worn in this country by a certain class of people, are now not common in standard business suits, but are frequently found in work clothes. European tools, however, often continue to *work* from the front, even after they have been in America for years. Most American tools avoid *working* directly facing the mark by taking *pit scores* or *insiders* from the side, approaching the mark diagonally or at an angle. For working the hip pockets or the side pants pockets, they like to be behind the mark, or slightly to the right or left as the case may be, facing the same way as the mark but well out of his line of vision.

Whatever the specialty of the tool, if indeed he has any, it is well known to the mob, and his stalls play to that specialty. Generally, however, he does more than just lift a pocketbook from a helpless mark held firmly but unconsciously in the *frame*. He does all the *locating* with *organized mobs*. He must have a good knowledge of people, so as to select victims who are carrying large amounts of money rather than those who are well-dressed but who have little cash. He must be very observant of small details which, added up, lead him to the consistently satisfactory *scores*. He must have a very fine sense of timing and strong *grift sense*. He directs all operations while the mob is *working*; the stalls follow his directions meticulously.

In other words, the tool is a practical psychologist. He listens to conversations in the crowd, and from them pieces together information he can use. He sees every move where money is involved. He notes the build, stance, dress, and manner of everyone he can see. He almost automatically separates local citizens from travelers; if he is in a *road mob*, he will take the travelers by preference (other things being equal) because they are likely to carry more money; if he is a *local* operator, he will want to avoid robbing local residents, since they may upset his arrangements with the police. He knows how to smell an officer of the law; some types he avoids religiously, other types he robs with pleasure. He recognizes other thieves, even though he has never seen them before, with uncanny precision. "Mobs recognize a frame anywhere they see it in a tip. Also, there are damned few who wouldn't recognize each other on sight." He registers any attention whatever from onlookers as he *works*. He knows how to be unobtrusive and almost a nonentity in a crowd or on a street-corner; he also realizes that he must be prepared to melt away into a crowd if he sees anyone who is looking too closely.

He is always alert, always under tension, though of a different kind, even when he is not *working*, for he is well aware that someone may tap him on the shoulder at any moment. Perhaps this perpetual tension is one of the reasons why a very high percentage of pickpockets are narcotic addicts—a higher percentage than has been encountered in any other *racket*.

There is a lot of nervous tension during the time you're stealing. I guess that is why there is a lot of junkies, because it releases that tension after the grifting is over. A lot of whiz that don't use junk will do outlandish things for the same reason. They have to blow off steam. Sex is one outlet. You can mark this down, too, as soon as the grift is over, they can't get along with each other.

However, as the tool we were using as a laboratory specimen *works* on the street, in a railway station, or at a racetrack, all these things are in the back of his mind. Principally, he is looking for *scores*. In this case, he sees a man leaving the betting window at the track. It is the $50 window. He knows that the man must either have made a bet or collected one. He catches a *flash* of green in the man's hand as it goes to his pants pocket, then the man moves into the crowd. Immediately he knows that this is a *fat* mark, possibly very *fat*. The chances are that this tool knows exactly the prices that all three horses paid in the last race, and he can figure instantaneously what a $50 ticket would pay on any one of them; besides, if the man is buying a $50 ticket, he must have enough money on him to make him worth while; in that case, the *flash* was not winnings, but the remainder of the roll from which he is betting. If he was cashing a $50 ticket, that would be all right too. And if he has bought one or more $50 tickets, the thief can cash them as easily as the purchaser can.

The tool catches the eye of the nearest stall, who may also have spotted this sucker. It is better not to *clip* him right here near the window, for such spots are often *covered* by track detectives, Pinkerton men, or, at big races, by out-of-town detectives who may not be averse to shake-down tactics. Besides, the man is striding off toward the stands. The second stall senses that the wind is up as soon as he observes the actions of the tool and the first stall, and even if he has not seen the mark, he knows that there will be *action* shortly. All three of them follow the mark separately but as swiftly as possible without attracting attention. The tool steps up behind his man, which act serves as an *office* to the stalls, who are walking just in front of the tool, one on each side. The mark suddenly stops to talk to someone. That might bring the entire party to a standstill. The stalls still have to get abreast of the mark in order to *make a frame*.

Of course, it would be quite possible for the three of them to *split the man out* from his friend momentarily and rob him in the flurry, or to rob the friend as well, but to do so smacks too much of the *hit and run* or *clout and lam* tactics of reckless *guns*. They slow their pace, the stalls actually blocking the progress of the tool if necessary, so that all three are walking, but not getting anywhere, especially if the crowd is thick. The mark leaves his friend and turns toward a ramp leading to the grandstand. They all sense this and the tool *offices* that they will *clip* him as he enters the ramp. They are now right *on his tail*, although no one except an experienced observer could tell this as they move through the crowd, which is a little heavier about the entrance to the ramp. We have slowed the *action* down abnormally in order to get some of the details in.

All this has taken perhaps a minute and a half or two minutes from the time the tool first caught the *flash* of money at the $50 window. The stalls have moved slightly in front of the victim, almost touching him with their elbows now, and the tool is directly behind him. The mark is entering the *frame*, but it has not closed yet, for the tool must *locate*. The stalls are already *shading* for him. In twenty seconds it will be *off*, if all goes well. The tool moves very close to the mark, *cutting into him* (making bodily contact) in such a way that the victim is not alerted; in fact, he probably is unaware of the contact. The stalls *shade his duke* with their *togs* while he runs deft, sensitive fingertips over the right pants pocket, then the left. There is the *impression* in the left side pocket, just as he thought, and some loose silver in the right. He wonders about the ticket, and checks both side coat pockets. There it is (probably), a thin piece of cardboard in the change-pocket just under the flap of the right *coat tail*.

He checks the *insider* and the *pit* too, for this is a substantial mark, and he might have a long, flat wallet *stashed* there. These pockets contain only what feel like letters or envelopes. Both *prat kicks* are checked; the right has some keys in it and the left a wallet. The reserve may be in that. The procedure of *locating* has taken about five seconds, and the stalls are watching the tool as they walk, slowing imperceptibly so that the mark comes against them, rather than their coming against him, but all four walking in what appears to be a normal fashion. The tool *offices* for a *left bridge* and a *left prat*, and the *frame* closes. Ten seconds more to go.

The stalls know that there will be a roll of cash in the left pants pocket even if the tool does not *office* for *scratch*, which he is not likely to do since he works closely with the stalls and since they would expect anything coming from the *left bridge* to be cash, anything from the *left prat* to be a *leather*. As they close the *frame* they block off the mark's hands (in case he should feel something and reach for his money) and the tool, coming behind and very slightly to the right, *gets his duke down* very fast under the *shade* which the *duke man* provides to the left. He goes for the left pants pocket first, for he knows there is considerable folding money there. Hooking his index finger just within the *crack* of the pocket, he takes up a pleat in the lining, then makes a dozen or so tiny pleats, folding the lining with great dexterity between his fingers. This is called *reefing* or *reefing a kick*. "I was taught to reef a britch from the bottom so a tweezer-poke would end up in the palm of your hand." His hand does not go into the pocket at any time, but the shortening pocket-lining moves the roll of bills upward so that it emerges at the mouth of the pocket. In fact, if the reader could see this take place, it would appear that the bills rise rapidly of their own volition and emerge from the pocket into the thief's hand. As the roll rises toward his hand, he *offices* "*come through*," then gives the signal for "*it's off.*" "*Cop,*" he says, and the *duke man* has the roll.

The stalls then rapidly *set up* the mark for a *prat score, shading the duke* again, and the tool *unsloughs* (rhymes with *plows*) the button on the victim's hip pocket; then, without breaking stride, he moves slightly to the right and *forks* the wallet from the left hip pocket with his middle and index finger, using his left hand. No need to *come through* on the *prat*. Another *office* that "*it's off,*" and the *duke man* has the wallet; he is careful to *shade* it, lest its passing to his hand give an onlooker a *flash* which might reveal the theft.

Now for the *ducket*, and the tool offices the stalls for a *right coat tail*, moves his right hand deftly under the mark's right elbow, which is blocked, lifts the pocket-flap and *pinches* the race-ticket between his thumb and index finger. He *comes away* with it swiftly, palming it himself without *duking it* to the stall. The entire act of theft has taken less than fifteen seconds. The *duke man* moves off to the left with the *scores* in his pocket. Simultaneously, the other stall *splits out* the tool from the victim, and all three are rapidly lost in the crowd.

For purposes of illustration, a standard, uncomplicated *touch* was used, in which everything went off according to schedule, the mark behaved like a little gentleman, and no emergencies developed. Even so, the *action* was still oversimplified because it is impossible to describe the simultaneous actions of three thieves and a sucker without becoming very complicated. Of course, this *score* could have been taken in several different ways, and any pickpockets who might discuss it would probably become involved in heavy argument whether it should have been done this way or that, whether or not the tool was left-handed (most good tools are ambidextrous), or whether or not the tool should have let the race-ticket go since he already had the money and wasn't even sure he was getting a race-ticket anyway. And perhaps some tools would have pocketed the *scratch* instead of passing it to the *duke man*. Also, we have used two stalls because we had them; in actual practice, one might have *stuck* the mark quite as effectively, though it might have taken longer and been more risky. Many mobs would have done it differently.

Actually, there is no such thing as a stereotyped *touch*. Every one is different, with many variables involved, some of which are the personalities and techniques of the mob which makes the *touch*, the nature of the victim, the degree and security of the *fix*, and the physical conditions under which the theft takes place. The important point is that each good mob is a fluid, adaptable unit of thievery, capable of scenting the quarry instantaneously, and of co-operating with a high degree of teamwork, feeling their way as they go and shaping their activities to fit the situation with great speed and cunning. This knowledge that they can *beat* a man, together with what appears to be an almost uncanny foreknowledge of how to do it, is what is known as *grift sense* or *grift know*. "A tool has to have grift sense, but he doesn't get grift sense until after he grifts. He has got to take a lot of pinches. It's not so much a question of dexterity, but he knows when to steal the poke and when to let it go." "Sometimes you get a feeling a mark might burn you. Then, even if you had the guy's poke topped, and were a smart tool, you'd let it go. That's grift know."

In the case of pickpockets, the sense of touch is an important adjunct to this *grift sense*, for the pickpocket receives and sends a constant set of signals to and from the victim by means of manual contact and bodily contact during the entire act of theft; some of these the victim responds to although he does not know their meaning; others he reacts to without being aware that he has received them. Likewise, a set of signals is constantly being exchanged by the mob members, some oral and verbal, some oral and nonverbal, some kinesic, some tactile, and some unconsciously sent or received; this aspect of highly developed tactilism and nonverbal communication among thieves has not been previously reported. It should be studied further by someone with special facilities for analyzing it; it might well throw some new light on the peripheral aspects of communication. Among thieves it is a vital part of communication, since the success of the theft depends upon it. Besides being heavily functional, it is so thoroughly integrated with ostensibly natural physical movement and verbal communication that it is difficult to isolate. The speed and accuracy by which communication takes place on this level are phenomenal.

Peripheral and Incidental Details of the Act of Theft

It might be of value to go back to the theft just described for a moment to see a few of the possibilities or variants in the pattern which such a mob as we are describing might have encountered. For example, when the tool *located* the *okus* or *leather*, we assume that it was a conventional-type billfold; "She had the okus topped, but she didn't pull it, as she made the fuzz and didn't even rumble the mark." It might well have been any one of a number of other types of pocketbook; these will be taken up separately in the chapter *Money and Valuables*. But it turned out to be a common *leather*, so we have no problem here. However, was it *on its feet* or was it *lying down* (or *laying down*)? If it was *on its feet*, it was standing in the pocket with the fold at the top or the bottom, and in a good position to *fork* or *spear*. If it was *lying down* or *on its side*, it was crosswise or on edge in the pocket, and the tool would have to *top it* or *top it up* before he *forked it*. The *sting* we described involved a wallet obviously *on its feet*, a situation which might make it easier for some tools, especially inexpert ones. "On its feet, it's pretty easy. It's when it's laying down that it's tough." A good tool, however, has only to *top it up* and thinks little of this maneuver.

Not for a pickpocket, and I'm talking about people in my class, it don't make no difference if it's laying down, on edge, on its side, upside down, or how it's laying, as long as he's in position and he's got the proper support, all of them are alike. As long as it ain't chained, as long as it ain't latched down, it don't make any difference whether it's standing up, laying down, on edge, upside down, or whatnot.

Or this *skin* could have been carelessly put into the hip pocket, or the pocket itself could have been shallow enough that the wallet was protruding from the *crack* of the pocket. The tool would think of this as a *pop up*, a *hanger*, a *kick out*, or a *kick in the ass*, the implication being that any slight disturbance of equilibrium would be sufficient to dislodge it. "Vulgarity in class mobs is just as taboo as it would be in front of your wife, or in my own home. I'd say 'kick out' or 'easy score'." (This informant refused to verify *kick in the ass* in the presence of a lady.)

The reader may recall, however, that our mark was an orderly fellow who buttoned or *sloughed* his wallet snugly into his hip pocket and that consequently the tool had to *unslough* the flap of the pocket before he could take the score.

At them tobacco auctions now, there's where you get a workout. Them hoosiers with overalls on over their pants . . . new overalls. And you got to unslough them two buttons on the side so you can get at any of their pants pockets. They slough them up and them new overalls are terrible, so stiff and slick. But you step up behind the right hoosier and unslough them two buttons and you got yourself a tobacco crop.

He does this, incidentally, with a quick, gentle upward flip of the first joint of the index finger, assisted in stubborn cases by the ball of the thumb.

Perhaps he couldn't *nail* this *hide* easily, but had some trouble *bringing* it (that is, getting it out) either because the pocket was tight or because, blessed be any saints who patronize thieves, the wallet was too fat to *come* easily. It is also possible that an inexpert or *rough* tool might *rumble* the *come on*, or mark, at the *come off*, or point when the wallet can be taken out. This would be more likely to happen on the *left britch score* when the tool is *reefing* the *scratch*. "He works it up and works it up, and right at the come off the sucker grabs for him."

When the tool goes after something in a pocket, he says that he *gets his mitt down* or *gets his duke down*. "I must have stalled for fifty mobs, but I never did get my duke down." When he gets what he is after, he says that he *comes up with it* or *comes away with it*. Some tools say that they *swing* or *swing with it*; this latter phrase is most often used by tools who have had experience with other types of thieving, especially shoplifting; women thieves use the phrase *swing underneath with it* or simply *swinging underneath* (the ultimate reference being to concealing an object under the skirt), and male thieves sometimes use the same phrase referring to concealing an object beneath an overcoat or topcoat.

Some tools, in thinking about a *score* or talking about it afterward, refer to themselves as *owning* it after a certain point in the theft, and show resentment if something happens to deny them the *score* at that point. "After I had it topped I figured I owned it." Even though the wallet is still in the victim's possession these tools behave as if it *belongs* to them, and are not likely to relinquish it unless the danger is acute. "I don't agree with this. That's not the psychological moment for him to say he owns it. I've topped a poke many times and had to let it go. A good tool would not say that when it was topped it belonged to him." An interesting case in point is the story told about a mob operating in depression days, when it was not unusual for a mob to board a streetcar or bus without fare, depending upon being able to steal it as they got on, or by the time it was needed; pockets were actually picked for metal coins—*ridge* or *smash*.

Back in depression days when I turned out, you'd get on a short car and fan a mark to see if you could find scratch. It takes a lot more dexterity to steal a small amount of smash than a lot of scratch. But during the depression you'd take what you could get. For nine cents at least you could eat. When you got on a short car the first thing you had to do was get the money for the kayducer. Many's the time we had to make it before we worked up to the center of the car where the kayducer stood.

This particular tool *fanned* a nondescript mark and *located* a paper bill in his side pants pocket. This was big game, for it might be a five or a ten. The mark wore an overcoat, and under that a long sweater which came down over his pants pockets. The tool *reefed the kick* and got the bill between his finger-tips; the mark sensed that something was amiss, and reached down on the outside, under his overcoat but outside the sweater, to check his bill. He took hold of it through the sweater and the pants, and felt the tool moving it away. "I had a death-grip on the scratch. The sucker had hold of it on the outside, but I had it on the inside. . ." There ensued an amusing miniature tug of war, which the mark lost since the tool actually had hold of the bill and the victim could not hold to it through his clothing; while the tool got the bill, the mark was not only *rumbled*, but he *blew* and caused the mob a little trouble, though they escaped by dropping off the car after the mark *beefed gun*, or announced publicly that he had been robbed. There are tales of this sort of incident ad infinitum amongst the *whiz*.

As a matter of fact, objects often leave the pockets in which they are carried with some reluctance. For instance, large rolls of paper money sometimes fit so tightly inside pants pockets that the tool has difficulty removing them. Sometimes he tries it one way and must *let it go* because he is not in exactly the right position, or because of circumstances he had not taken into consideration, like the cut or tightness of clothes, the build of the man, etc. "If a mark looks like he's going to rumble, a careful tool lets him go. There is a lot of people in the world and a lot of pockets, so he lets him go if he seems like he's going to look around."

In such cases, he may *office* the stall or stalls to *let him gee*, and then *put up for him* again so that the tool gets a different *crack* or *slant* at the mark. If the tool who *gets his mitt down* is a competent *mechanic*, he will find a way to take it, even if several tries are necessary. Sometimes very large rolls of bills are taken from very tight pockets without the victim being even slightly aware that he is being robbed. For instance, one informant recounts an incident which involves the removal of a large roll from a man's pocket under quite different circumstances. The roll had been secured with a rubber band, which became disengaged as the tool was working on the roll, which then began to swell. As he brought it up in the pocket, it became larger and larger, and consequently more difficult to move upward. When it emerged, all pressures were off it, and it expanded suddenly, filling the tool's hands to overflowing. The tool *officed* "*cop in your hat,*" to the astonishment of the stalls, who had never heard such an *office*. One of the stalls subsequently covered it with his hat until it could be removed from the immediate scene of the theft. "If this ain't nothing but one-dollar bills," he said, "we've got all the money in the world."

There are, too, cases where objects other than money or wallets are mistaken for valuables, and time and energy wasted before the pickpockets discover their mistake; American pickpockets working in England and the Colonies where pipes are very commonly smoked always note the difficulty they have in mistaking tobacco pouches for wallets—and fat ones too.

Right-handed people usually carry their money on the left side. But in areas under the British flag this don't run true to form. I think it is because they are great pipe-smokers and carry their tobacco in the most convenient place and carry their dough in the right britch or in a couple of extra pockets they have, with the flaps buttoned down. I must have had a split-basket full of them tobacco pokes. We were hustling four handed—two guys and two twists—and all you have to do in a case like that is fan the mark and take the leather. But nine chances out of ten them tobacco pokes was made out of leather and very fat, and were standing on their feet right in the left prat. I took off a basket full before we found out that they had tobacco in them.

Then we had to go back and look for tweezer pokes, and we usually found them in the right britch.

Money, too, sometimes comes in large packages; I have a record of one *touch* which netted several thousand dollars which were being carried to a bank; the money was wrapped in newspaper and fitted tightly into the owner's overcoat pocket; he was accompanied by a guard. The theft, while not easy, came off without trouble, and the owner never realized how he lost the money. One of his employees (suspected of carrying on an affair with the owner's wife) was accused of taking the money from the coat before the owner departed for the bank, was tried for the theft, and was acquitted. The mob attended the trial with considerable interest and one of them, now dead, told me—for what it may be worth—that if an innocent man had been convicted, he would have found a way to clear the employee by mail without endangering the mob; this would have been quite possible, since he could have shown an intimate knowledge of the movements of the victim and his guard which no one but the people who stole the money could have had. Note that this thief, with considerable character, albeit unappreciated by the dominant culture, had no sympathy whatever for the victim, but did not want an innocent man to suffer for something he did not do. This, along with many other attitudes, will be discussed in the section dealing with ethics and morals of the subculture.

The stalls performed smoothly and effectively in the *trick* at the racetrack, which we described in detail above; in fact, any self-respecting tool could probably have *handled* the mark we picked with half as many stalls. But we had them, so we used them. We put the mark in a *vise* and held him there so that the *action* could be properly described. However, had one of the stalls *turned the mark into* the tool a bit roughly, or in such a way as to arouse his suspicion or even his attention, he might well fear that he had *crumbed the play*. "I came through too soon and crumbed the play." If the mark had become suspicious, i.e., if he thought of his wallet or perhaps checked it with his hand, or if he showed any sign of being annoyed or specifically aware of the presence of pickpockets, the tool would cease operations or postpone them, because the sucker had been *rumbled*. If the mark showed definite symptoms of suspecting theft from his person, the mob would realize that he had *tumbled*, or that he had been *ranked*, a term used mainly on the

West Coast. "He ranked that move." "I don't think that is right. It's from the point of view of the mob—it's one of the mob that ranks him." "We framed for that sucker and I was about to beat him for his poke when some broad ranked him." In such a case the mob would probably *let him go* (or *let him gee*) unless he was known to carry enough money to make it worth while to *tail* him until the tool could get another *slant* at him. Sometimes the sucker is not *rumbled*, but an onlooker is *ranked* (usually the fault of the stall for not properly *shading the duke* of the tool) with the result that there are witnesses who may report the theft and support the mark if he *beefs gun*. In such cases, when it is possible, the tool returns the money or wallet to the pocket of the victim, who will then be easier to *cool out*.

Perhaps the mark only *rounds*, or turns to look at the tool, although he is unaware of the theft; this can be serious if the theft is completed, for the victim then can possibly identify, or *make*, the tool if he is arrested; good tools never *give up their kisser* to a mark who *rounds*, and are reluctant to go back for a second *crack* at a mark who may have seen them clearly enough to make identification. However, if the *frame* is properly set up, the tool knows that the mark is never going to see the man who robbed him. Stalls, of course, do not have the same problem, for they do not get into the victim's pockets, although they seem to be arrested as often as tools, if not oftener; also, they are very likely to have the wallet which has been passed to them.

While the tool is most likely to sense suspicion on the part of a mark, or the realization of a bystander that theft is in progress, the stalls too are always alert for this; when they sense it, they try to ascertain whether or not the tool has also sensed it and, if not, they alert him by an *office* or signal, which may vary from mob to mob. The tool himself, however, must make the decision whether or not to go through with the *touch*, and the stalls accede to his judgment; if they sense that he is going right ahead, they perform their work even though they may think he is making a mistake; while they relay to him any information which may indicate a *rumble*, they must have confidence in his judgment.

An experienced tool makes these decisions in a split second, and his accuracy in making them is easily checked by the amount of time he spends in the clink. The tools with *class mobs* are usually most conservative, or as *safe as kelsey*, for they know that there are always plenty more pocketbooks to be taken, but that one false move may put them behind bars. One of the informants who contributed to this study had his last *square pinch* (an arrest for a theft he was caught in the act of committing) in 1939. Good tools become supersensitive to any reaction by the mark which may indicate suspicion; often they concentrate on the back of the victim's neck (when they are working from behind, as they usually are) and one informant says he photographs the back of the victim's neck in his mind, never to forget it; certainly he remembers it during the time he is working in a given crowd on a given day; how much longer he can recall it is, of course, a matter of opinion. Some thieves have phenomenal memory for people, comparable to the ability of those few detectives who merit the name of *camera eye*. Some pickpockets register the build, the stance, and other physical characteristics of the victim so perfectly that they automatically avoid him after he has been robbed. Some memorize one detail, such as the pattern of the man's necktie, and register that automatically whenever they may see it again in the crowd. Both stalls and tools have need to be sensitive to identification, but the decision to rob a man is, in the last analysis, made by the tool, and he must be able to avoid repeating on a mark, even though the stalls should be so stupid as to put the man in the *frame* without realizing that he has already been robbed.

CHAPTER VI

DIFFERENT TYPES OF MOBS

A mob is a working unit of pickpockets. The minimum is two; a lone pickpocket, working without any support, is hardly classed as a mob. He is usually referred to as a *single o tool*, a *single handed tool*, or a *single o cannon*. Mobs are usually referred to by the number of persons composing them; that is, they are *two handed*, *three handed*, or *four handed*, which is the maximum number used in this country, with perhaps some temporary or unusual exceptions. In general, mobs are also known as *tribes*, *troupes*, or *teams*, the last two being terms often used by the police, though not exclusively so. Sometimes a *team* is *two handed*, while a *troupe* is *three handed* or larger. "So this dick come over, and I know that this troupe over here got nailed and that troupe over there got nailed. Right out from under me. . . . Well, that don't make no difference. . . . I got to make a living." Within the profession, mobs are classified in numerous ways, several of which will be discussed in this chapter.

In order to avoid confusion, perhaps we should indicate immediately that all mobs belong simultaneously to more than one of the categories which we are setting up. Thus there are *three handed local mobs*, *road mobs* that are *four handed*, *organized mobs* that work *locally*, *class mobs* who work *on the road*, *jig mobs* who operate on a *knockabout* basis, *cannon broads* who work *two handed*, either *locally* or *on the road*, etc. Likewise, several different kinds of pickpocket may be found in any given type of mob. A *mocky jew mob* might *fill in* a *jig tool*, a *hungry tool* might work with any kind of mob, a *class cannon* (white) might work with a *jig mob* on *put ups*, or a *makeshift mob* may operate with two bums for stalls and a pretty good *wire*. *Rough tools* may be *class cannons* and *careful tools* may never make the grade or vice versa, depending upon personalities. These terms will all be explained as the chapter progresses.

Furthermore, the mob in its various forms is the heart of the pickpocket subculture. It would fall within Trager's Cultural Index No. 2, Association. In the pickpocket subculture it appears that the mob is often more important than the family as a stabilizing influence; sometimes mob and family are combined, as we shall show. These two are the only formal aspects in the subculture, with the family usually being secondary. In fact, because of the importance of the mob in the economics and technology, it is the primary and basic associational factor in the subculture; all other aspects of association are peripheral and relatively non-essential except when they impinge upon the activities of the mob. Thus the pickpocket's loyalties, as well as his fortunes, are tied up with a fundamental type of association which, to members of the dominant culture, appears to be loose, ephemeral, and highly insecure. Yet the thief respects it and participates in it because it is all he knows; furthermore, tradition says that it works; and so it does, within limits.

Travel

Perhaps the first major division made by pickpockets themselves is on the basis of travel. If a mob goes out of town to *hustle* and if it has a policy of traveling from place to place, working in each *spot* for varying periods, it is known as a *road mob*. "Road mobs that are always on the tear, always hustling, they never take time to enjoy their money; so it don't do them no good, 'cause they are always on the hustle." If it stays more or less permanently in one locality, working that city or the immediate vicinity, it is known as a *local mob*. While there are skilled operators in each type of mob, there is a certain status enjoyed by *road mobs* which *locals* do not generally share, largely because there is a much higher percentage of *class cannons* among *road mobs* than among *locals*. Also, there is a certain social distinction observable, with some *road mobs* wondering how their *local* brethren stand the boredom of a permanent life in one city; at the same time, other *road mobs* develop the same aversion to travel that some legitimate traveling salesmen express; they envy anyone who can settle down—or at least they say they do. Actually a pickpocket who has been on the road for years is seldom happy to live and work permanently in one city, though he may do so for various reasons. Likewise, *local* pickpockets, once established, do not seem to gravitate to the road, with its hazards and uncertainties. As a matter of fact, one can discern two different kinds of thief and two philosophies of thievery underlying this dichotomy: the *road man* is the more venturesome, the more restless, the more interested in change and variety; also, because of the stresses and strains of *road work*, he is usually a sharp, alert thief, with an eye to all the angles; sometimes he has auxiliary *rackets,* such as the *hype* or some form of the *short con* which he practices occasionally, or on which he can fall back in an emergency. The *local,* on the other hand, likes his security and is sometimes incapable of facing the hazards of *road work.* Some are simply afraid to work outside their own city. It is obvious that, while many *locals* enjoy a high professional standing in all ways, some *locals* may be simply lazy, dilatory, or somewhat shiftless professionals who make a good thing of police protection in a given locality.

Now you take Willie Anderson. He never left New York in all his life. He wouldn't get out of the subway, and you couldn't make him get out of the subway. The only time he ever got out of the subway was when he went out on the road one time. I was with the String Kid. We was going to Jefferson City, Missouri, and he was doing the pinching. Willie and his mob was all on the same train. They was four handed and Willie Anderson is doing the pinching for this mob. So we're in Kansas City, and here's a guy that got on at Topeka and I want to make a play for him. Because the presidential special train would stop at every capital, you know.

So this guy is an Associated Press correspondent, and he's got a billfold like that. It was an insider. Willie had him spotted, too. When this guy come off the train, Willie was figuring on getting that for hisself, see. And he couldn't get up there to the steps where the correspondent was leaving the coach. I wiggled through there . . . . I'm as good as the next one, you know. It was perfect for a fast and furious. The Kid got right in there, too. So we clipped this guy and the score was six or six and a half.

We walked away. We jumped in a cab and went downtown and went in a restaurant. That's the only score I wanted to get, you know. I didn't want to be around there after that. We went on down there to the restaurant and in a few minutes Willie came in. He said, "Well, I have had nothing but bad luck. I've made more money in New York in one goddamned day than I could make on the road in all my life. This is my first, last, and only time. I'm going over and get me a plane." And he did. This was at Topeka, Kansas. He said, "You knew I had that mark spotted. I wanted to get that score."

I said, "Yes, but I've got to make a living too. Do you need anything? Do you need any money?"

"No," he said, "I don't need anything, but I'm going back to New York and if I leave again, it'll be in a wooden box. I'm not going on the road any more." And it's a fact, he never did.

Road mobs are usually *organized mobs.* That is, they specialize their duties and responsibilities down to fine details. They adjust their number to the minimum (usually two or three members) and each member is a specialist in his work. One of them is always a *steer*, a specialty for which a *local mob* has little necessity. Some mobs call him a *folder man* because he handles the timetables and rail or bus schedules. The *steer* plans the itinerary and handles the details of transportation; he knows all the events en route which the *road mob* should *make*, he knows what cities the mob should *buy through*, and he has a vast personal knowledge of persons and places which are important to the mob if they are to work efficiently. He must be able to read and should read the newspapers. Also, since the *road mob* must arrange the *fix* as it goes, he has the duty of contacting the detectives, the *fixers*, or other intermediaries in each locality in order to arrange for the mob to work for one, two, three, or more days under police protection. The details of this will be discussed under the chapter entitled *The Thief and the Law*. Also, if the *road mob* decides to work *on the sneak*, that is, without advance arrangements in any given locality, the *steer* must be prepared to handle any trouble which arises as a result of this lack of protocol. Of necessity, he either carries a part of the mob's total emergency capital or *fall dough* (sometimes amounting to several thousands of dollars) or he knows where and how he can get it into his hands with a minimum of delay.

Usually a good stall is also a good steer, as a rule. He knows all the get ons, he knows all the fixers, he knows all the transfer points, he knows the country, he knows the topography, he knows the geography, he knows where you're going, he's got all your plans laid out. He knows that Jim Sweeney's the fix over here, and Jack Little's the fix over there, and who can get you here, and who's bondsman, and this and that and the other thing. He knows all these things. That's what makes him so valuable to a mob, because actually stealing a pocketbook . . . there's a million guys that can steal a pocketbook. But it don't mean nothing. They just keep the wolf from the door, that's all.

The *steer* is usually also a stall. If the mob operates *two handed*, the other member will be a tool. If the mob is *three handed*, there will be two stalls and one tool. Often one of the stalls is a woman, and on occasion the tool may be female.

A woman stall uses her arms and elbows to keep a mark in position, the same as a male stall. But of course there's a sex angle that comes in there with a woman, where it doesn't with a man. Of course . . . a woman stall she uses her buttocks in order to distract his attention . . . to keep his mind where she wants his mind to be. That's about all there is to it.

Usually, however, *road mobs* use the woman, if any, for *stalling*, as previously described. Rarely both stalls are women, except in a *four handed* mob, which is less common now than formerly.

If the stall handles the mark right, there's no question about what the tool . . . the tool's work is easy then. The hardest work, the hardest part of the whiz is the stall. That's the hardest part there is. Once a stall becomes a good stall, he very seldom becomes a wire . . . because he's so much in demand, there's so many mobs that are willing to fill him in that he can be filled in without dough, without fall dough.

A single handed pickpocket, male or female, while actually a functioning unit—and usually a very efficient one—is not referred to as a mob. However, he—or she—may be quite versatile because the *single handed worker* must operate without a stall; also, he is more flexible since he does not have to get other people, and usually highly individualistic people at that, to agree upon an itinerary, working hours, and other technical matters. It is also to his advantage to work alone, especially if he is expert, for he does not have to divide the proceeds of the day with anyone. A *single o tool* traveling over the country has an additional advantage, especially if he is not well known to the police, because he does not attract so much attention, nor does he run the risk of being arrested because he is with someone else who is known. He often has auxiliary *rackets* such as the *hype* or the *heel*, at which he may be quite proficient. Many police officers have never seen a pickpocket working alone, and so do not look for one. The reason for this is that such pickpockets are rare, are difficult to see working because there is no *frame*, and are not often booked by the police. *Road mobs* also, it should be noted, are not so common as they were in former years. The following statement will give a good general distinction between *local* and *road mobs*:

There's a lot of guys that are local pickpockets. You know what I mean. I don't know whether it's fear or what it is, but they don't want to get out of town. They just stay in one locality. But then there's other mobs, you know, that want to work on the road all the time. You work on the road, you get all the spots . . . where you pay off, you know. And you can always find somebody to pay off. There are some pickpockets that never leave the town right where they are. I don't know whether it's fear or what. But they just will not leave town. It's the same in Philadelphia, or Cincinnati, or any town.

There's just some guys that have got the fear. They must have fear, because . . . well, there ain't any way they can leave there. Of course, they get pinched here and there, and that's to be expected. There's some kind of a fear that if they get away from where they're known. . . . Let me explain this to you. Every good cannon, he's got a bondsman, you know, and there's nine out of ten of these guys I'm talking about have got a bondsman and they're afraid to get away from him. They can't get out . . . see, it's some sort of fear. One of the best in the country I know of is in Pittsburgh, and he . . . I mean he's really good. He's tops. This guy, he is one of the best, but you just can't get him out of Pittsburgh to save your neck.

Local mobs, on the other hand, are not so closely *organized*. They may be *three handed* this week and *two handed* next week. They may use this tool now and have another one later. They may be *pick ups* or *pick up mobs* in that they get together a varying personnel to work at irregular intervals anywhere that the picking seems good. "Yeah, strictly class mobs. I'm not talking about makeshifts and pick ups and this and that. I'm talking about knowing what you're going after." Because all members live in the same vicinity, it is easy to operate on this rather casual basis. Their relations with the local law are generally quite good— otherwise they would be in prison. In fact, it has been said that some detectives protect certain *locals* in order to use them as informers or stoolpigeons. *Local mobs*, especially the lower-class ones, do not always pay for police protection, but count on the fact that they are not well known and the fact that they prey largely on transients in large cities to keep them from the attention of the police. Some *locals* operate on a small scale, irregularly, in certain cities for months or even years without much difficulty. Other *local mobs* are very well *organized*, and have a minimum of turnover in personnel.

Working consistently in a certain area has great social and personal advantages for this type of thief, since he can maintain a home and numerous contacts with people who are useful to him or with whom he likes to associate. His *connection* for narcotics is also usually local, and he fears to go away from a safe and reliable source for drugs. He can work regularly or irregularly, with the same mob, or as a temporary *fill in* or *pick up* for several mobs if the occasion arises. "He was telling me about a character he filled in with—you wouldn't know him—one time in St. Louis." It is notable, also, that there are a few very capable women working *single handed* on a *local* basis, though few old-timers still work *single handed* on the *road*. For instance, a "sharply" dressed Negro woman, uniformed as a maid and using a child as a front, can get in some very effective work on crowded buses or city railway systems. This is known as *grifting with a squealer* or *hustling with a brat*.

There is also a sort of in-between type of mob which operates locally but which also covers the surrounding area in short trips, or makes occasional trips to large gatherings such as political conventions, inauguration ceremonies, etc. although they do not travel consistently or far from home. These are known as *knockabout mobs*; as a general thing, they do not have any particular specialty, nor do they have a restricted territory away from home "Knockabout mobs are usually low-class. One good guy and a couple of bums."

Professional Status

Mobs are also classified according to the professional status of the members. Thus a *class mob* will be composed of *class cannons*, and usually exclusively so, since this type of operator will not take the risks of working with inferiors, or with people whose reputation for integrity (according to the standards of the subculture) is not established. "Class mobs don't declare you out, because you have your fall dough up. You never discharge a man. He always discharges himself. If he's always late, he discharges himself and he takes down the fall dough." These mobs are contrasted to *pick ups*, *makeshifts*, *locals*, etc., which reflect lesser stability and lower professional rating. A *cannon mob* is usually a highly *organized mob*, though not necessarily a *class mob*. Says a con man, "Never play for a lop-eared apple; they love to be trimmed by a cannon mob." The designation *cannon* itself has a kind of internal or built-in status, since it has, within the past twenty or twenty-five years, supplanted older terms such as *dip* (used today largely by Britishers or Colonials, policemen, and men on some other *rackets*), which simply means a pickpocket. "Dips very seldom make a roper. Once a dip, always a dip." *Cannon*, an intensification or augmentative of *gun* was, and still is, used with some sense of indicating a better-than-ordinary pickpocket. *Gun* still used largely by old-timers, derives from the Yiddish *gonif* 'thief.' We see a similar process operating among Negro pickpockets, who use the term *shot* to refer to the same class of professional which white thieves call a *cannon*.

Racial, National, and Sex Classifications

Racial, national or ethnic classification is reflected also in the names applied to types of mobs based on these divisions. All-Negro mobs are called *boon mobs*, *burr heads*, or *jig mobs*, especially on the East Coast. "There's jig mobs. The jigs, they work a lot different from us. I mean, you stick one for me and I'll stick one for you." Although some individual Negro pickpockets are not only expert professionally but in every way *class cannons*, Negro mobs generally speaking do not have a very high rating in the fraternity of white pickpockets, or among the few topnotch Negro operators, for that matter. Here the status depends not upon race but upon professional reputation, it being rather a sociological and economic accident that so many of the less accomplished pickpockets belong to the Negro race. Negro mobs, also, lack the specialization and organization necessary to effective operation. It is common for white pickpockets to disclaim any race prejudice, acknowledge the abilities of certain Negro *shots* with whom they have worked or with whom they have associated, and then to discount all other Negro operators.

I said, "There's one swell jig," I said. I can borrow money from him and he's a nice guy; and he had a broad, oh she was a beautiful broad. Must have been part Polynesian, or something. She had jig in her, you know, but she must have been part Polynesian, or something like that, for she was a very beautiful woman. Maybe part Chink or something like that, with them almond eyes. And my girl, she said to me, "You mean you let a nigger set down at the table along side of me?" I like to . . . lost my own broad over that.

Likewise, Jewish organizations are referred to as *mocky mobs* or *mocky jew mobs*. "Mocky is not a Jew. It's a Sixth Avenue Jew. There is lots of very fine, high-class Jews on the whiz." There are a few good Chinese and Japanese pickpockets, but not many. "Shorty the Jap was one of the best cannons I ever knew." A very sharp observer among pickpockets tells me that he suspects that Orientals have a dislike for bodily contact with Occidentals which keeps them off the *whiz*. Although some American Indians are expert thieves along the traditional lines of their own subculture, I have never heard of one becoming a pickpocket.

There is something of the same ambivalence of feeling about Jewish mobs that we have noted above regarding Negro mobs, except that it is notably less prevalent, with many Jewish operators working with Gentiles, and vice versa. There are also numerous Roman Catholic pickpockets, though no mobs organized on this basis have been observed; it is notable that there is a sort of mutual recognition or tolerance of religious scruples amongst Jews, Gentiles, Greek Orthodox, and Roman Catholics. A Roman Catholic, for instance, will be permitted to drop out of the mob while a Catholic priest is being robbed (much thievery takes place in the crowds at various shrines and religious congresses) and such a scrupulous pickpocket naturally wants no part of the proceeds from this theft. Likewise, if a Rabbi is being robbed, Jewish members may be excused, though it is reported that they do not so generally respect the cloth as do the Catholics.

Nationality also plays a part in labeling mobs, such as *spik* or *spick mob* (Cubans, Puerto Ricans, or Mexicans) or *old country mobs* (Europeans not yet Americanized); usually these *old country mobs* consist of Germans, Russians, Austrians, or other Central Europeans. These are much less numerous than they were twenty-five or thirty years ago, although there still are some, and individual *old country guns* still operate or *fill in* with modern native American mobs. There are also many French-Canadian mobs operating in Canada, with some crossing the border into the United States. Montreal seems to be the headquarters for pickpockets in Canada; in fact, it is known as the "Home of the Chirps." French-Canadians, however, do not rate very high professionally among *class cannons* in this country, nor do Latins, the Mexicans rating highest in this group.

Women are accepted on an equal footing with men so far as mob membership is concerned, and there are some all-female mobs who as often as not specialize in other peripheral *rackets* such as the *boost* and *binging hangers*, which will be discussed in a later chapter. All-women mobs are known as *moll mobs* or *twist mobs*. Some of them are highly effective and seem to have less trouble with the law than male mobs or than women who work with male mobs.

You meet some good women on the whiz. Two Jewish gals, Sarah and Rachel, and the best broad outfit I ever seen. I was coming down the elevator one time in John Wanamaker's and got to the bottom and heard a woman scream. She fell over in a dead faint. Some big pigeon-breasted gal. She screamed because her pocketbook was open and they didn't have a chance to close it. So I closed her pocketbook up and helped her off the elevator. And got her outside and then called a floor walker and everything. They said, "We'll take care of her, she just fainted."

I said, "I don't know what happened—high altitude or something."

I seen those two gals, so I tailed them on out. I got outside and said, "How about my end?" I was just kidding, you know.

They said, "What are you talking about?"

I said, "I know you beat that broad." And two nice looking gals—I mean real nice looking—and both about five foot or along in there.

They said, "Then come up the street if you are that smart. Come on up the street and we'll turn that thing over." So we turned it over and they had a pretty fair score—$150 or $170, I forget which. So that's the reason this broad fainted, you see; she had that money in her poke. So I got their address.

I monkey around with this one, this Sarah. She had a guy, but I didn't have no gal. I was on the outs, you know, so I went up to her apartment. We had coffee and drinks, and this and that. I monkey around with them for quite awhile. There was nobody with them. When they worked, they wouldn't take me, they wouldn't take you, they wouldn't take nobody. They were strictly two handed. They knew each other's actions. They could beat a man, they could beat a woman, they could beat anybody. They were moll buzzers and whiz at the same time. They could handle anything that came up and boy they had a ton of money. They had the swellest apartment you ever seen. Rugs that thick on the floor; some of them must have cost $1500. And closets full of groceries and everything. Of course, they boosted all that stuff.

Occasionally one encounters a *single o broad*, and she is likely to be very skillful. Some of these are well up in years. In this connection I have a report showing the intrusion of a young woman from the dominant culture into the criminal subculture, but only insofar as her criminal techniques are concerned; she was entirely self-taught, but her methods were sufficiently effective to impress the skilled international operator who discovered her; she had no contacts with other professionals, although she had observed them working in crowds in the city where she lived. She will be described in the chapter on *Skills and Training*.

Working Habits

Some mobs are known by their tactics, especially when these are rough or unorthodox. Thus a *heist mob* is one which brooks no interference and robs the victim willy-nilly. The irony of this label is broad if we stop to recall that real "heist mobs" are stick-up gangs who rob banks and payrolls and armored trucks; they operate with violence and at gun-point. They belong to the *heavy rackets*, which are at the opposite pole from the pickpocket. The hyperbole here is characteristic of the pickpocket's imagery; an operator who tugs a bit hard at a victim's wallet, or who purloins a pocketbook without first establishing the appropriate misdirection is likened to a tough stick-up artist who uses naked violence. These mobs may simply be clumsy or inept; on the other hand, they may feel so secure in the *fix* that they need not be subtle; or they may simply not care. They do not constitute the upper echelons of the profession. They are also known as *clout and lam mobs*, *hijackers*, or *rip and tear mobs*. "It was pitiful the way the mob got away with the rip and tear stuff." *Hit and run* and *root and toot* are also used, though some *whiz* claim that the last is more of a *con* term than a pickpocket word.

Places to Work

Pickpockets also classify mobs according to the places they work, or the kind of work they do. Thus a *third rail mob* is one which consistently works the subways; this is largely New York usage, and these mobs are fewer now than formerly. In all large cities there are *jug mobs* who work the banks; these mobs are usually transients, although some *local mobs* will work *jugs* at certain times and under certain conditions. "In L.A. I filled in with a jug mob for a while." *Jug mobs* are selective workers; that is, they watch the customers withdraw money from a bank, or have information that a certain customer will withdraw a considerable sum of money and then *take him out* (*bring him out*) where they rob him. A mark who is robbed on the basis of advance information is called a *put up*. Because this is delicate work, the professionals who do it are usually *class cannons*, and they take very few *scores*, perhaps only one a day or less. "Only mobs with class can stand that jug grift. They can afford to wait. They don't have to get that touch every day. Those junker mobs have to keep it coming in. If they take ten scores of $25, that's $250, but they get the town all heated up. Only class mobs have money in reserve and can wait for the one or two big ones."

The mobs who formerly infested railroad and bus stations and who rode the trains are now practically nonexistent; in fact, one now seldom sees a *whiz copper* or pickpocket detective in a railroad station; ten years ago all stations were heavily protected. "This old kayducer was as right as rain and would not start his elevated train unless there was a whiz mob on with him, and at that time, he would not have to hold his rattler long." Likewise the *circus grift* and the *carnival grift*, while still surviving here and there, are nothing like what they were before World War II, when some of the big circuses carried their own *whiz mobs* to trim the crowds along the way.

Kinds and Varieties of Pickpockets

There are many different kinds of individual pickpocket as recognized by the profession. These have certain predominant characteristics of technique, personality, or behavior recurring with great enough frequency to constitute recognizable types. There are, of course, many more kinds of pickpocket which are not recognized as types, or only partially recognized; these are individuals who get a name for certain things within a limited circle, or who fancy themselves as specialists in this or that, or who believe that they constitute a special breed of cat for personal reasons. There are also several other types of pickpocket which cannot be included in this study.

The pickpocket is essentially egocentric almost to the point of megalomania. When we consider the high percentage of illiteracy or semiliteracy among them, we can understand why many of them have horizons sufficiently limited to throw their own self-image into high relief. No pickpocket thinks of himself as an inferior operator; in fact it is a safe guess that there is no pickpocket who does not consider himself near the top of his profession and who does not rationalize this assumption in one of several ways. Most pickpockets are able to observe and recognize this tendency in others, but never recognize it in themselves; in this way they prove not only their basic humanity, but verify the pattern which most of the professions follow, and with good precedent, for thievery is very old. The fact is that the pickpocket has to believe that he is one of the best; if he admits his own limitations, he loses his nerve (*blows his moxie*) and will eventually find it impossible to work. His constant preoccupation with thievery and its imagery in his own thoughts, together with the perpetual rehashing of each *touch* with his partners (*cutting up touches, chopping them up*, etc.) tends to reënforce in his own mind the infallibility of his technique, the daring of his nerve, the irresistibility of his personality. "We're very fortunate today to hear about this, Doc, because Doc always enjoys chopping them up. He likes to hear them." Among *class cannons*, however, braggadocio is notably infrequent, and the individual will have an impressive external reserve.

In any consideration of these types, the question of status is inevitably intruded, and that question becomes increasingly complicated if we attempt to discuss it with deference to all points of view within the profession. Therefore, we shall assume something approximating the point of view of the *class cannon*, simply because that kind of individual has more perspective than, say, a *hit and run* pickpocket from Harlem who works with anyone who will *throw the hump* for him. To attempt any sort of representation of all or even several points of view in this study would complicate it out of all proportion to its practicality. Also, indications of relative status, as they are expressed, will be understood to be statements colored by the entire class-consciousness of the top men in the profession; they are not intended to reflect either favorably or unfavorably on any other levels of professional operators whose point of view, unfortunately, cannot be included here.

Since there is no convenient principle of analysis by which we can subdivide the various types, perhaps an alphabetical one is as good as any. Furthermore, this method will avoid the necessity for putting one type above another, unless that type has definite status-value.

A *bang up* operator is an accomplished one. This implies that his excellence lies in his techniques; he may or may not be a *class cannon*; that is, he might be skilled and capable, but lack status for some other personal reason, such as having a reputation for cheating his partners. The term, as I have recorded it, usually applies to tools, as a *bang up wire*, a *bang up tool* or a *bang up hook*, but may refer to stalls also.

Cannon and *cannon broad* or *cannon moll* we have discussed briefly above in connection with types of mob. This label carries status, though perhaps not so much as it did several years ago when it was new as a substitute for the older *gun*, which has gradually weakened and generalized; it also included some other types of thief, but *cannon* reënforced the older term, made it sharper and more specialized, and it immediately became acceptable to the more competent professionals. Within the past few years it has become increasingly popular, but may eventually go the way of *gun*. A *careful tool* is one who works gently but expertly, who takes no chances, who lets every questionable victim go, for he would rather lose a *score* than endanger the mob. "Some careful tools reef every score." "He was a careful tool. He didn't take so many scores, but he'd go for weeks without a rumble." There is a distinction between a *careful tool* and a tool who is cautious; the latter may be neither expert nor recognized as a good operator; he may simply be timid or fearful.

When a pickpocket works with a carnival, he is known as a *carnival louse*, a *carnival cootie*, a *carnival bum*, or a *sure thing grafter*, which is an older and less pejorative term, though it is rapidly becoming synonymous with *louse*. "Show me a sure thing grafter and I'll show you a carnival louse." This term has a definitely negative status-value and is always applied by others to someone not present, or someone who is being abused; a man might use it ironically or humorously about himself, but hardly seriously. Probably the negative implications of the term stem from the fact that *carnival bums* often cannot work except under the protection of a carnival and all that this implies; they are looked down on for this reason, as well as because carnivals do not attract the highest type of *grifting* personnel. This stigma does not apply so strongly to pickpockets who *work* the *circus grift* (now almost obsolete) or who *work behind the big top*. Here there is a marked difference in status between *circus grifters* and *carnival grifters*.

When a pickpocket is unduly careful or shy about making close contact with the victim, he is called a *center fielder*. This is especially applicable to a stall who fears to take his share of the risk, but who always wants his share of the take. "Sometimes we call a center fielder a 'mile away' or we say he's 'sneeze shy.'" Note again the degree of hyperbole involved here; the distance involved in the operator's relation to the mark is a few inches or at most a foot or two, but the image visualizes him as working out in center field or within a mile. *Sneeze shy* implies that he has an inordinate fear of arrest. Some mobs refer to a *center fielder* as *playing safety first*, which is a kind of play on another baseball term, though the addition of the *first* has its sarcastic implication.

When a pickpocket is financially embarrassed, he is said to be *c.o.d.* This is especially applicable to one who has just been released from prison, or who has just been *filled in* in an insolvent condition. The implication is that, as soon as he arrives, the mob starts paying his way. "When I filled him in, he was strictly c.o.d. but when I took a fall he didn't spring with a dime." Of course, any thief might find himself in this condition temporarily, but if he turns up *c.o.d.* consistently, he soon loses status, even though some mobs might feel an obligation to use him as a *pick up* for a few days to enable him to get on his feet. This is called *giving him a day's work*, even though he might work as an extra man for several days, or even weeks.

When a pickpocket operates consistently on a *petty larceny* basis, or is never anything more than a very small-timer, he is called a *doormat thief*, the sarcastic implication being that he steals doormats (or that he can't even steal a doormat), though of course such a profession or specialty is entirely mythical. A *dynamiter* is a very *rough tool* who may get by without too many *beefs*, but whose technique associates him with the "tear off Kids" or the *snatch and grab* type of theft. Note again the hyperbole; an operator who does not observe the proper finesse is imaged as blasting the wallet away from the victim. This type of tool naturally does not expect immunity, but he had better operate under very sound *fixing* arrangements or have excellent stalls, or both, unless he wants to spend half his life in *stir*. A tool who is *dynamite*, on the other hand, is tops, and is anything but a *snatch and grab* man.

Anyone asleep in a public place is, in the thieves' argot, a *flop*. While this may seem to the lay reader an unconventional situation in which only bums and riffraff would be involved, let him be assured that many otherwise decorous people doze in public; this is particularly true of senior citizens who find that, once they sit down and relax, the next step is a nap. Pickpockets are ever watchful for these marks, and there is a specialty in the *racket* which preys exclusively on *flops*. "He hustles the flops." He is called a *flop worker*, and he prowls the parks, the subways, the railroad stations and, more frequently, the stations for subways or elevated trains. Some invade hotel lobbies; in fact, I have in my files some photographs of a dozing postprandial mark who is being stripped of everything including his wrist watch and jewelry. These *flop workers*, while recognized as part of the profession, are not highly regarded by better-class pickpockets, who think of a mark as someone who is up on his feet and going somewhere; in fact, many of the best operators cannot work successfully on a victim unless he is moving naturally. "That's the psychology of it. He [the *flop worker*] can't stand my racket. He said, "How in the goddamned hell can you put your hand in that man's pocket when he's walking and talking?' And I can't see how he could put his hand in a man's pocket when he's sound asleep." A *forty-second street thief* is one who cannot *work* anywhere but in one city or one locality. Perhaps this is because he cannot *work* unless he is *hustling behind a shade*, and the only shade he knows how to manipulate is in one locality. Perhaps he has a psychological block against *working* in other localities. "A Forty-Second Street thief might work in New Orleans or Los Angeles, not necessarily in New York. He is a one-spot hustler, and he's afraid to grift when he's not in that spot."

Among old-timers, a *grifter* denotes a pickpocket or *sneak thief*, and some still so call themselves. The term *grifter* has, however, in recent years so generalized that it now includes all sorts of non-violent criminals from carnival *flat jointers* to *big con men*. The *grifter* in this older sense is the *gentle grafter* of the fiction of O. Henry, written shortly after the turn of the century before *grifter* had become sufficiently popular to have replaced *grafter*.

We have already mentioned *hijackers* (or *high jackers*). The individual tool using very rough techniques is called a *hijacker*. This may be regarded as a specialty by some pickpockets—usually those who have little else to claim as a specialty. "Johnny may not be a good sneak, but he's one hell of a fine hijacker." A *home guard* is simply the name which *road mobs* apply to a *local* pickpocket; it is not a term which *locals* would apply to themselves, except whimsically. "They will say about home guards, they'll say, 'Pay no attention to him . . . he's just a local character.'" A *hungry tool* is one who is always working; he is said to be *money hungry* because he thinks only of making money. There are also *hungry mobs*, though this classification is largely accidental in that two or three *hungry* operators work together, probably by choice. "A hungry tool doesn't necessarily mean that he is determined, but it means that he is money hungry. He could be ever so determined to take his score and still not be money hungry."

When a tool is very fast and dextrous—but not *rough*—he is called a *lightning tool*. "Joey Fay is a lightning tool. That's why they call him the Electric Kid." This is a label which indicates professional status, especially when used by *class cannons*. The Eastern police use the term *live cannon* to distinguish a pickpocket from other related operators; while it is not a pickpocket term, many pickpockets, especially those in the East, know it and may use it ironically or humorously. Says a detective from a pickpocket detail: "In New York City a live cannon is a pants pocket worker who hustles crowds, while a lush-worker rolls drunks." In this quotation we see another police word, *pants pocket worker*, which is used by pickpockets seldom if at all. An accomplished tool, smooth and fast, is called a *live wire*. "Abie Lesser was a live wire if I ever seen one."

Another term for an excellent tool is *mechanic*, a term preferred by the more conservative old-timers; this word, meaning a skilled worker, has spread throughout the underworld from safecrackers to professional gamblers. A woman pickpocket is, of course, a *moll*, or *moll whiz*. "Some say Owney Madden's broad was a real moll whiz, but when I knew her she was mainly a booster." In this connection perhaps the term *gun moll* should be mentioned ("The sharpest gun molls are mockies"), although it has left the underworld for Hollywood and the crime magazines, where it is often erroneously used to mean a girl accomplice of a *heavy worker* who carries his pistol, and sometimes uses it; in fact, this character has been created out of whole cloth and has no counterpart among the thieves who call themselves *guns* and their female accomplices, *gun molls*. As has been pointed out, the *gun* element stems from the Yiddish *gonif* and does not, as Hollywood likes to believe, mean "pistol."

A diligent and skilled operator may be called a *money getter*, especially if he is a tool; this term is complimentary, whereas *hungry*, discussed above, is not; the difference lies in the attitudes implied toward money and work by the two words. At the risk of seeming facetious, we might say that a *hungry tool* devotes his life to the taking and hoarding of money; a *money getter* can take it or let it alone. Actually, the *money getter* is more of a "playboy"; he likes to spend money as well as make it. When a pickpocket (usually a tool but not always) who normally works with a mob decides to work by himself now and then, he is said to be *muzzling around*, and such an operator may be called a *muzzler*. This indicates only occasional departure from the normal relationship of tool and stall and a *muzzler* should not be confused with a *single o tool*, who works consistently alone. This term is interesting in that it is probably borrowed from a certain type of sex pervert who gets gratification from manual and bodily contact with women in a crowd; while the similarity in movement is perhaps close, there the anology ends, for pickpockets as a group are overtly and conventionally heterosexual, with little understanding and no tolerance for so-called perversions of any kind. The following quotation is characteristic, even to the point that the informant thinks that *muzzlers* (the sexual kind) must be homosexuals because they are perverts. "No, a muzzler ain't a faggot. His line—I'll tell you— he's a guy that will muzzle around single o."

A very small-time pickpocket who fears to take risks is referred to as a *petty larceny bum*, often shortened to *petty larceny*, as "He's petty larceny." This kind of thief likes to keep his *scores* within the limit for petit larceny, thereby avoiding the much heavier penalties incurred for grand larceny; in many states anything over $20 constitutes grand larceny. Obviously, no professional pickpocket can accept a $20 limit on the proceeds of free enterprise and maintain his self-respect. When one pickpocket reaches for a term of deep contempt for another, it is likely to be *pocketbook snatcher*. "Sheeny Augie . . . that pocketbook snatcher." *Poke glommer* is also used, with the added pejorative implications.

All pickpockets like to think of themselves as specialists of one kind or another, the specialty sometimes changing from time to time. Sometimes they fancy their specialty lies in the particular pocket which they can pick best, or which they find easier than others. Really topnotch thieves, I have observed, have few illusions about a specialty, but are completely versatile. Therefore, one wonders if the concept of specialization may not actually be a rationalization of one's limitations. The terms *prat digger* and *prat worker* reflect this situation. Both mean a tool who specializes in hip pockets. Some pickpockets have never seen anyone rob any other kind of pocket, and perhaps do not even know that it is practical to try to do so; such an operator would see nothing derogatory in being termed a *prat worker*, but when either *prat worker* or *prat digger* is used by a *class cannon* to refer to another pickpocket, the term definitely suggests his limitations. Following are three quotations from different types of pickpocket which show varying attitudes toward the *prat digger*, and at the same time reveal something of the techniques and professional status of the speakers. "Kid Shelton had fingers five inches long. He was the sharpest prat digger I ever stole with." "A prat digger isn't a good one if he can't make a bridge or a pit." "We have summer cannons [in New York City] who are hooks and can nail a prat poke when they don't have to go in under a tog." A *producer*, on the other hand, is a pickpocket, usually a tool but not necessarily so, who has a reputation as a money-maker without meriting the label *hungry*; he is a good man to have in the mob.

When a youngster who has just been *turned out* begins to feel overconfidence in his own abilities, or when a newcomer to the *whiz* talks too much about his exploits, he is called behind his back—and on occasion to his face—a *sensational punk*, which we might render into the language of the dominant culture as "the boy wonder," although the argot phrase has more bite and more sarcasm than the legitimate idiom. A Negro professional is called a *shine cannon*, which is generally a term used by whites showing acceptance and sometimes respect; it is not applied to every Negro who calls himself a pickpocket. The good Negro pickpocket prefers to be called a *shot*, and is so designated by his own race. A *sneak tool* is a very capable operator who normally works with a mob, but who can operate by himself after the fashion of a *solo cannon* or *single o tool*; with a *sneak tool* it is more than just *muzzling around* now and then, for he can operate alone much of the time, even though he has stalls with him. He seems to rely more on his own skill, daring, and *grift know* than he does upon his stalls. He is not a lone wolf, but rather an aggressive, productive worker who does not always depend on the support of the mob, even when the stalls are present. Another name rarely used for a stall is a *stick*, so-called because he *sticks the mark* or *sticks the mark down* so that the tool can do his work. "You see, you got only a second. You got to come away with it when the stick comes through." Another kind of stall is a *straphanger*, which term adequately suggests a dilatory, inactive, uninterested, nonaggressive pickpocket who moons along, unaware of what goes on around him; he resembles the typical *sucker* straphanger in a subway or elevated car. Usually this term is applied to a stall, but it may also refer to a tool, in which case he is about as ineffective as a tool can be. A pickpocket who cannot go under a topcoat or overcoat is called a *summer cannon* or *summertime tool*; during the winter these tools like to stall for someone who can go under the *togs*, or go to the South or Southwest where they can find marks who are not unduly encumbered with outer vestments. "Now, of course, if a guy's a summertime tool and one of them guys that we call, pardon my French, a half-assed pickpocket—half the time he sees a kickout, a guy's poke sticking half out of his pocket and he's falling down drunk hanging on a lamppost, and he walks over and gives him the Mary and calls hisself a pickpocket."

When a pickpocket *works* the subways, especially during the rush hours, he is known as a *third rail*; this is New York and Boston usage largely. Note here again the implication of power and violence which the pickpocket focuses in himself, the third rail being actually the center rail which carries the tremendous voltage necessary to run the subway system.

If one pickpocket says of another that he *wears the gloves* he means that the one referred to is afraid to take hold of a situation, he is not aggressive toward the mark, he is a *center fielder*, a *mile away*, or *playing safety first*. When this term is applied to a tool it is very sarcastic, for it evokes the ludicrous image of a thief performing this most delicate of all thieving operations with gloves on. A successful professional, either stall or tool, may be called a *winner*, but one hears the term more often than not applied to tools, probably because the tool must *produce* if the mob is to make any money, and any success that the mob has directly reflects his abilities. And, of course, any pickpocket is a *whiz* or *whizzer*, though this is usually expressed as being *on the whiz*, which is the name for the profession. "I never knew he was on the whiz." "If you have a hot thimble on you in Boston and somebody puts the finger on you for being whiz, they can do you in."

There are, of course, many more names applied to individual pickpockets, the number and variety being limited only by the experience and observations of the various groups. Those included here are pertinent because they have been in use for some years and are, generally speaking, known throughout the fraternity. Also, they reflect many variations in the behavior pattern which could not be illustrated if this study restricted itself to standard or classic examples such as those used in the chapter on *The Act of Theft*.

CHAPTER VII

THE MARK

Who Is a Mark?

Generally speaking, a mark is simply someone with a pocket-book; for those professionals who are strictly pickpockets, a mark is a male who has a pocketbook, for pickpockets as such avoid robbing women, although some related operators, such as *hanger bingers*, prey on women exclusively, and some pickpockets also rob women as an adjunct to the *whiz*. It might seem strange that a pickpocket, strictly speaking, should avoid stealing pocketbooks from women, but this is the case. All *class cannons*, for instance, express extreme distaste when robbing a woman is mentioned, though they readily recognize that there are other types of operator who do this with enthusiasm, and usually give them their due as professionals.

This preference for the male mark and distaste for robbing the ladies has, I am sure, no relationship to chivalry, but its reason may not be immediately obvious. I have heard it suggested by a certain type of psychiatrist that the pickpocket suffers from a latent form of homosexuality, and that he unconsciously identifies with the female; since the act of theft is symbolic of the sex act, the pick-pocket chooses male victims in an unconscious and symbolic expression of homosexual urges. If this were true, we would then of necessity, I suppose, have to assume that all male *hanger bingers* and *moll buzzers* (who rob women exclusively) are submerged heterosexuals. But what about the female *hanger bingers* and *moll buzzers*? Are they possibly latent Lesbians? And what about the female pickpocket, the *cannon broad*, the *moll whiz*, the *gun moll*? These operators prey predominantly on men, although some, like those noted above, have other side lines which they ply when it is convenient. Are these female pockpockets, in contrast to the female *hanger bingers*, only fulfilling an unconscious heterosexual urge when they *fork a leather*, *reef a kick*, *pinch a poke*, or *plant their prat* against a mark?

Of course, we do not know precisely why some people become professional thieves and others do not, but I think it is just as reasonable to look to their conformation to an ancient behavior pattern as it is to explain their aberration on the basis of neuroses which are present (theoretically, at least) in the dominant culture, but may be absent or partially absent from the subculture.

If we look into the literature of thievery, as well as into the social history of the dominant culture, we quickly see that, until the 20th century, the males of the dominant culture carried most of the money, if not all of it. The classic pickpocket or *cannon*, male or female, was primarily after money, although until the last ten years or so he also took watches and jewelry. He developed techniques by which the male of the dominant culture could be robbed of his wallet, and, although his techniques changed with the times as well as with the costumes worn and the nature of money or valuables, the psychology of his approach was consistent, his attitudes were passed along from generation to generation, he acquired status, and he conformed to the pattern of this group of specialists.

If we look into the literature of roguery of the 16th and 17th centuries, for instance, we see the prototypes of the modern *cannon* and *cannon broad* operating along classic lines all over Europe. They were particularly prevalent in England, and Spain was overrun with them. The men in these dominant cultures were armed and were likely to deal summarily with a pickpocket if they caught him; therefore there was status in robbing him, and this type of work was likely to "separate the men from the boys" rapidly and effectively. The use of female stalls was common among these pickpockets, and some of the women stalls became excellent tools, even as today.

With the great westward movement to the New World, these types, among many others, found sanctuary as well as prosperity all the way from French Canada to the Argentine; it is historical fact—as well as folklore amongst modern pickpockets—that thieves were members of the "first families" of Virginia. In the cities of the New World, the pattern of the European dominant culture was altered in many ways, but it remained the same in at least one respect; the males carried the money, and the females who had any money remained at home, or appeared only with male escorts; in any event, they did not go about as modern women do with a *hanger* which may contain a considerable amount of cash, since the role of modern woman has changed and she often handles the business and banking for the family. Therefore, the traditional pattern for pickpockets remained the same until the 20th century and, in many communities, until our own generation.

Furthermore, there were in Europe lesser thieves who preyed on women; they lacked the skill or the courage, or both, to tackle armed men; they stole jewelry, trinkets, shawls, clothing, etc. Many of them, as today, combined these crafts with shoplifting. Naturally they were not averse to purloining any small change which the lady might carry also. They became organized and prospered in their small way; they included among their victims not only women, but cripples, drunks, persons not mentally sound, and males of the lower or tradesman class who might carry small amounts of money and were not usually armed. To these peripheral thieves we must look for the patterns which give us today the *moll buzzers*, the *hanger bingers* (which professions have become profitable only in recent years), the *lush rollers*, the *jack hustlers*, the *mary ellen workers*, the *bollix workers*, the *coin throwers*, and other types of thief who, while related to pickpockets, are not strictly speaking pickpockets at all, and are not accepted by the *cannons* of today as pickpockets. They still lack status.

Thus we see the practical reasons why the mark selected by modern *cannons* is usually a male, and it becomes clear that we do not need to depend entirely upon an unconscious maladjustment, sexual or otherwise, on the part of each individual thief to explain this phenomenon.

Modern pickpockets classify marks largely into three classes. An *egg* is a young man, around thirty. A *bates* is a man over forty. "I'm by myself and there's about twenty people loading on this coach, and I kept pushing and he wasn't no bates. He was about forty years old. A bates is a guy over forty." A *pappy* (or *pap*) is an elderly man. "A dip rumbling an old pap at the get-on." These divisions do not, in my opinion, reflect the latent homosexual preferences of the thief, so we will examine them in the light of the behavior pattern. If it does not at first make sense to classify the victims of theft from the person on the basis of age, we should recall that this type of theft is intimate, personal, and very much dependent upon the reactions of the victim. The speed of walking, the way he wears his clothes, the amount of money he is likely to have, the degree of his alertness, his possible reaction to a *rumble*, and many other factors figure into the attitude which the thief may take toward him as a possible victim. Older men can be robbed, usually, with less risk than younger men because their reactions are less sensitive. There is an old saying about a mediocre pickpocket that "he has gone over to help an old man on a bus."

Middle-aged men are likely to carry the most money, and their prosperity often can be judged by their clothing, luggage, and manner; young men often do not have much money, and they constitute a certain risk for thieves who eschew violence, for a young man's reaction times are sometimes fast, and he may possibly grab the tool and punch him in the nose. However, these are in the main superficial considerations; men of any age may have money, and if a pickpocket senses the fact, he will try to find some way to take it; where *class cannons* are involved, they will take it from anyone, anywhere. One of the distinguishing features about *class cannons*, also, is their ability to see beneath a mark's exterior and to smell money where the ordinary observer would think there is none; one of the largest *scores* I have recorded was taken by a *class mob* from a farmer in overalls at a county fair. Sometimes laborers, such as painters, yield very fat wallets.

While marks are not generally classified according to their work or profession, this sort of designation is used when the type of work the man does is obvious from his clothes, his uniform, or other identifying factors. Thus a Catholic priest is called a *buck*, and some tools will rob him as quickly as any other *sucker*; others will not. A farmer or yokel is called by old-timers a *rufus* (obsolescent) or a *hoosier*. "So he froze there, and he can't get his hands up. And I think he is reaching for something, you see. So I'm afraid to take my eyes off the hoosier." "We was dressed just like all the rest of them hoosiers, you know. . . . Overalls on and hip boots and everything, flying right round with the rest of them." A physician is a *croaker*. "Now that's the guy that's standing in front of the truck. As soon as I step in this croaker's office, I know I'm pinched. Just one foot in the door and I can feel this guy behind me." A laborer such as a construction worker, miner, or truck driver is a *working stiff* or *red neck*; he becomes important on pay-day, but at other times is not so interesting. Officers of the law are, of course, usually recognized and named according to their branch of enforcement. Any officer, in uniform or out, is called a *copper*. In uniform, he is a *bull* or *harness bull*. A plain-clothes man is *fuzz* or *fur*, perhaps from *fuzzy tail*, a cat. Any kind of federal officer is *whiskers*. A man from the pickpocket detail is a *whiz copper or whiz dick*. A small-town policeman is a *fly cop* (obsolescent) or *clown*. They all carry some money.

Some mobs have a strong prejudice against robbing any *law*, whatever he may be; this is especially true of pickpockets who work locally and have to deal with the *law* in one way or another. Others, especially *road mobs* composed of expert operators, rob any officer of the law with pleasure, provided they are out of that *law's* jurisdiction. Of special interest as *suckers* are the Western and Southwestern deputy sheriffs and special police who frequently attend race meets, rodeos, exhibitions, state fairs, etc., in full Western regalia. When these men are away from home, they are very attractive to *road mobs*.

One informant reports an ironical story in connection with making a *sucker* out of the *law*. He was stalling for a tool on the *road* and they visited a large political convention. There were *whiz dicks* there from all over the country, ostensibly to recognize and pick up thieves; among these was a *whiz copper* from the tool's home city. The tool recognized the *dick* before the detective saw the tool and his partner. The temptation to rob him was great, so they watched their chances and followed him into a narrow ramp leading to a stairway which was at this time teeming with people. It was a simple matter to *put up for him* and the tool extracted his wallet, which contained his badge and credentials as a police officer. The wallet contained about $200—and some photographs. One of these photographs was a picture of the tool's beauteous girl-friend in the near-nude, autographed in intimate terms to the detective.

Types of Mark

Marks are also classified according to race or nationality. A Negro is usually a *shine* or a *jig*. "We made a beat on a big jig, that's all." On the West Coast a Japanese is called a *special*. "Then we nailed that special at a rat-stop just outside L.A." A Chinese is called a *monkey* in the same area, or by pickpockets who travel through that area. A Mexican or Central American is a *spik* or *spick*. He may also be called a *greaser* in the Southwest. A mark who resembles types commonly associated with certain nationalities may also be indicated by names for that nationality, as in "Why don't you touch up the prats for that big Dutchman?" and so on through as many national types as any mob thinks it can identify, such as Irishman, Hunky, Frog, etc.

When a mark looks *easy*, or proves to be *easy* after the *touch*, he is called a *soft touch*, or a *soft mark*. This may refer to the personality of the mark, but more often to some peculiarity of his clothing or wallet; that is, his wallet may be protruding from his hip pocket, or *scratch may spring* very easily from another pocket. Some mobs sarcastically refer to a *soft mark* as a *cousin*, either before or after he is robbed; this is probably the same as English *cozen*, more widely current in Elizabethan times than now, although Yiddish *kashn*, a fool or a sucker, is suggested by some operators who know Yiddish; earlier, the Jewish form may well have influenced the English term.

Marks may also be indicated by the section of the country from which they seem to hail (as *rebel* for a Southerner) or from what they are carrying (as *kiester mark* for a man carrying a suitcase) or from what they are doing (as *flop* for a mark who is dozing). A *fat mark* is one who looks as if he has money, or who is observed to have money. Or he may *be there*. "I seen him fanning this impression every once in a while. 'This fool must be there,' I says to Turkey." A *nervous mark* is one who is constantly shifting position, or who is difficult to approach closely; some marks cannot be robbed for this reason.

Here's one thing. There's some people that'll never lose their pocketbooks. They're just that nervous temperament, that nervous type of people that you can't get close enough to. If you can get close enough to a guy.... Everybody in the world that'll allow you to get close enough to them will lose their pocketbooks, if they ain't thinking about it. If they got their mind on it, that's a horse of a different color.

When a mark complains to the police, he is said to be *beefing* or *beefing gun*. Also, a bystander who observes pickpockets at work may *beef gun*. Sometimes these citizens report vociferously and enthusiastically on what they see. Anyone who complains about the depredations of pickpockets is said to be *yelling*, even though the *sucker* never raises his voice. "We was ripping the tip wide open and the Track was yelling murder." A *rapper* is a mark who prefers charges against a pickpocket; sometimes he can be bought off with a return of his money. "If the law won't take, the next thing is to try the rapper." When a mark discovers he has been robbed, he is said to *blow*; when he notifies the police, he is said to *cry copper*, *holler copper*, or *beef gun*. When a *rapper* cannot be halted in his determination to send the thief to jail, he is called a *righteous mark*. Usually his "righteousness" gains the mark nothing but expense and trouble, for the pickpocket operates rather securely under the *fix* and some technicality often lets him out; occasionally a witness or victim will sustain his *righteous* mood long enough to withstand the many delays which the attorney for the pickpocket knows how to engineer, and a pickpocket goes to prison for a year or two—except in these states where there are "habitual criminal" laws; there a *righteous mark* can send a thief away for years or for life, it he has much of a record. Usually, however, the efforts of a *righteous mark* backfire to his disadvantage and to the thief's advantage. The mark loses his time and effort, in addition to his money, and the pickpocket knows how to wear him down; he knows that the mark has nothing material to gain by having him convicted, and that many marks are most sensitive to material values.

Sucker trouble is a run of bad luck with marks, although this does not necessarily imply arrests or complaints to the police. The mob may simply *rumble* a number of marks consecutively or *hip* them (very slightly arouse their suspicions) or have trouble *handling* them. "They must've had money on their minds. We didn't run into nothing but sucker trouble." Sometimes *sucker trouble*, however, goes beyond mere lack of success. If a mark succeeds in catching the tool's hand or sleeve, the tool says, "He grabbed me by the throat," regardless of what part of the anatomy or the clothing the mark was lucky enough to grab. Sometimes tools use this phrase to indicate that the *sucker* became suspicious, and *throat* becomes an abstraction which may be expressed in such phrases as "He had me by the throat." When a mark actually grabs a tool, or catches him in the act—a very rare occurrence with expert pickpockets—the tool says that the mark *comes down on him.* "He come down on me before I knew what was happening." Only inexpert tools get into such a position, since even a competent *single o tool* knows how to prevent the mark from grabbing his hand at all times; with the interference of a skilled stall in *mob work*, it is known to be virtually impossible for a mark to catch the tool in the act.

If and when the mark does catch the tool with the *score* in his hands, the smart tool will *fling it* or *go to the floor with it* or *go downstairs with it.* That is, he will swiftly drop or throw the wallet at or near the victim's feet in the hope that someone will believe that it fell there or was dropped there by the victim himself. However, the psychology of marks being what it is, the victim is usually the first to stoop to retrieve his lost wallet, at which moment one or

both stalls *split out* the tool, who fades away into the crowd before the mark can *put the finger on him* or identify him to police,
witnesses, or himself, for future reference in the *line up* in case the
pickpocket is arrested. For the moment the mark is, as the saying
goes, "in pursuit but don't know which way he went."

Of course, the mere fact that a man has been robbed of his pocketbook does not cleanse him of all sin. Consequently, many marks
show a high degree of larceny themselves, and while perhaps they
would not commit an overt act of theft, largely because they neither
know how nor have the nerve to do so, they sometimes show their
dishonesty in many ways, and the pickpocket naturally uses these
manifestations for the generalization that all marks are dishonest
anyway, and so deserve to be robbed. For instance, one *cannon*
took off a *score* of $1600. The theft was reported in the papers as
$160. The pickpocket grew curious about this discrepancy and
phoned the police reporter to find out if an error had been made in
reporting. The reporter verified the amount reported lost as $160.
"I think that mark had been stealing money," commented the
thief, "and didn't dare let anyone know how much he had in that
wallet."

Instances where marks claim less than they lost are relatively
rare, however. Usually it is the other way, when there is any difference between what the mark claims he lost and what the pickpocket finds in his wallet. Many of them claim more than they lost
in the hope of recovering more, or to cover up shortages of one
kind or another in their business or domestic finances. A man who
has lost heavily at gambling, for instance, may claim he was
robbed, especially if he had no business using the money he carried
for gambling purposes; often he will do this, even though no one
has picked his pocket. Every police blotter carries such cases—
in which the police do not believe the man's story but cannot dis-
prove it, or in which the man overlooks inconsistencies in his fabri-
cation and trips himself up.

Some marks deliberately go out to "frame" a pickpocket in
order to recover money they have lost, or claim to have lost. I
have been told that this is one of the big problems in some New
York police stations, since New York has a law which permits the
thief to make restitution without compounding a felony, the
restitution being made by the court and not by the thief, after
a considerable time has elapsed and after the victim has proved his

claim to the money. Theoretically, the return of the money does not influence the judge or jury, but actually it probably results in lighter sentences, more probations, etc. Also, it encourages the victims of pickpockets to take more interest in prosecution, for they may then establish a claim. However, some marks like to make claims (bona fide or otherwise) that they have been robbed, and then hope to state their testimony in such a way that the court will order restitution from money (not necessarily theirs) found in the pickpocket's possession.

In some police stations, there is a constant trickle of what we might call "professional suckers" who visit the station daily or whenever they hear a pickpocket has been picked up, and attempt to "identify" him as the man who robbed them. Sometimes this pressure is sufficient to induce the thief to go into his *fall dough* in order to pay off the "victim" privately and eliminate him as a possible prosecuting witness; these "victims" like to study the suspect and feel him out regarding his resources and reactions to making restitution; they know that the pickpocket must have some other complaints against him too or he wouldn't be a live suspect; they also realize that some pickpockets, having stolen dozens of pocketbooks and not knowing how many of these bona fide victims might turn up as *rappers*—with each wallet potentially constituting a separate offense—might figure that it would be better to plead guilty to one *score* of, say, $200, make arrangements for restitution, and perhaps get a lighter sentence, or, in rare instances, a probated sentence. With this conviction, the other complaints are likely to lose freshness, and will probably not be pushed at all. This type of *sucker* is interesting because he has all the inclinations of a criminal, and would like to have a *racket* of his own, but being of the dominant culture, he lacks both the technological equipment and the organization (both of which he would have to acquire in the subculture) to systematize his larceny.

Mr. Danny Campion, for many years chief officer on the *whiz detail* and later on the *con detail* in New York City, once told me that one of his worst headaches came from these *suckers*, who pestered his office daily in the hope that they could find someone whom they could "identify" and seek restitution. Mr. Campion, being the kind of man he is, heard the *sucker's* complaint, listened to his descriptions of the man who robbed him, let him see the suspect, and then with a few shrewd questions separated the phony victims from the real ones—and there were a few real ones.

Campion's reputation for fairness was such that he often defended thieves who were unjustly accused by the phony *suckers* in these cases. In fact, if Campion thinks a suspect is not guilty, he will take the stand as quickly for him as he will against him if he thinks he is guilty, and many an innocent man owes his freedom to the fact that Danny Campion got on the stand and testified to what he honestly knew and believed, rather than to what the prosecution wanted him to establish. His reputation over the years as a skilled and honest detective—a reputation not so easy to establish and maintain in these days—is formidable among both the underworld and the upperworld of New York City, and has been set forth many times by writers more competent than myself.

The great majority of marks, however, do not have any angles nor do they want to cheat any poor thief who has to work hard for a living. They just report what they lost, and they usually know exactly within a dollar or two. I have on occasion been present when members of different mobs were reading the newspapers and checking up on which mobs got which *scores*. As one thief read aloud, the others would comment, "That was us." One man would say, "And we got that 160-buck score", another would say, "Here's one for $440. Anybody claim that one?" When no mobs present acknowledged it, there was speculation regarding which other mob might have taken it off, and there was no implication that this might be a phony *score*. The thieves depended on the accuracy of the *beef*, the reliability of the newspaper account, and the testimony of those present. Everything seemed to check out neatly.

The mark, then, is simply a man with a pocketbook. He is preferably from the dominant culture, for pickpockets do not like to rob anyone from the various criminal subcultures; in fact, if this happens inadvertently, the victim usually gets his money back either directly or through an intermediary. Although some bitterness naturally develops between pickpockets and marks who *beef* or prosecute, I can find little of the hatred of marks which is sometimes reported. Actually, the pickpocket likes prosperity and is never happier than when every mark has a large roll. His thieving is detached and impersonal. However, he has absolutely no scruples about taking those rolls, and no feeling of regret or guilt after they are taken. A mark is simply fair game.

CHAPTER VIII

MONEY AND VALUABLES

The Mark and His Money

The mark's pockets are important to the pickpocket only because they contain money. In fact, the pockets have become so symbolic of both the mark and his money that a mark is very often—perhaps predominantly—referred to by pockets, as a *left britch*, a *kick out*, or an *insider* which was taken at a particular time or place. In fact, the mark is thought of in terms of the pocket for which he was robbed, and the whole mob shares this imagery. If further identification is necessary, the thief making the reference will name the amount of the *score*, and then everyone remembers exactly the situation, together with many peripheral details.

I have observed that competent pickpockets seldom if ever forget the size of a *touch* taken recently, and many operators remember the size of *touches*, especially large or troublesome ones, over a period of many years. They also recall with great fidelity other details of the wallet—its kind, its condition, the presence of other papers which might be of value to the thief, the presence of papers which would be of value only to the mark, etc.

This memory for detail of all kinds extends through the criminal subcultures, and is especially evident in those groups where literacy is not high, or where little if any use can be made of written notes. Hence, pickpockets not only remember the amounts of their *scores* with great fidelity, but also retain telephone numbers in their heads without benefit of notes, remember street addresses almost indefinitely, register the times of arrival and departure of trains, retain the license numbers of police cars or other vehicles in which they have an interest long after they have made the observation, and recall the numbers of many persons they have met in prison long after their release. Good pickpockets are especially sensitive to faces, and are doubly so if those faces happen to be on detectives of the pickpocket detail. This memory seems to be effortless and automatic; perhaps either one has it or he fails to make the grade as a professional.

It is a funny thing, but I always remember scores. That is, within reason. At the end of a week I can tell you every score we took off, and where we took it, and how much and all that. I don't try to remember them. I just know. Some scores, lots of them, I guess, I remember for years. I just have to think of something to call them to mind, or we are cutting up old ones and somebody says, "Remember that mark in the fur coat that we had to frame for five times?" And somebody else will say, "You mean at that Euclid Avenue get-on?" And I'll say, "Yeah, that 85-dollar poke." But if you asked me how many 85-dollar scores I ever took off, I'd be lost right away. Of course, there are lots of small ones lost in the shuffle. But if somebody said something that brought them to mind, I would remember them, too, I think.

Pickpockets refer to all money taken from a mark as a *touch* or *score*. These are general terms. They are then broken down into wallets or pocketbooks, cash (in the form of a roll, or loose in the pocket), and valuable papers of one kind or another. Of pocketbooks there are several kinds which are classified according to their construction. The ordinary billfold which men normally carry, folded double, in the hip pocket, is called a *leather*, and this term covers a number of minor variations. Synonymous terms are *hide*, *skin*, or *poke*. There are also *okus*, *oakus*, and *hocus*, which are all related to *poke* through the ancient pseudo-Latin thieves' slang, now gone legitimate, *hocus pocus*. The relationship is phonic, and appears to have developed in modern times because *poke* suggested *hocus pocus*, not the other way around. *Poke* is probably the most popular word used by pickpockets. It appears in Western American thieves' argot during the last quarter of the past century. Perhaps its use was reënforced by the nonargot usage widely applied to the sack or pouch in which the settlers—and especially the prospectors and gamblers—carried gold in the form of coins, dust, or nuggets. Old-timers may still refer to a billfold as a *book*, clipped back from pocketbook. A *sock* is, in general, any device for carrying money on the person, including conventional type pocketbooks.

An *accordion poke* is an old-fashioned type of wallet with many folds and compartments; it usually occurs as *cordeen poke* or simply *cordeen*, with the initial "a" assimilated with the indefinite article having the same phonemic value: "He had a cordeen poke on him." A type of pocketbook which closes with small clasps is called a *tweezer* or *iowa tweezer poke*, or more often an *iowa tweezer*, though some operators favor *tweezer poke*. "Suppose it's a tweezer poke. How's that gonna be, whether it's upside down or not? What difference does that make? Suppose it's an ox tongue, suppose it's one of them old Iowa tweezers? It don't make no difference. As long as he's got pants on." This type is encountered

amongst the older gentry in rural areas, and may yield a phenomenal amount of money. "It's a square poke built on a kind of
frame. Buttoned down in the middle. You can't tell how much
money is in it [by touch] because of the frame." "Richard Dick
cracked he blowed his tweezer shooting the trotters and they went
sour on him." Another kind of wallet reported consistently in rural
localities, or amongst retired farmers, stockmen, etc. who have
moved to the settlements is the *ox tongue*. This is a long tubular
pouch, often made of horsehide, and closed with either drawstring
or clasps; it is generally carried by the kind of citizen who does not
like to be caught short of cash on his person. When a wallet is taken
from the hip pocket, it is known as a *prat poke*, but there the system
ends, and wallets taken from other pockets are called *scores*, as
pit score, bridge score, etc. When it is empty, it is *dead*, or a *cold
poke*, or *clean*. Anyone stealing an empty wallet says that he
drew a blank.

An *insurance man's poke* or an *insider* is the long flat wallet
carried inside the breast-pocket of the suit-coat. "And here's a guy
I picked up about the third race, at Lincoln Fields. He had one of
them . . . I call them an insurance man's poke." "So this guy is a
used-car dealer, and he's got a billfold like that. It was an insider."
A woman's purse is a *hanger*.

Regardless of the size of the *leather*, it is known as a *big one* or
fat one if it has a good deal of cash in it. A *nice score* is a good one,
but not so large as a *big one*. A *banner score* is the largest one taken
during the day, the trip, or the season, according to the range of the
discussion. "Banner score is an Eastern expression. When you get
into the Western or Midwestern, it's a 'red one' or a 'darb.' That's
in speaking of the score itself, not the day's grift, not of the spots
you are working but the individual score."

Money does not have to be in a pocketbook to interest a pickpocket, but it takes a more skilled tool to steal cash, either loose or
in a roll, that it does to steal a wallet. In other words, many a lesser
light can steal a wallet, especially a *prat poke*, but it takes a competent professional to *reef a kick* and remove a roll of bills. Paper
money is known, in general, as *scratch* or *soft*. "We turn out two
stiffs and a wad of soft." Some old-timers still use *rag* in the same
way that *soft* was used above. "That working stiff had over two
C's in rag on him." If the *scratch* is in a roll (and *scratch* often
implies that it is) this situation is emphasized by the term *bundle*,

and sometimes *bundle of scratch* is heard; if not, *bundle* alone conveys the meaning that it is rolled, folded, or wadded up. If it is a good *bundle*, the mark is said to be *loaded up* with *scratch*, or *loaded down* with it. On the East Coast the term *nipple* or *knipple* is heard as a synonym for *bundle*. If the *bundle* consists largely of small bills, it is called a *michigan bankroll*, or a *mish*. (There is a saying that there are more bills in that kind of bankroll than there are rabbits in the state of Michigan.) "He comes up with a bundle of scratch as big as your fist, but it's a mish—all aces." This term also indicates a fake bankroll, sometimes carried by small-time gamblers, with a newspaper core and a few bills on top. The type of bankroll sometimes carried by professional gamblers or conmen with small bills inside and a few *coarse ones* on top is a *boodle*. Single bills in the pocket, or several together which do not constitute a *bundle* are called *pieces*. "I fanned his left bridge and it felt like he had several pieces there." A *piece* also indicates a hundred dollars, as does a *bill* or a *c note*. The other well-known slang terms for various denominations of bills are in use by pickpockets, and have been for long years before they emerged into somewhat general usage: *ace*, a $1 bill; *fin*, a $5 bill; *sawbuck* or *saw*, a $10 bill; *double saw*, a $20 bill; *half a c*, a $50 bill, etc.

Metal money is of no interest to pickpockets today, but there was a time during the depression when most of them learned to steal carfare after they got on the bus or street-car. Also, up to the time that gold money was impounded by the government, pickpockets were glad to pick up $5 or $10 gold-pieces along with other money in a mark's pocket. Gold coins were known as *ridge* and silver change as *smash*. Both these terms are sometimes used by old-timers to indicate silver change. *Smash* is sometimes dropped by pickpockets to distract the attention of people on a bus or in a station, and modern *donicker hustlers* drop silver half-dollars or dollars likewise, but under different circumstances which will be described in Chapter XII. When pickings are very slim, or when there are many *scores* with only a dollar or two in each wallet, pickpockets refer to this type of *grift* as *dribs and drabs*. When they are making only a little money, or when they are making it very slowly, they say they are *grinding it up*, or *grinding up nickels and dimes*. These last two phrases are seriously used by the small-timers who actually do operate on a slim margin, and by the more successful operators as a form of hyperbole or overstatement to describe some bad luck or a time of financial difficulty, especially a desperate attempt to raise money after a *bad fall*.

Perhaps it should be noted again that all pickpockets look on the mark as fair game, and there is no conscience about stealing his money. It has been said by various writers that pickpockets develop a hatred for the mark which they nourish as a sort of rationalization of their theft. I have also been told this by operators on other rackets; in fact, confidence men say that a *cannon* hates a mark so badly that he cannot bring himself to talk with him, and hence seldom is able to become any kind of a *con man*, even a *short con man*. Investigation does not bear this out, however, for several pickpockets have to my knowledge become successful confidence men. Pickpockets do not verify either directly or indirectly the generalization that they hate marks, though of course there is no sympathy expressed for them either. They regard a mark as a fisherman thinks of a bass.

Jewelry and Valuables

Sometimes wallets contain papers which are valuable or negotiable. Certain kinds of checks, for instance, can be cashed, either by the thief or by someone to whom he sells or gives them. As a rule, however, the better class of pickpockets do not want to become involved in cashing a check, however negotiable it might be, as for instance a government check or a payroll check on a large company. They know that they are not specialists in this *racket*, that people who cash federal checks can be handled in federal court, and that it is better to pick another pocket than to take the risk. These checks are called *stiffs* or *paper;* government checks are *whiskers* or *whiskers stiffs*. Sometimes these are left in the wallet when it is dropped into a mailbox, to be returned to the mark.

Occasionally there are other papers which interest the pickpocket for one reason or another. There may be one or more stock certificates which the pickpocket cannot cash, but which the victim might pay to have returned; if these represent a large enough amount of money and the operator knows enough about handling such a situation, he may collect a hundred dollars or more, but this is rare. The same is true of deeds to real estate and other valuable personal property. Here is an example showing how such cases might be handled to the profit of the pickpocket. This type of operation would, however, be attempted only by a very capable mob.

I'll tell you what we did one time. We was at Lincoln Fields Racetrack then, and the tool nailed a guy there, and he had a long poke, about that long, you see? When we opened it up and looked in there, and there was about two hundred and a lot of horse pedigrees in there . . . all on onion skin, you know. And they was all original—they wasn't no carbon copies. So we figured, well. . . . And he had two hundred and he was an owner. An owner and trainer, too. Back of Lincoln Fields there was a bunch of old buildings there, and they had sheds . . . storage sheds in behind them, you know. So I go down there and I plant this poke up there in that storage shed. He had his badge in there . . . his owner's and trainer's badge and everything. Next morning in the paper came out in the morning edition of the *Tribune* and offered $500 reward for the pocketbook, so we figured it over for a while and we figured what the heck, we have a chance to get that $500. Probably more than we'd make today, anyway, so I go up and get his room number in the Morrison Hotel, see. So I went up to that floor in the Morrison Hotel and I found one of them linen closets, one of them supply closets, and I put the leather underneath a bucket. I goes up there and knock on his door. See what kind of a guy he is, you know. I said, "I seen your ad in the paper this morning."

"Look," he said, "There's no amount of money can replace those"—they call them pedigrees, you know—"there's no amount of money can re-place those."

"Well," I said, "some people contacted me this morning. They told me they could replace them for you, with your pocketbook intact," I said, "but without any money."

"Oh," he said, "I don't want the money back. That don't make any difference," he said. And he ran his hand in his pocket. He said, "Here's five one-hundred dollar bills. I'll give you that, if you can just get those pedigrees back for me. That's the main thing."

I said, "You don't mean no monkey business?" And I put my hand in my pocket like that. I said, "You see what I got here."

"Yeah," he said, "I know, I know."

I didn't have nothing. No gun nor nothing. I said, "OK, I'll go see those people. I'll be back in ten or fifteen minutes. I wouldn't want you to call up."

He said, "I wouldn't call nobody." So I stood outside the door for a while and listened, you know—to see if the guy was calling anybody. Then I tiptoed down the hall to that linen closet. And I tiptoed back and knocked.

I said, "Here you are. Gimme the money." I said, "Here you are." He was tickled to death to get them, and I took off like a big bird.

As a rule, smart *cannons* do not destroy or meddle with valuable personal papers. They *turn over* the wallets at specified intervals.

"So I went up to the kip to turn over this poke, because I didn't want to open it on the street." "They said, 'Come up the street if you are that smart. Come on up the street and we'll turn that thing over . . . so we turned it over and we had a pretty fair score." "He had the pokes in his coat tail. So we're going out to turn them over, and of course when we hit the spot where we should turn them over, why there was nothing to turn over." While empty *leathers* are *dinged* at the end of the working period (whenever the mob stops work to *turn them over*) in some safe and convenient place—that is, disposed of so that they will not turn up to enrage the victim or embarrass the pickpockets—those wallets containing valuable papers are sometimes returned to their owners, with the money taken out, of course. There are several ways to do this, perhaps the safest being to drop the wallet into a down-town mailbox, knowing that the mailman will turn it in to the post office, and that the identification contained in the wallet will assure delivery to the rightful owner. This is not done for reasons of sentiment, or fair play, or consideration for the *sucker*. It is done for reasons of public relations, since a victim who has lost, say, $80 but has received back irreplaceable papers might be a reluctant witness against someone accused of stealing pocketbooks; also, when the *fix* is in, a citizen who has just lost several valuable papers becomes an insistent and difficult *beef* for the police to deal with. If they are able to return the wallet (and the post office will usually turn in the wallet with a report to the city detectives) he feels quite good even though he has lost his money. This is called *cooling the mark out*.

Wallets are disposed of by competent *cannons* in places where they will not be likely to come to anyone's attention. This means behind billboards, in garbage or trash receptacles, in the storm sewers. Some mobs visit a moving picture theater once or twice a day and there in the security of darkness, *turn over the leathers*, divide the *knock up* (the day's take) equally, and carefully deposit the *dead skins* under a seat near the back of the theater where they will not be found immediately. Some operators follow a pattern in disposing of wallets; others vary their methods so as to avoid leaving a trail of any kind. There is, in a certain Midwestern city, a crack in the foundations of the State Capitol; I am told that it has been the custom for many years for pickpockets to drop empty wallets into this apparently bottomless receptacle. Such a custom also expresses, in an insolent sort of way, the attitude of the members of the subculture toward the institutions of the dominant culture.

In fact, by asking what pickpockets find in wallets besides money, one might get at some index regarding what members of the dominant culture value most. The report is dismal, the most consistently recurring nonmonetary items being contraceptive devices, usually described as in a "beat up" condition. Many men carry photographs of their children; sometimes they include their wives, but more often "some broad" in whom they are currently interested. One tool reports, "Doc, sometimes I find poetry, beautiful poetry, wrote by some broad, I guess. It is a shame to go to the sewer with it."

Occasionally there are articles of a pornographic nature, as can be seen by the following account:

One time in Evanston—that's right up the Lake from Chicago—I seen a fat mark come out of a jug, and I give the hook the office, and he cut into him and so we nailed him. After he was beat, he says, "Kid, case that Bates and come back. This is a big one." So I put the tail on him and he went right up into the elevated station and grabbed a train for Chicago. No, he never blowed, or nothing. So I kept the meet back on the main drag with the wire. The hook says, "Kid, if this one is as big as I think it is, we can knock off work for today. It is a heavy one." So we are afraid to carry it around so we go up to my flop and he takes it out. It's one of them flat insiders. And it's that thick. With rubber bands around it both ways. And what do you think was in it? Money? Not one nickel. We turned it over . . . and Doc, if I didn't know you was a broad-minded man, I wouldn't be telling you this. That son of a buck, he had it full of pictures. Dirty pictures. If he had one, he had a hundred. If he had one picture in there . . . dirty, filthy pictures, all photographs. . . . Doc, I never seen nothing like that before. Did I look at them? Well, yes, I admit I did. [Here the informant gives an embarrassed description of what he saw.] So I looked at my partner and he looked at me, and I says, "I'm going to tear this thing up and put it down the donicker. If either one of us ever got snatched in the neck with this on us, we'd get life."

In former times—up to about ten years ago—the jewelry of the mark was always interesting to pickpockets. Today very little of it is stolen, the exceptions being the weaker or borderline mobs who need it to eke out the cash they are able to steal, and, among capable operators, the theft of some particularly valuable piece, such as a good diamond or a fine watch. However, with cash plentiful, what good pickpocket wants to take the trouble and risk of pawning jewelry, when he can steal the money direct and leave no *tail?* The answer is that the theft of jewelry is now obsolete, and a knowledge of how to steal it expertly is largely restricted to mature men who learned when the practise was still popular. Nevertheless, a change in social conditions or in our economy might possibly motivate a return to the practise, and therefore, it may be pertinent to discuss briefly the argot as it concerns the theft of jewelry; this also has some historical and etymological significance, for terminology is sometimes transferred to situations where jewelry is no longer involved.

Jewelry is still lifted in most foreign countries. In fact, while studying the contraband drug traffic in Mexico, I suffered the loss of a Phi Beta Kappa key which was *binged* off my watch-chain; I suspect that this thief was after the watch and chain, but it is possible that he loved learning for itself alone, and that he coveted the key as a fetish rather than for the gold it contained. In either case, I suspect that he overvalued it; but we must remember that in Latin cultures the arts and sciences are much more highly regarded than in our own.

The most commonly stolen articles of jewelry were, some years ago, watches or the watch and chain complete. Watches were called *soupers* (from the old fashioned large-model timepieces which were stolen for their gold cases, known as *kettles*) and the spelling (amongst those who can spell) is *super*, for the relationship to *kettle* is not recognized. A pocket watch is also a *block*, while the watch and chain is a *block and tackle*; the complete *outfit* is also called a *front*. The watch by itself is sometimes called an *onion* or *thimble* by old-timers. A gold chain was a *slang*, and the common phrase was *souper and slang*. This was also called an *outfit* or *sling*. "His prats were clean, so I nicked his sling." "The Yellow Kid got his start and his monicker peddling cheap soupers to Loop bartenders. He was just a punk and he said his brother was a dip. Some said he just bought the soupers from some fence, but anyway he sold the story and not the souper." The Yellow Kid, we might add, must have sold his story rather than the watch his brother was supposed to have stolen, for hot watches in those days were a dime a dozen around the Loop, and the bartenders there were highly allergic to the purchase thereof, or even to taking them in trade. However, the Kid's subsequent rise to eminence as a big-time *confidence man* would seem to lend some credence to this legend, which is believed by many old-timers.

Watches were, of course, valued for their gold and the works were usually *dinged*, while the cases were sold to dealers in old gold. They were generally classified as *red outfits* or *white outfits*, according to whether or not the watch and chain were of yellow or white gold, or silver. Many thieves simply *binged* or *banged* the *souper*, that is, twisted it off the chain by spreading the ring which went into the watch-stem. Good wrist watches are sometimes taken today by *flop workers* and others, who peddle them intact.

Any kind of jewelry, usually exclusive of watches, was—and still is—referred to as *slum*. This term is borrowed from the old-time circus *pitch men* and carnival *flat jointers*, who applied it to the very shoddy jewelry they used in their *rackets*. If there are diamonds in it, it may be called *ice*; a pearl necklace, which is sometimes worth stealing even in these days, is a *bead rope* or a *rope*. A man's tie-pin, seldom worn nowadays, was a *prop*. If it had a diamond setting, it was referred to as a *stone*. "A stone is the softest touch there is, unless it's anchored." By *anchored*, the thief means secured by a guard or lock (*anchor*); while this will prevent the ordinary pickpocket from removing it with his fingers in most cases, it is no insurance against those who carry *nippers* with which to snip off the stem of the pin. The necktie or scarf from which a stickpin is taken is a *choker*. A watch-charm or any minor bauble such as a lavaliere or ear-pendant is a *dangler*. Anything of inferior quality, or any imitation of the real thing is *shag* or *crow*. "Ella Boze knew that skin was crow, or Sophie wouldn't've been wearing it." Handkerchiefs, especially silk ones carried in the breast pocket, were also sometimes stolen. They are still called *wipes*. "English Alfie used to say that in them days they nailed wipes . . . used to get sixpence for them." Also, *fob workers* used them in removing money from the *jerve*. "A fob-worker uses a wipe to clout coins."

Stickpins are stolen in a number of ways, but perhaps the quickest and easiest, not to mention the safest, is for the tool to open a newspaper and pretend to read it in front of the mark. The center fold of the newspaper is gradually eased up under the mark's chin, which act is not likely to attract attention in a crowded station or on a bus or subway car. The center fold is then hooked under the setting, slight pressure upward on the paper removes the pin from the tie, and it slides down the center fold into the tool's hand, into his pocket, or into the hand of the stall, which is waiting at the bottom of the fold.

The stones in stickpins were named according to their quality and value with terms like *nigger head* (a flawed diamond), *cat's eye* (a stone with a yellow cast to it), *fish eye* (an imitation diamond), etc. *A chip* is a diamond weighing less than 25 points or, some say, less than ¾ carat; an *old mine stone* is a diamond or, on occasion, another type of gem, cut in such an old-fashioned way that its value is affected.

Rings were also taken, often right off the fingers of the marks who wore them—a sort of theft still common in some foreign countries; in fact several years ago, there was an Austrian exhibition-pickpocket performing in this country who did spectacular work on public dance floors and on the public stage, removing rings, wrist watches, stick pins, and all kinds of jewelry from both men and women without *rumbling* them. At least once on a large hotel dance floor he removed many sets of suspenders from the male guests, who had to hold up their pants while they walked to the bandstand to reclaim their supports. The stones in rings were also classified, and the settings are of some interest, since the stone may be removed from the setting if the ring itself cannot be removed from the finger, or the settings may have a value as gold. Thus we had such terms as *egyptian setting, tiffany setting, basket setting,* etc., which were not argot words originally, but rather technical jewelers' terms borrowed through the *fences* or pawnbrokers who dealt in stolen jewelry.

The close-in, delicate work done by thieves who stole jewelry from the person is verification of the pickpockets' own classification of their craft as essentially a *sneak job,* and the closer a *cannon* is to the *sneak,* the more successful he will be. This attitude toward the mark, this way of approaching the job, this extreme delicacy of touch, this lightning speed coupled with the ability to conceal one's movements from others, this ability to melt into a crowd without attracting attention are not simply the skills cultivated independently by maladjusted personalities who take to thievery as an expression of frustration or conflicts or sexual rejection. These skills and the attitudes behind them are almost standardized; they are used with some variations and modifications against many different dominant cultures; they appear to represent the distillation of skills, techniques, and abilities passed down through millennia in a subculture which specialized in a certain type of theft from the dominant culture.

It should also be noted that some pickpockets are still on the lookout for marks carrying small packages or pouches of *stones*; these may be unset diamonds as they are bought and sold in the jewelry business. Most of these thefts occur in the East, and especially in New York, where unset diamonds may be transferred by dealers or buyers in considerable quantities.

The Mark and His Pockets

The pickpocket, and especially the tool, almost literally lives in a world of pockets, or *kicks*. His waking hours are filled with schemes to get into them; his working time is spent actually doing so; when he is not working, he is dreaming about the *big ones* in someone's pocket somewhere, to be taken somehow. The tool especially, with his highly developed sense of touch, has a knowledge of the insides of the world's pockets which is almost fantastic; some tools register even the body-oils of the mark which permeate the cloth of the linings and alter the consistency of the clothing. "Everybody's clothes are different. The oil from your body gets into the linings, and a tool has to be wise to that." However, most of this esoteric knowledge is useless to anyone but the tool, and he uses it for a very brief instant while he is inside; furthermore, most of it is incapable of articulation in clumsy words, and must remain forever sealed in the nerve-endings of the tool's fingertips. "Every man's pocket is different. There is that oil in the skin that gets into the pocket. Some people get their clothes cleaned often. Some never get them cleaned, so the pockets are all different. Some reef up fast, others won't."

The mark's pockets are all duly located and classified; because of the almost universal wearing of standard, mass-produced suits by men in the United States, this classification varies little; in fact, for practical purposes, it never varies at all. With the male wardrobe being what it is, we have only pants, coats, and, now disappearing, vests. The vest pockets, however, may be almost eliminated from the pickpocket's list for the simple reason that only one, that one sometimes found inside a vest and comparable to the inside-coat pocket in position, is commonly used to carry money. It is called the *insider*, and marks are known to carry one or two large bills there, presumably tightly buttoned up and safe from all harm. "It's always good to try the insider—there might be a big bill there." Rarely outside vest pockets are referred to as *vest jerves*, and the lower ones are called *downstairs*. "As you say, the vest kicks are of little importance and only real old-timers would call those kicks by any name at all." The term *insider* also applies to any other secret pocket built into the lining of the vest, which pocket may also be called a *plant*. To the pickpocket, incidentally, the term *insider* has become an abstraction meaning possession of anything, not necessarily something which can be put into that pocket. "How'd you like to have a Cadillac in your insider?"

This leaves us the pants and the coat, in the summer at least. In the pants, the side pockets are called *britch kicks* or *britches* (often pronounced *bridges*) and by a few old-timers, *breeches*. These are usually referred to as the *left britch* or *right britch*, as the case may be. The hip pockets are *prat kicks* and are likewise the *left prat* or *right prat*. In the plural they are simply *prats*. Hip pockets may also be called *kiesters* or *kiester kicks*. The watch pocket just under the belt-line on the right in the front of the pants is a *fob*, *jerve*, or *britch jerve* (often pronounced *jarve*); in and around Philadelphia, this pocket is known as a *dibby*.

The side pockets of a suit-coat are called *coat tails*, comprising a *left tail* and a *right tail*. Negro pickpockets favor the term *tail pits* for these pockets, and this term is being accepted by some white *cannons*. These terms are often shortened to *tails*, as in "I fanned his tails and the only thing there was a pack of butts." Rarely one hears the side coat pocket called a *sack*. The most important pocket in the coat from the pickpocket's point of view is the *coat pit*, or the inside breast pocket, usually on the right-hand side of the coat. Here the long, flat wallets are carried. "To score on a coat pit, you got to get the tog up under his chin." This is often shortened to *pit*, which also means a shoulder holster for a pistol worn under the coat or under the shirt; sometimes, to avoid confusion, this is called a *gun pit*. The little ticket pocket either inside or outside the suit-coat is a *coat jerve*. The outside breast pocket is a *wipe kick*. "Few scores come from the wipe kick, but a lot of ticket snatchers get scores from that kick on the tracks."

Today, most *bridges* are cut with the *crack* (which is the opening to any pocket) running parallel to or congruent with the side-seam of the trousers. However, in some custom-made trousers, in riding breeches or jodhpurs, and in many makes of overalls or workpants, the *bridges* are cut with the *crack* running parallel to the waistband, or cutting diagonally across from the corner of the *jerve* to the side seam of the pants; this type of pocket is called a *top britch* or an *uptown britch*.

The outside pockets in an overcoat are called *side kicks* (from which we get a venerable American idiom) and the coat itself is called a *tog* if it is a topcoat, raincoat, trench coat, or other lightweight garment. The outside coat pockets are *tog tails*, the inside breast pocket a *tog pit*. An overcoat of full size and weight is called a *benny*, cut back from one *Benjamin* of Biblical fame, but *tog* is generally used to include an overcoat too. The side pockets of a sweater are called *patch pockets* (this term is not used with reference to men's coats, contrary to standard usage) but the term is also applied to the pockets of a woman's suit; hence a *patch pocket worker* is not a "purebred" pickpocket, but rather a *moll buzzer*.

There are marks who attempt to influence fate and gimmick up the law of averages against theft from the person. These unscrupulous persons are held in great contempt by the *class cannons*, although their precautions to protect valuables may thwart the lesser brethren. The most common protective device used by marks is a *spike*, *nail*, or *dipsy*. "Sometimes you have got a dipsy to beat." This is a simple safety pin put through the pocket from the inside of the coat or the pants, and thought to preclude removal of the pocket's contents, since the pocket is securely pinned shut. However, a good tool can open one of these in a second or two extra, and its presence only makes him the more interested in the *score*, since it would not be *nailed down* if it were not of some size. Some marks, especially those fresh from the soil, have their wives sew their money—that is, their big-money—into their inside coat pocket, or into a side pants pocket, but this only tips off the tool that there is a good *score* there, and causes him no great inconvenience. Some marks use a *chain* or *string* on their wallets, and although these chains may look formidable to the layman, a good tool takes them by *banging* or *binging* them, that is, twisting off the ring on the end of the chain; although watches are seldom stolen by pickpockets today, any tool who has had experience at *banging a souper* (twisting a pocket watch off its chain) will have no difficulty with a chained wallet.

For a mark to wear a topcoat or overcoat in cold weather is not considered unethical, but all models approved by pickpockets have a *slit* in the back to facilitate walking and to enable the tool to get up under the *tog*. Marks who insist on carrying a fat wallet underneath a long, slitless coat may possibly find that an enterprising tool has found it necessary to make a slit where there was none before. It should be added that *class cannons* frown on the use of the razor blade except under the most drastic circumstances, and even then some of the more orthodox refuse to approve it.

One instance, however, has come to my attention where there just wasn't any other way. A *road mob* was attending a large convention of organized labor in the balmy weather of fall before the *togs* came out. However, the skies opened with the convention, and it continued to rain steadily. Even so, the pickings were quite good until some enterprising hucksters appeared on the streets with truckloads of large plastic ponchos which sold for a dollar. This was an irresistible bargain, and soon everyone was parading the streets in long, crisp draperies which could not be raised quietly to get at the pockets beneath. And so the mob held a conference and decided to use the blade, to operate swiftly and efficiently, and then to depart before public relations problems began to pyramid. As a result, within a few hours there appeared many victims unconsciously wearing the badge of their condition in the form of a slit in the rear of their ponchos. The tool, particularly, expressed some professional revulsion at having to pass these people on the street and observe the marks of his own lack of professional conduct; he did concede under pressure, however, that there was a certain convenience in being able to spot at a glance marks who had already been robbed; this was especially handy since it was raining and since everyone looked pretty much alike in their uniform ponchos anyway.

To summarize, there is no safe pocket in which to carry money or valuables—if there are pickpockets about and if there is enough in the pocket to interest them. Their delicate sense of touch enables them to *fan* and judge the number of bills with some accuracy, though of course they cannot foretell denominations. This exploration is done on the outside of the victim's clothing. Contrary to popular belief, the professional pickpocket seldom, if ever, actually goes completely inside the victim's pocket; that is, his whole hand does not disappear into the pocket. While there are many ways of robbing a pocket, most skilled tools do their work with two fingers, which always work very near the *crack* or pocket opening. "Your fingers are in the pocket, but yet they aren't," is the substance of what several tools say about this, especially when talking about *reefing a britch kick*. For the *prat kick* there is even less penetration of the pocket. Says one tool, "For a prat poke, I just top it up, and pinch it, and let the mark walk away from it." Says another,

"Unless it's a prat poke standing on end—that's the only kind I'll fork—I reef it. When it starts out, I let the mark ease it the rest of the way out by his own movement. We are both walking and the stall too, you understand."

I have noted that some psychiatrists and psychologists suggest that there is some sexual symbolism about both pocketbooks and pockets—as of course there may be about many other things—with the pockets representing the female genitals and tying in with the theory relating theft to the sex act. While this is, of course, not impossible, I have not observed any verbalizations or attitudes which would lead me to agree; in fact, female pickpockets use the same techniques men use (would this imply latent homosexuality?) and both seem to use them as a practical matter. As a matter of fact, both men and women *on the whiz* seem to be universally and overtly heterosexual; I have never heard of a successful professional *cannon* who was overtly homosexual.

CHAPTER IX

THE THIEF AND THE LAW

The Traditional Pattern

There is ancient ritual governing the relations between the dominant culture and the subcultures which prey upon it. Part of this ritual embodies not only the rules of combat between culture and subculture, but the code of chivalry as well. Therefore, much of this chapter will deal with Trager's Cultural Index No. 9, Defense, which includes, among thieves, dealing with the enemy on a fiscal basis.

To the layman the relationship between the thief and the law appears to be more simple than it really is. He looks upon anyone who transgresses the law as open to arrest, prosecution, conviction, and punishment. Therefore, if a thief steals Mr. Smith's pocketbook, the police will naturally try to catch him, if Mr. Smith will only report the theft. Should Mr. Smith be so fortunate as to capture the thief red-handed, the police will naturally arrest the man, the courts will prosecute him, and, assuming that Mr. Smith's complaint is bona fide, a jury or judge will convict the thief and send him to prison. He serves his time, learns his lesson, and sins no more. If everything worked out this way, the dominant culture could control the predatory subcultures without difficulty, and what is more, it could exterminate them, for *no criminal subculture can operate continuously and professionally without the connivance of the law*.

This does not mean that the entire system of law enforcement, including the courts, is corrupt. In fact, the connivance of the law with any kind of crime seldom involves a substantial number of officials in any department, except in instances of extreme municipal corruption, some of which have been exposed in recent years. In the case of pickpockets, a very few officers, perhaps only one or two, are sufficient. The *fix* cannot normally involve too many people, for its profits are then split too many ways. A small number of unscrupulous public servants, however, can operate, within any department, an arrangement whereby certain types of professional crime is protected within certain limits. Beyond these, the criminal must be prepared to go to court and perhaps do time.

The *fix* as a widespread arrangement between police and professional criminals has been demonstrated many times by competent investigators; it is almost a national institution. The overall pattern is well known. In this study we are considering the *fix* as a general mechanism, and we do not have any specific city in mind. However, in order to keep our perspective, we must remember that the wide-open days for pickpockets are over. This is partly due to better law-enforcement in general, partly to pressure from merchants and the press to eliminate pickpockets because they tend to give a town a bad name and hurt business, and partly to the fact that the number of pickpockets appears to be steadily decreasing. The pickpocket is not one of the pillars of underworld society as he was a generation ago. He does not have the income to corrupt the law on a very large scale.

In addition, we must bear in mind that the law does not operate in a vacuum. If police, for instance, are carefully selected, thoroughly trained, and adequately paid, the protection of crime decreases markedly. Police practices and the courts reflect, to some extent at least, a cross-section of public opinion. They become corrupt, usually, in inverse proportion to the participation of solid citizens in local government. This is why we see, in many American cities, a cycle of advancing corruption, an overthrow by a reform administration of aroused citizens, complacency, and an eventual return to corruption. Good government exists only as long as good people work to keep it that way. The pickpocket, who has a fine nose for any degree of corruption, can always find certain cities where he can purchase some degree of protection, either before he starts to work or afterward in the event of arrest. Likewise, he tries to avoid those cities or those districts which are known to be *wrong*, or where the police will not have any part of protecting him. It is significant that in our own times one major *racket* practiced by one subculture has been stamped out because public pressure forced police action on a national scale. This is kidnapping, which was an adjunct to the *heavy* subculture. Arrest and conviction are today almost foregone conclusions. These are the real deterrent factors. It is well known that no one can get away with it any more.

As a sidelight, it is significant that special classes of law-violators or "criminals" created by new laws or special laws like the income-tax laws or the prohibition laws are not accepted by the already existent subculture as bona fide professional criminals, unless they have previously operated on a professional basis and have their roots in the subculture. Because they are derived from different strata of the dominant culture, it is not likely that they will ever crystallize into anything approximating the traditional criminal subcultures. Their only bond in common is conviction for a similar offense.

Likewise, the "occasional" criminals—members of legitimate society who have been sent to prison for law-violations seldom connected with organized professional crime—have little chance for acceptance amongst professionals, though some eventually become professionals. As a group they are regarded as *squares*, and are just *suckers* or marks or *chumps* who happen to be in prison.

The ancient tradition of connivance between the law and the criminal element is well known. It was well established in Europe as a principle before America was settled; there it operated on a small, tight scale, since crime was not very big business. However, with the settling of the New World and the consequent flooding of new areas with people of all shades of opinion about crime, together with large numbers of professionals who came either voluntarily or under the deportation laws, the professional criminals not only increased in numbers and spread over a very large geographical area, but infused themselves into the dominant culture in a way which made it difficult to tell a member of the subculture from a member of the dominant culture without close examination.

In fact, in some entire frontier communities in the 19th century the criminal subculture became temporarily the dominant culture; the dominant culture was able to reassert itself only through the activities of vigilantes and other quasi-legal citizens' groups who used armed force, or the threat thereof, to force the subculture back into a subordinate role. This upsurge of the subcultures into political and economic power has left a mark on many American cities, where there are still privileges and advantages accruing to members of the criminal subculture.

As professional crime in the 20th century became big business involving an incredible national gross, and as the prohibition mobs learned how to apply organization to the aggressive invasion of areas of the subculture not previously subject to their control, they were able to exert such pressure that law enforcement became, at certain times and in certain places, subject to control from the underworld rather than from the dominant culture through legally constituted channels. The story of wholesale graft and corruption which has come to light in cities like Chicago, New Orleans, Detroit, New York City, Jersey City, Miami, Los Angeles, Boston, Memphis, Kansas City, Cleveland, Denver, and many others is now a matter of well documented record. Anyone who reads is familiar with these scandals, and anyone who thinks about the problem can deduce that these outbreaks of public indignation and reform are perhaps only minor ripples on the surface. The investigations of the Kefauver Committee and later the O'Connor Committee within the past several years leave one feeling that the criminal subcultures are better organized, more prosperous, integrated more closely with certain elements in the dominant culture, and perhaps more powerful than at any time in the past.

The Pickpocket and the Fix

Although the thief as a class is perhaps not so important, relatively speaking, in the criminal subculture as he once was, and the pickpocket is a minor sort of thief, there is still protection for him under the large umbrella of the law. The pickpocket takes hundreds where other types like racketeers, professional gamblers, *confidence men*, bookmakers, numbers racketeers, narcotics wholesalers, etc., take hundreds of thousands and even millions. No one would call a pickpocket a "big shot," though some individuals may be personally highly respected in the subculture and may have some very good connections both in other *rackets* and with the law. However, the protection of pickpockets appears to be neither as brazen nor as extensive as it was in former years.

If we contrast, say, Chicago now with Chicago in 1900, we get the idea not only that the number of pickpockets is drastically reduced, but that their quality is upgraded so that only the better class can work under protection. In 1900 anyone who thought he was a pickpocket could *get his duke down* and see how good he was. If there was a *beef*, and there was certain to be, it could be handled through the several powerful saloon-keeper-fixers who were the guardians of "clean" politics in those days; two of these who have seldom been equaled and never surpassed were Bathhouse John Coughlin and Michael Kenna (Hinky Dink). Their regime came to an end only within the past few years, with the death of "The Bath." They protected legions of pickpockets. Meanwhile, generations of detectives, brought up rigorously in the tradition of the *fix*, did the best they could to handle the demands for work permits by pickpockets, and took their *end* in what is euphemistically called *stem court*—a procedure by which a pickpocket is accosted, arrested, charged, tried, convicted, and fined all in the course of a few minutes by one or two detectives. This is all done on the *stem* or street, and the open-air atmosphere of the procedure gives it not only its name, but labels it with an informality and casualness which has, from earliest times, characterized the relations between the Chicago police and the underworld.

And then, around towns like Chicago and Detroit. Now in Detroit, it used to be 25 bucks every time they saw you. A lot of times you'd be on the nut 125, 150, or even 200 bucks before you ever made a dime. I've gone out to get my supper and got on the nut for 100. Before I ever got to a restaurant and back, I'd get seen by different mobs. When I say mobs in that respect, I mean mobs of coppers. They'd throw up their hand at you. Well, you better put 25 down at Billy the Bum's for that team of coppers, and you got to remember who seen you and who didn't see you, because if you didn't, you'd get a tamping the next time they seen you. You gotta have a pretty good memory.

Naturally, most pickpockets would like to work permanently and perpetually under the *fix*. That would be an ideal situation from their point of view. They could rob all and sundry, and the *beefs* could echo to the high heavens, but no one would ever be sent away for this crime against property. "You gotta get a beef unless you ding the poke. What are you gonna do, go back and hand a guy his plane tickets? Say, 'Here's your plane tickets, I got your poke'? What are you gonna do?" There is nothing that so quiets the feelings of insecurity in a pickpocket's soul as the knowledge that the law will go as far as possible to protect him should a victim of his depredations have the temerity to *beef gun* or *beef whiz*. "Elmer Fink was brushed off for his okus in the alley; he beefed gun and yelled that he blowed a greasy fin. He beefed whiz and wanted his cush back that was never taken." However, this complete, all-purpose type of *fix* is increasingly difficult, for several reasons.

First, as we have said, the pickpocket is not in the big money, relatively speaking. Therefore, he can *fix* only one or two officers rather than the whole department, as was the case in some cities in the past. Second, the *beefs* come in to the department, and the *fix* soon becomes obvious if the detectives who were *fixed* do not produce some pickpockets. Last, the old-line type of detective who accepted the *fix* as a natural part of his due is passing, and in his place come better trained, better paid officers who are perhaps not so vulnerable, or who know how to "take" in less obvious ways. All this adds up to the fact that the *fix* is no longer as easy or as secure as it once was.

Modern pickpockets, therefore, while they would theoretically like a permanent and secure *fix*, are of two schools in actual practice. The first likes to *fix* in advance and to work only in those localities where they are protected, and only for a short time at that, for they will shortly attract notice, and ultimately bring trouble to their patron saint at headquarters. Members of this group like to make all arrangements in advance and pay as they go; thus they are able to stay out of jail for remarkably long periods of time. The other school reasons that it is impossible to arrange an *airtight fix* in many places anyhow, and so why not go right ahead and work *on the sneak*? "Fixing in advance ain't worth the trouble outside of a few few spots. Not many more coppers like the old coppers." As soon as any *fuzz* that can't be brushed off lights on them, they offer to pay, not only for past sins but for future indulgences. "You'll make any fuzz that might be flying around. That's how it got its name—fuzz flies around and it is catching. Fuzz will light on you, so that is it. Fuzz and fur." It used to be that *working on the sneak* worked often enough to make it practical; today it is risky business, although some mobs seem to survive fairly well under it. There are some who develop a kind of professional ambivalence, *fixing* in advance in some places at some times, but *working on the sneak* at others.

There are various ways of approaching the *fix*, whatever school of thought one may subscribe to. In some communities one can deal directly and unashamedly with the detectives; in others, there is a local *fixer* who handles such matters for the political organization which is in power, and he sells protection on a highly systematic basis. In some cities there are several *fixers*, each of whom handles the *fix* for different types of *racket*. In no case is the *fix* absolute and secure; anything might happen to *curdle* it, in which case the pickpocket would have to be prepared to take his medicine. "Memphis, Tennessee, was known as the rightest town in all the world at one time, when Mike Haggarty was doing the mending. They had the cannon, the heavy, the con, and the bawdy houses in full swing. And then the fix curdled . . . just went sour."

Neither officers nor *fixers* like to deal with amateurs, beginners, or inept operators; they will protect only smooth, well-known professionals who can be counted on not only to work with a minimum of disturbance, but who will protect the *fix* on whatever level it operates if things go against them. For a professional thief to talk to a grand jury is regarded as subversive by both the law and the underworld.

There are advantages and disadvantages in both systems. The *fix* applied directly to the *whiz dick* and his partner is simpler, quicker, and often cheaper than the other way around. This is known by old-timers as *fitting the fur*, or *fitting his mitt*. However, such a *fix* is usually good only against arrest by these two officers. They will not pick him up unless he gets caught red-handed; if the thief must be arrested to keep up appearances, the officers will find a way to turn him loose afterward, charge another nonpaying thief with his offenses, and perhaps send off the other fellow to do some time, just as a lesson to those who don't pay off.

If the pickpocket is arrested and comes to trial, the *right* officers will do all they can to have him acquitted; if he must be convicted, they will use their good offices to get him a probated sentence (which may be vacated later on by a beneficent judge) or, at least, a light sentence. Trying a protected *cannon* is uncommon, for usually there are many delays and maneuvers between arrest and conviction, and *whiz dicks* are very sharp about helping their clients. For instance, persons who have been thought to have an ironclad case against a thief caught in the act may appear to press the charge in court, only to find that they have come to the wrong courtroom or the wrong court; sometimes they have been notified of the wrong date or time. And so—what court would hold a poor thief if the prosecuting witness or witnesses did not appear against him?

Whiz dicks are also expert at coaching witnesses and complainants, and a little friendly talk with a *beefer* may convince him that he has so weak a case that it isn't worth while to prosecute; his coöperation is often fostered by the return of his money, or any part of it necessary to calm him down, for both the *whiz* and the *fuzz* are thrifty and do not believe in returning any more than is necessary. Then there are also cases wherein the mark is rampant with righteous indignation; he has some political connection, and is determined to send the *whiz* to prison. In cases like this, the *fur* may feel him out to see how much more he lost than he actually did; in other words, if he lost $65 and his wallet comes back with $165 in it, his ulcers may recede in jig-time. It is always understood, however, that if a case becomes too "tough," the thief must take his chances in court, and perhaps serve his time.

When the *fixer* handles all arrangements, there is broader coverage, the price is perhaps somewhat higher, and the risk of *curdling* is probably smaller. The reason for this is that the *fixer* works through the organization and can have influence upon a considerable number of people, even unto the judge himself. Police officers can, if necessary, be handled from above, and the *fixer* is not nearly so vulnerable to personal pressures as are individual detectives. At the same time, the organization has to be even more careful than individual policemen about backing inept operators or professionals whose word is not good; in the event of a political shake-up or an investigation, such thieves might be very unreliable and could testify against the officers or the courts where they were protected. This almost never happens.

There is an added advantage in working through the *fixer* in that whichever party is in power usually carries sub rosa connections with the party out of power, and sometimes the party out of power retains one or more fixers who play "footsie" with the *fixer* for the party which is in power. Therefore, when a mixed ticket has been elected, a *fixer* may be able to bring influence to bear on members of both parties; an individual *whiz dick* would find this delicate work beyond his simple talents. However, the services of a *fixer* come high—higher than most *whiz mobs* can afford today.

Experienced *cannon mobs*, whether they be *locals* or *road mobs*, regard the *fix* in the light of insurance. It is an operating expense which must be met if they are to work. Also, because they are not in the really big money, there is a limit to how much they can pay and still make a good living. It seems to be generally agreed that $100 a day per man is about all any *whiz mobs* can pay and still operate profitably. If this goes directly to the detectives, that kind of *pay off* is rather profitable for the officers, unless they must split the *pay off* with several other people. "Because there was such a big pay-off there, you always had to work about three-handed to get that dough for the fix." Even so, no officers in any city dare give any mob more than two or three days' work a month because the consequent *beefs* become too embarrassing. "Then we could work until it got too hot, and by 'too hot' I mean there'd be too many beefs coming in and the chief'd tell the dicks, 'You'd better bring somebody in here or get yourself another job. Go to work on one of them coal trucks or something.'"

If the money goes to the *fixer* and eventually into the pot where all such funds accumulate, it is not enough to be very impressive in these days of big-money *rackets*. The party organization is also sensitive to public pressures, and too many *beefs* can generate *heat* which can cut off protected thieving entirely, or reduce it to occasional arrangements for conventions, race-meets, etc., when there are many out-of-town marks to be robbed. "Things are getting warm here for strange whiz mobs. In fact, the place is on fire."

There is another factor in the *whiz* which makes it harder to protect than, say, the *confidence games*, professional gambling, and prostitution. This is the fact that the victim is a bona fide victim. That is, he does not need to participate in any such dishonest schemes as he is a party to if he is taken on a *con game*. He is not trying to cheat anyone else. He does not necessarily have any larceny in him as does a *sucker* who, say, is trying to beat a rigged gambling house. A citizen who has lost a wallet comes into court with clean hands and with no lack of sympathy from the jury and the press. There is nothing that he has done, or tries to do, which makes him fair game. His only offense was to possess a pocketbook. As one *class cannon* succinctly puts it, "He must have pockets in his pants. He must be over nine years old and under ninety, and he must have pockets in his pants. There are no other requisites."

The Fix and the Fall

Whatever method of *fixing* any individual pickpocket or mob may use, the transaction demands cash on the line. Therefore, successful pickpockets must have money available at all times. This cash reserve is called *fall dough*. "Say for instance, it's a three-handed mob and you got three grand fall dough up." Sometimes it is all carried by one member of the mob, especially a woman; sometimes each member carries his own, with the understanding that all or part of it is at the disposal of any other member should a *fall* occur. In *organized mobs* there is usually a specified amount, shared equally, available at all times. Sometimes it is in a bank account in the name of a friend or relative who could telegraph it instantly if it were needed. Pickpockets like joint accounts with someone they can trust—or think they can trust—so that money is available to them at all times. The pickpocket often thinks of any cash reserve as being *in his seams*. "Now maybe this mob has got six thousand dollars fall dough, two grand apiece. You haven't got that in your seams, you've got it someplace where you can wire and get it or telephone or something."

The phrase *in his seams* refers to an ancient custom of sewing money into one's clothes. It is still actually done by many thieves, who will fold one or more large bills lengthwise and sew the money under the overlap in, say, the side seams inside a trouser leg, or in the cuff, or inside a coat lining. This is hazardous, however, for the *fuzz* has learned that pickpockets have this quaint habit and may cut up a suit of clothes in a search for the *stash*—once such a common practice in the Middle West (reputedly originating in Cedar Rapids, Iowa) that it had a name, the *hurdy gurdy*, now gone the way of the flapper and the model T. "Guns always have jack sewed up in their seams, but in Cedar Rapids, Iowa, they took all your rags and cut them to pieces, if you were a whizzer. They made you swim the Cedar River. The cannons called it the hurdy gurdy."

Today the smart *cannons* working on the *road* carry enough *fall dough* for emergencies—say $1500–$1800 in a *three handed mob*—and then keep the rest in reserve where only they can get to it. "Your cousin—that's the guy who's got your fall dough." *Locals* do not need to carry so much, since they are known to the local police and probably to any local *fixers*; they can easily get their *fall dough* from a joint bank account or a safety deposit box. All pickpockets like to have a *bail piece*, which is especially useful to *local mobs* if they have a *fall*. This type of security is called *colat*. It is the deed to a piece of real estate which is completely unencumbered and can be transferred to a bondsman in order to get out of jail quickly.

Since the *fix* is never entirely reliable, the thief must always be prepared for a *bad fall*. This means an arrest in which the *rapper* means business and the circumstances prevent the *fix* from working freely. He may find himself dealing with *wrong coppers* who cannot be *fixed* by any means at his disposal. If the pickpocket has a previous understanding with the police, he says he is *doing business* with them or *working right*; in fact, he will always try to *do business* whether he succeeds or not. "Most of them work right." "Well, I wouldn't say he worked right."

There's no such a thing as working right in New York. You might get a couple of dicks right. You might get a certain spot that's protected by whiz coppers and you might get that spot right for certain trains or buses or something like that, but as far as working right in the city of New York, there's no such thing as working right.

Usually he has no fear of *buttons, harness coppers, harness bulls,* or *harness cops.* These uniformed officers do not have the specialized knowledge necessary to cause him trouble. So he avoids them and they usually do not know he is around; in the event of a *beef* on the street, a *harness bull* may be called to investigate and may even make an arrest. However, the stalls are so adept at *splitting out* the tool that usually the *chump* cannot get at the tool or even identify him successfully enough for prosecution; in fact, if the stalls do their work, it is virtually impossible for the mark to see the tool's face.

Plain-clothes men are the nemesis of the pickpocket. They come in four or five varieties. First, there are federal officers; these men are seldom interested in pickpockets, except insofar as they might lead to bigger game, and they appear to make use of pickpockets sometimes as informers or in other capacities. For instance, informants have reported that men who identified themselves as federal agents have asked their coöperation in locating pistols on the persons of people in inaugural crowds, and marking such individuals on the shoulder with talcum powder, a small can of which was supplied each tool. It would be hard to devise a more effective and discreet method of "frisking" a crowd than this.

City detectives are the most dangerous to pickpockets, especially the pickpocket squads found in larger cities. Usually they have had long experience in dealing with pickpockets and know many of them by sight. Sometimes these squads have men on them who are known as *camera eyes*; that is, they can memorize any face and recognize it anywhere, even after years have elapsed. An honest *camera eye* is a boon to law enforcement; a corrupt one becomes a *right copper* with almost unlimited opportunities. We might use two different types of *camera eye* to illustrate our point. The first is *camera eye* Wilkerson, of the Detroit force, recently gone to his reward. He had a phenomenal memory for thieves. He constantly refreshed this faculty with a pack of playing cards on the backs of which were embossed photographs of thieves he thought he might forget. From time to time he revised his Rogues' Gallery so that he was always discarding those he had perfectly memorized and adding those he wanted to learn. His reputation as guardian of the financial district in Detroit was always good. He was what thieves call a *wrong copper;* that is, he did not take the *fix*—at least not from pickpockets. At the same time he did not maul them around or beat them up, although he would pick them up to see if they could yield any useful information.

Here is what happened when Camera Eye Wilkerson picked up a pickpocket. Reports on his methods indicate that he was almost kindly in his manner, but very shrewd in catching and convicting pickpockets.

The mob had a meet at 4:30 to work that slave grift. He walked right up and said, "Don't run or anything. I just want him." That was me. "Now look," he says, "don't go and get no bondsman or nothing. Or get no writ or nothing foolish like that. You guys go on and don't worry. I'm taking this man in, but he'll be back tomorrow night."

So I thought, "What the hell does he want with me?" Well, we went down to headquarters and he locked me up. But first I should tell you he mugged me with a special camera he had and took my finger prints. Then he left me in the holdover overnight. Next day he come around with a lot of pictures. Different guns, you know.

"Do you know this fellow?" and "Where is he now?" and stuff like that.

I told him, "Look, Mr. Wilkerson, I'd like to help you, but I just don't know." That went on for a long time.

Then he said, "Well, you don't seem to know much of anything, do you?" and he had the guard take me back to the holdover. Later that night they turned me loose. He had the financial district there, you know. And he told me, "You stay out of my district, if you don't want to get locked up." Strictly an honest copper.

The other specimen is *camera eye* McCarthy of the Buffalo force. He had all of Wilkerson's ability without Wilkerson's ethics. He worked with the former Chief of Police "Honest Jimmy" Higgins to compile their famous *pocket gallery* of thieves, at one time the best portable *rogues' gallery* available. Eventually McCarthy went to prison for taking the *fix*. He did not wait for thieves to *do business* with him; he stood for the kind of free enterprise which carries the sale to the customer. Using his phenomenal memory for thieves, he picked them out anywhere and *put the shake on*, or requested a contribution in the form of a direct capital gain. If this was not forthcoming, he would run the man in *on his record* and perhaps *work him over* just as a lesson in manners.

Both McCarthy and Wilkerson were reputed to be able to do

that phenomenal act—*make a man on his merits*, that is, spot a criminal by his dress, manners, appearance, behavior, etc., even though he was unknown to them personally. Actually, there probably are no such detectives, with all due credit to Wilkerson and McCarthy, whose lightning memories made it appear that they could *make a thief on his merits* when actually they were recalling his face or other aspects of his physique. "No, there was no mark beefing. No, here's what happened. They just made us on our merits and came right over."

Private detectives are also on the lookout for pickpockets, largely because private agencies are hired to guard certain meetings such as conventions and sports gatherings, the presence of pickpockets being likely to dampen the good spirits as well as reduce the prosperity of any crowd. The reputation of Pinkerton men seems to be enough to keep most pickpockets away from gatherings which they protect. In the past, private agencies commonly hired pickpockets or thieves who could be released from prison on parole, and these men *put the finger on* their confreres so that a private detective could make the *sneeze*. This is still practiced, but apparently on a lesser scale. The Pinkerton Agency is perhaps the best known of the private agencies, and I understand that it hires few if any pickpockets today, though it uses some for undercover work. "Molly Matches, a noted woman cannon years ago, had four boys and they all became guns: Edwin, John, Michael, and Vincent. They all turned turtle and joined out the Pinkerton Detective Agency. They protected the race tracks everywhere. They took their end off of touts." "But this Pinkerton wanted to shake him down . . . take money from him for coming on the track, in addition to the admission fee. They all got up and testified that they had given money, you know, at times and at every racetrack where a Pinkerton operates . . . and the jury acquitted him . . . and there hasn't been a Pinkerton since that protecting a racetrack in this state." The agency is called *the eye*, from its trademark, the all-seeing eye, and its operators are sometimes called *pinks*. "That pink was an ex-cannon himself."

Store detectives (sometimes ex-*whiz coppers*) are also dangerous to pickpockets, especially since some pickpockets are also shoplifters, and the *store dick* likes to *nail a cannon* or a *cannon broad* whenever the opportunity presents itself. "Here's a mob working over here and they get busted. They get nailed, see." I have observed that sometimes *class cannons* tend to risk their liberty by stealing some trivial article in a store, when they could steal the money more easily and buy the articles; however, it is against the principles of most *whiz* to pay for anything that can be stolen.

The police in any small city or town used to be *fly cops*, but now they are called *clowns*; as a rule they do not give pickpockets much trouble since they do not know how to *spot the frame* in a crowd, and they do not have the experience with thieves to recognize them by sight, nor to deal with them systematically as do big-city *fuzz*. However, if a thief *falls* in one of these towns, he may be in for very serious trouble. When there is no *fixer* or *fixing* done by the police, these places are called *sucker towns*, and buying one's way out of trouble may be not only expensive if it can be done, but impossible to do. The reason for this is that neither the institution of the *fix* nor the machinery for operating it have been established in these communities.

The pickpocket calls any kind of policeman a *shamas* or, if he is giving an *office* to his partner, a *sham*. This derives from the Yiddish term for a sexton or the watchman-janitor of a synagogue, and seems to have originated amongst pickpockets, then to have spread to the usage of many other types of thief. A *burglar copper* is a detective who is always on the alert to pick up a thief and *shake him down*. He may also be called a *shake artist* who knows how to make the *whiz* pay off or *give up*. If he is especially avaricious, old-timers will call him a *panther*, and the act is called the *shake*. *Shake artists* are also called by some operators *thieving coppers*, although usually that term means only that a detective can be *fixed*, and not that he goes out *on the shake*. "Personally I can't say that I have, although I know of numerous instances where they were on the shake." When a pair of *whiz dicks* systematically gives a pickpocket the *shake down*, they are called a *shake mob*. "So they took us over and put us in the jail, and these dicks put us both in the same cell. I guess it was about 2 o'clock when this happened. No shakedown, no nothing."

Note that this *whiz mob*, after being *shaken down*, solicits police coöperation, but does not get the *shade* it wants.

So we stuck with him. In that fourth race he took out another five-hundred dollar bill and he's got this on his vest insider. I said, "Alec, this man is there." And he puts that poke down in there and he buttons it up and he buttons his vest all up and everything and he gets a five-hundred dollar bill out in his duke and he goes up and he marks down three on his program so I figure he's gonna bet $300 on it. And he liked the horse I liked, so I said, "Well, we'll get them tickets anyway." You've gotta take anything on a racetrack. So Alec put up for him and I took them. Then he gets up to the window and some way or another, I don't know why, but he changed his mind and bet $200 on the horse. But he blowed them other tickets in that third race and he ain't gonna blow these tickets. He holds them in his hand. He goes to the left britch with that $300. I office Alec and step in behind. Well, he takes his hand off it and it belongs to me. . . . I take it. So he steps this way and I step that way, and I don't take but two steps and a guy tapped me on the shoulder, and he says, "Well, you beat the guy for his tickets in the second race and you just beat him for $300 now. Don't you think it's about time you come up with something?" They was two of them, dicks.

I said, "I beg your pardon. I don't know what you are talking about."

He says, "You wanta go to the donicker and get the shit smacked out of you or do you wanta cut up that $300 with us?"

I said, "I'll cut up the $300 right here, if that's what you want."

He said, "$100 for him, $100 for me, and $100 for you and that little guy with you."

I said, "That's kind of rough, isn't it, Jack, when you aren't giving us any support?"

"Well," he said, "we're giving you a passup. . . . That's enough."

I said, "You ain't no local coppers."

"No," he said, "we're from out of town. We come out here to see that nobody got hurt."

I said, "Well, you didn't help that guy, he just lost $300. You think you could help square him around so we could get that thing he's got inside there?"

He said, "No, he's lost enough now. You let that guy alone. If we see you around again, we'll snatch you—you and your partner too."

On the whole, *right coppers* are those who can be *fixed* and *wrong coppers* are those who will not *take*. "Inspector Hunt was the right fuzz and was the man fitted for all grift at the Exposition." "You can't do business with a wrong copper, and the more you try, the worse off you are." As a rule, a *wrong copper* will not have anything to do with the *fix*, even if it is handled from above; his more larcenous fellows know this, and he is usually protected from contact with the *fix* which might embarrass him to the point of talking before a grand jury; sometimes *wrong coppers* are assigned to beats where their talents can be best used without interfering with official policies; again, they may work in the midst of the *fix*, either not seeing it or pretending not to, in order to keep their jobs. Also, if we include uniformed police, the *wrong coppers* are heavily in the majority, and the fix is often manipulated by a small, tight group of officers, some with excellent political connections higher up, who control it with a close hand. There are, conceivably, policemen in some cities who not only do not know how the *fix* works, but who do not even believe in its existence.

It is said that a few detectives will go beyond the concept of the *right copper* and the *shakedown copper* and actually assist the pickpockets in their thieving. This is called *grifting with a shade on your tail*. That is, a detective will escort a *whiz mob* in the crowd and, if they have *sucker trouble*, or if any mark catches a tool in his pocket, or if any bystander *beefs gun*, the officer steps in, *splits out the tool* and settles any argument about the ownership of the mark's pocketbook by returning it to him, or retrieving it off the ground where it has usually been thrown at this point, and, if necessary, browbeating the *sucker* enough that he is not likely to *beef* at headquarters. Usually the officer simply steps in, shows his badge, and asks, "What's the trouble here?" If the *chump* is brimming with righteous indignation, and has the tool *by the throat*, the *dick* calms him down a bit if he seems too conscientious about having the tool arrested. "I only knew one gun that would hustle with a dick." "There used to be a team of whiz dicks out of Phila—father and son. They had their own mob and they grifted with a shade on their tail."

Some pickpockets, noting the quieting effect which the detective's badge has upon the *sucker*, provide themselves with such a badge either by surreptitious purchase or by pilfering the wallet of some unfriendly *fuzz*, and use it exactly as a detective would use it. The stall can carry the *buzzer*, or wear it, and *split the tool out* with great effectiveness in the event of a *tumble* by impersonating a detective. "Tim Bairdon used to grift with a buzzer on his vest." "Button is right, but I wouldn't say it's a common term. Maybe shake guys would use it." *Buzzer* is a Western term; *button* is used in the East. "It was tough on him because they found that button on him." Sometimes other criminals make up *shake mobs* and prey on pickpockets if they can get away with it.

They could have been a shake team. Counterfeit coppers, I mean. But they were wise to the whiz. No, they didn't flash no button. And they never touched us, never laid a hand on us. And never asked who we were. But they made us first because neither one of us looked at them first. Not until afterward. . . . Well, I fanned this guy with the scratch, and that's what

I'm looking for. The tip was thinning out fast, and I was reefing the kick. I always look around, but I didn't have much time . . . and it was in my hands, see, and I was so anxious to beat him. . . . Well, anyway, I didn't look around before I took the score and when I looked up, there they was, looking right at us. One of them said, "Where you fellows from?" and I started to walk away. So he said, "Hey, you fellows will have to get out of here." And I kept on walking.

So the other one said, "Don't run, or I'll shoot you." So I stopped. I could tell he wasn't a dick by his methods. They were so different from a guy who's going to make a pinch. A dick isn't going to shoot you if he is going to make a pinch. It was so different that I knew what they wanted. And I knew they seen me take that bundle of scratch.

"Well," I said, "what do you want to do about this?"

And so he said, "This ought to be worth something to you."

"How much do you think it ought to be worth?" I says, and he didn't say nothing, so I says, "Fifty bucks?" And he took it, and we went on. If they had been real dicks, they couldn't have been righted up for no fifty bucks, especially when they knew we had that bundle.

In some cities, where the *fix* is controlled from above, the pickpockets who have paid their fee to their *connection* are ordered to report at a certain corner at a certain time on the dot, and to stand under a certain sign or beside a certain fireplug. While they are there, the pickpocket detail comes by and memorizes their faces so that they will not pick them up in the ensuing two or three days during which they will be working; thus the *fuzz* knows the *whiz*, but the *whiz* cannot identify the *fuzz*, which gives the police organization a certain security; however, most *class cannons* know all the important *whiz coppers* in the country just as well as the *whiz coppers* know them, so this maneuvering is largely ritualistic. It should be added that *whiz mobs* working under protection do so only at intervals, and for short periods of time as a rule. Thus there will be a wave of *beefs* while the mob is working for two or three days, then it will subside when they stop. Newspaper publicity and the *heat* from headquarters will simmer down also, as the *beefs* cease, and everyone will say, "Well, the pickpockets must have left town by now."

Sometimes in certain communities there is an *airtight* arrangement under which the pickpockets who pay off are protected, while it is said that those who do not may be arrested and *framed* with the charges which have accumulated as a result of the depredations of the mob which is *paying off*. Sometimes these "innocent" pickpockets—innocent in that they did not commit the thefts they are charged with—are actually sent to prison and this is thought to serve as a good lesson to them to clear with headquarters at all times. Even more frequently, it provides the pressure which detectives need to force pickpockets to turn stool pigeon, and the pickpocket is sometimes saved at the brink when he decides to work with certain detectives who want him to supply information on other types of underworld activity, or to turn in other thieves. Sometimes *locals* watch for *road mobs* and *tip off* the police to reduce competition. "The law didn't know us in Miami, so local whiz must have tipped us off."

A *whiz mob* which is working under police protection or with police coöperation says it is *hustling with a shade, working with an edge, working with the odds,* or *hustling with pro,* the latter being an East-Coast phrase. "To grift with the pro is to grift right." *Pro* is short for *protection,* and a *shade* refers to a *shade the best of it.* There is also a pun on the use of *shade* as something with which a stall *shades the duke* of the tool so that he can work safely.

Hustling with a shade or hustling with pro wouldn't necessarily mean full protection. It would be used as only partly protected. And it could be used in this sense: if you got a passup by some whiz copper, but not all of them, you might have a shade; I might have a shade the best of it in a certain town and another mob goes in right behind me and they get knocked off as soon as they see them. Well, they give me a passup for they might happen to like me, and dislike the other guy. So shade or hustling with a shade I wouldn't say was full protection.

A pickpocket may also think of himself as *grifting right* if he has police protection. *Right* in this sense is a loose term with a multiplicity of usage according to the situation. The thief may take a *right fall* (be arrested for a theft he actually committed, not one for which he was *framed*); he may receive as a result a *right rap* (a sentence which he actually deserved because he committed this particular theft); if possible he *rights up* certain detectives who are known as *right coppers* because they can be *rightened up.* After he has done this, he says that he *has them right.* If the *sucker* really gives him trouble, he may be able to *right the case* (buy off the officers, the judge, the victim, or, on occasion, the juryman who can make the difference) even though he was *grabbed right* (caught red-handed) in a *right town* (one where the *fix* is well established). "A bum rap is harder to beat than a right one." The term *wrong* is an antonym of *right*, and can be used in many situations to mean exactly the opposite of *right*.

When a pickpocket takes a *right pinch*, he is arrested for a *touch* or *score* which he *took off*. This is not a *shakedown*, but a bona fide arrest. "I never did have a right pinch on the whiz." The *whiz copper* may *claw him down* on the street, or in a city bus, or anywhere he catches him *dead to rights*, in which case the pickpocket will try to find out if the officer will *cop*. "That big fink with the stash will always cop." The tool will probably try to *ding the poke*, or *throw it* or *drop it*, or *go to the floor with it*, but if the *sucker* is very quick and the officer is right at hand, he may be *sneezed down*, or arrested practically in the act. If the officer proves to be unsympathetic, or unresponsive to the aroma of fresh, crisp paper money, this may be a *bad fall*.

The *dick* takes both the *chump* and the *whiz* to headquarters, where the victim swears out a warrant. If the tool has been successfully *split out* from the mob, he can count on them to go into action immediately to help him. Of course, if the whole mob is taken, that can be very bad. Let us assume that his stalls were not *snatched in the neck* along with him, and that they are still free. He is locked up in the *can*, the *bucket*, the *boob* (from *booby hatch*), or any other jail, lockup, holdover or place of temporary confinement.

He is booked for grand larceny, along with any other charge that may stick. He is *printed* (his fingerprints taken) and *mugged* (photographed), and the *whiz coppers* go through their files to see what kind of record he has. They may recognize him immediately, and go directly to old files which contain his record; if not, they may have to look him up in the *hall of fame* (the "Rogue's Gallery") to identify him positively and to find out how his record is filed, since pickpockets do not always give consistent names and residence addresses, with a view to confusing the police. This is no longer a very effective device, however, and the *dicks* will soon identify him positively, connect him with his past record, and may as likely as not take him to the *cop out room* for a little questioning. This will deal mostly with the whereabouts of other wanted characters, and possibilities of linking this pickpocket with other *touches*, the number and identity of his partners, etc. There will also be explorations of his resources, and if he does not offer to *grease* anyone who craves *greasing*, he may be delicately reminded of such possibilities. Or, if he happens to be in the hands of thoroughly ethical and high-minded detectives, all his overtures will be ignored, and none will be made in turn. During the questioning he should be coöperative and voluble; otherwise he may have his skull *dusted* with a blackjack several times over lightly, this being repeated at intervals sufficient to give him quite a headache. Or, he may be beaten about the hands with a nightstick, which is bad for his dexterity, or *worked over* in a hundred different ways. On the other hand, pickpockets are recognized by the police as strictly nonviolent, and usually reasonable; they probably receive a minimum of brutal treatment at the hands of the police, for things can usually be worked out on a live-and-let-live basis. If a *cannon* has a *right pinch* by *wrong coppers*, however, he will probably go to prison despite any *fixing* efforts he may make.

If he is an old-timer with a high sense of ethics, he will tell nothing under pressure, or at least nothing that is true, or that will hurt anyone; if he is human, he is very likely to say some things he will later regret, and he may even *cop out* or agree to plead guilty (*cop a plea*) in return for a light sentence, a suspended sentence, or some other deal which would seem to benefit both the dominant culture and the subculture simultaneously. Pickpockets, however, seldom plead guilty, especially those in the upper brackets. They usually manage to work out something which seems better all the way round.

In this case we will assume that the tool admitted nothing; meanwhile the stalls are zealously seeking sanctuary and indulgence from the factotums of the *fix*. They will do anything to *shake the rap*. If they are a *road mob*, they will probably already have the name and telephone number of some good Samaritan who, for a slight consideration, will go to work on the case. If they are *locals*, they already have *connections*. A bondsman is the first *connection*, for without bond, the tool must remain subject to questioning in the *cop out room*, either until he *cops out*, until the detectives conclude that he will not supply the desired data, or until they are convinced that he will coöperate on a sort of fiscal basis, and that he has the resources to do so. The chances are that if the *dicks* were susceptible to *fixing*, they would have responded to his first overtures with money on the street when he was arrested; however, negotiations sometimes cannot be carried on there and must be completed at the police station, though all concerned will agree that this is not the best place. The stalls, of course, must work very discreetly, or they, too, will be entertained in the *cop out room*, with all the de luxe treatment afforded visiting pickpockets.

As soon as a bondsman with proper political connections is located, he takes over. He knows how much *fall dough* is available and works accordingly. If it seems that the case will really go to court, he will get a lawyer, and a good one; if it appears that the officers may be prevailed upon to withdraw the charges for a certain generous portion of the *spring money*, and the *sucker* can be persuaded that it is better to have his money refunded in toto, with perhaps some lagniappe, the local *fixer* may *square the beef*, and things may not be so bad as they seemed.

Once a good lawyer enters the case, the detectives know that it will be fought hard; they also know that the pickpocket must have some cash reserves, or the good lawyer would not be so likely to be there—though in rare instances some thieves have credit with attorneys. And so the *fur's* reasoning may be that it is foolish to let the lawyer have all the *fall dough* and run a good chance of seeing the pickpocket go free in addition. Therefore, all other things being equal, they may be inclined to cut in on the *fix money*, even though they may have to split it with others. If they will *stand for* the *fix* in any form, they will be interested; if not, they are *wrong coppers* anyway, and, unless an angel intervenes, he will go to trial and perhaps to *stir*.

On the other hand, there may be factors which make it difficult, embarrassing, or even impossible for the detectives to *fix* the case, even though they might be willing to do so. Newspaper publicity has to be considered. The identity, personality, and status of the victim are important in some cases. Is the grand jury sitting? What is the complexion of the judge who will handle the case? What will the prosecutor do? How close are elections? These are all peripheral details.

Of more central significance are questions like these: Is there a *flyer* out for this man? This is a police circular carrying photographs, fingerprints, past record, and charges for which the man is now wanted; if it is in circulation, some other police department may claim the man anyway and extradite him for trial somewhere else. Is there already a *floater*, or *sticker*, out for the man in this city? That is, has someone else already sworn a warrant for this man's arrest, and can it be served? If so, is there any advantage of substituting one mark for another? Will the *fix* in his case *curdle* if the previous warrant comes to light? Also, there may have been a *buy* recorded by the narcotics squad or the federals, who may have recently had an undercover agent or a stool pigeon dealing with the mob if they are addicts. Sometimes there is a "detainer" issued for a thief on the basis of a "wanted" request from another city, or on the basis of such a warrant as was just described. This is called a *reader* or a *dipsy*. "The rapper didn't show, but they held me on that Cohen dipsy." Did any other complaining witnesses appear or attempt to identify the pickpocket when he was *lined up* at police headquarters? Was he given more than one *line up*?

These matters are of importance both to the detectives and to the lawyer and his client, but from different points of view. Furthermore, there is the question of how much influence the bondsman or other *fixer* has with this city administration, and especially with the prosecutor and the judge who will try the case. Does the *fixer* have an *in* or an *iron bound in* with the local political organization? Will the *fixing* of this case put pressure on the administration to *stand for* other rackets not now protected? "A burg that will stand for the cannon will stand for any racket."

All of which leads to this question: Will this case have to be *fixed* on an individual basis, or is there already a well-established, well-oiled graft-machine set up to process all *fixed* cases? If it is to be handled on an individual basis and there is no working organization, it may be quite expensive—if several people who are not normally *on the take* have to be approached and bribed. Or, on the other hand, it could be surprisingly cheap, if the two detectives would accept $100 apiece to present a shaky, uncertain, or confused case for the prosecution, or perhaps advise the prosecutor that there is no case, and persuade the *sucker* that he is lucky to get his money back. If there is a working organization, there will be something of a standard fee, and this pickpocket will be processed like all other *fixed* cases; his case will attract little attention, and he will probably go free.

Meanwhile, the tool has *sprung*, thanks to the work of the bondsman. If the bond is high at first, the lawyer will work to have it reduced. If it can be reduced low enough, the pickpocket always has in the back of his mind that intriguing thought of *taking a powder, taking it on the a.d., taking the fence,* or *taking it on the lam.* In other words, should he jump bail, then later on pay his lawyer and reimburse the bondsman? This is bad for the credit, and is done by smart *cannons* only rarely, and in cases which look so shaky that there is a good chance of conviction. Jumping bail always makes it more difficult for him to get bond next time. Probably he will simply *sit on the beef,* that is, hang around town without working and await the disposal of his *case;* to a thief, a *case* has a more specialized meaning than it has to the layman, since he looks at it in a highly subjective way; it means to him trouble with the law that can't be *fixed* easily, and is likely to get to the court-room. "At one time I was sitting on seven cases at once," may sound like a statement by a versatile judge, but it simply means that a foolish pickpocket had attempted to work while on bail for the first *case,* had another *fall,* needed more money, and worked while on bail for the second *case,* etc. until he had pyramided his *sucker trouble* into a major disaster. In such a case the sensible thing is to *cop a plea* and get safely into the penitentiary, though few pickpockets would see it that way.

While the tool is out on bond, he should be sensible enough not to try to work, or at least not to work in the same city where he is on bond. If he is clever, he may *hopscotch* a little in the vicinity, working carefully in other towns where he is not known, always remaining available for trial when his case comes up. Perhaps his bondsman has been able to *square the beef.* Perhaps one of the stalls or a representative of the bondsman has been able to *shake the rap* at considerable expense so that the charges will be withdrawn. Perhaps some *polly* (politician) can be interested sufficiently to intervene with the judge, who will do what he can to lighten the sentence, probate it, or even vacate it completely in his chambers after the jury has passed a verdict of guilty. Maybe he will get off with a *bit,* which is a jail sentence of usually 30 to 90 days, or a *sixer,* which is six months in jail. In some states he might get a *gag,* or indeterminate sentence. Maybe he will get *settled,* or sent to prison; among pickpockets this term does not carry the implication of a long sentence or a life-term which it has among some criminal groups; it usually means two years, with good time off. "I was hustling for eleven years before I ever got settled." However, under the "habitual criminal" statutes in some states, getting *settled* for a pickpocket with a long record may mean life, or the equivalent, and some very expert *whiz* are doing very long sentences today in those states where this type of law is in effect.

Should our man go free, he will rejoin the mob—which has in the meantime been *grinding up nickels and dimes* to fight his case— where his post has probably been temporarily taken by a *fill in* who will take his share of the *knockup*, but will not have to contribute anything to the ransom of the tool. Should he get *settled*, he will go sadly to serve his time, and the news will go around the hangouts that the mob has *dropped one*. And perhaps for a while thereafter that particular city will be regarded as *hot* for the *whiz* and may be avoided for a time by all except the more incorrigible, or those who spend their *fall dough* lightly.

CHAPTER X

SKILLS AND TRAINING

Since it would be impossible to present the behavior pattern throughout the entire subculture, with all of its ramifications, this book has been concerned almost exclusively with the technology of pickpockets, or, in a broader sense, the ways they make a living, together with those peripheral activities which are functionally related to making a living. Sometimes it has been difficult to draw the line between what is functional and what is not, in which cases the policy has been, usually, to omit this peripheral material. It would be manifestly impossible to cover all phases of the life pattern of a specialized group of thieves in a study so limited in both size and scope. In this chapter, then, several of these peripheral areas will be considered, but only insofar as they contribute to the general picture of making a living. If the reader will recall Trager's Indices to Culture cited earlier, he can easily fit these activities into the general pattern of the subculture, as contrasted to that of the dominant culture.

This area of the subculture is comparable to *Education* in the dominant culture; most pickpockets have certain cross-cultural traits, since they are all, to some extent even if that extent is minimal, exposed to the education system of the dominant culture. The slight degree to which most of them respond is evident from the high incidence of illiteracy among them. This lack of response to the education system of the dominant culture is a result of several forces. First, the traditions of the subculture are all against it; there is, from birth on, a suspicion and distrust of the dominant culture which is intense; thieves tend to resent any attempt (however well meant) by the dominant culture to educate the children of the subculture in the ways of the *square John*; this suspicion is intense in direct proportion to the lack of formal education experienced by the parents.

The following comment by a professional shows the dichotomy between the institutions and values of the subculture and those of the dominant culture. It also shows the conflict in the mind of the father over denying his boy the advantages of the dominant culture, at least while he is a child.

153

I had that problem occur just a short while ago. You remember I told you we've got a little boy. And here some time ago, just a few months ago, he wanted to join the Cub Scouts. And I always had an idea when them things come up, I'd call a spade, a spade. I mean it's all right to think that, but when the time comes, it's a little different. So he wants to join the Cub Scouts. And he's with my mother, his grandmother, and we're not rich or anything like that, but I'd say he's got a very good home. And he wants to join the Cub Scouts, the junior Boy Scouts. So I know that the Cub Scouts make stool pigeons out of all those kids. All them organizations do. They make the cop on the corner look like something, but they don't tell them that when they grow up, he'll put them in the penitentiary, if he gets a chance to do it. And I know that they're going to train him to be a perfect little stool pigeon. So I turned that over in my mind for two or three days. After all, it's going to affect his whole life. So I finally come to the conclusion, well, let him be a stool pigeon, if he wants to be, but at least let him be normal. Let him get what the other kids get and when he is just a little older I can tell him straight, "Now that cop out there, he's a dirty son-of-a-bitch. He'll put you away. That's a kind of an oath he took to get that kind of a job, and he wouldn't only arrest you, he'd frame you and put you in prison."

Second, the educational system of the dominant culture teaches little for which the subculture has any direct use. Perhaps a bare minimum of reading is harmless, since it permits reading of form-sheets and train schedules and, on occasion, newspapers; enough writing to correspond is also accepted, though not considered essential, for communication is mainly verbal in this subculture; and the *grapevine* (a loosely organized but very effective arrangement for transmitting messages for great distances by word of mouth) has worked effectively for centuries, so why discard it?

True, some thieves later in life realize some of the advantages of literacy, and learn to read and write fluently—sometimes in prison schools.

Well I'll tell you there's a lot of guys, ashamed as I am to say it, well I ain't ashamed to say it though because why should I be? It's their own damn fault if they ain't got any education; they've been in enough joints. Half of them have spent half their lives in the penitentiary. And can't spell "cat." And they got a library there and schools and everything. I don't know; it's just that "dese," "dose," and "dem" kind of guys are ignoramuses. They know all the answers, as far as their racket is concerned. They don't know anything else. You know there's pickpockets that will freeze themselves to death and not steal an overcoat? In the winter time. If they can't get the money out of the leather to go buy an overcoat, they wouldn't step inside a joint and beat it for an overcoat. They think that's beneath them.

But pickpockets with the attitude of this informant are rare. Most of the skills they need are manual, psychological, almost intuitive. They have to learn to *work on the sneak*, and the public school system seems to neglect or omit entirely this phase of the thief-child's development.

Last, almost everything taught in the public schools is directly opposed to the values and techniques of living in the subculture. Everyone is taught to conform, to coöperate, to take orders. "I learned to stall and I learned to hook, too, and I broke in many a stall. A lot of stalls won't break in, you see, because they're thieves and they won't be told. That's the reason they are thieves. They don't want people to tell them what to do. So if you can't tell a man what to do, then he can't stall." Public education teaches property rights which are quite the reverse of most of those recognized by the pickpocket. It attempts to instill respect for law and order. It tries to develop in children the desires and abilities to function in the dominant culture. It develops attitudes and motives which, viewed by the pickpocket, are not only useless but definitely subversive—if one is going out on the *whiz*.

And so there is a general disregard for public education, and all the institutions associated therewith. As a result, pickpockets have little incentive to keep their children in school even for the minimum number of years required by law, and they are inclined to wink at truancy, general incorrigibility, and delinquency. These children are often problems in the schools, for the parents regard the teacher as a kind of female *hack*, *screw*, or *shack* (prison guard) and are likely to encourage or approve anything Junior does to make trouble for her. If he gives her a hard enough way to go, they feel that this indicates promise for the future; if he is by chance expelled, that is fine with them. He can learn rapidly then to work with his elders. On the other hand, there are a few enlightened pickpockets who send their children to school and even to college, for they want them to have a better life than their parents had.

Of course, not all pickpockets come from pickpocket families, or even from families of the subculture; some come from the dominant culture, are rejected by it or reject it, and by chance or by choice find a way to associate with members of the subculture; these associations are usually with children of the subculture, often enough older than the child of the dominant culture to be looked up to, identified with, and finally associated with professionally.

While juvenile cross-cultural ventures from legitimate society into the pickpocket subculture are not common, they do happen.

Most often, however, the pickpocket is born into a family living within some criminal subculture; from earliest consciousness he learns the attitudes of this group, cultivates hostility for the dominant culture, and shows vocational aptitude in various techniques calculated to separate members of the dominant culture from their money. Once an individual has grown to adulthood in this subculture and acquired professional status, only the most unrealistic type of thinking on the part of members of the dominant culture would expect him to change his ways. One hears of religious conversions which have suddenly changed the lives of pickpockets and made them pillars of the dominant culture; I do not know of any such cases personally, nor have I reason to believe that they exist on a bona fide basis. Likewise, I have never known psychiatry to create a similar conversion and adjustment, once the pickpocket has become established.

In fact, I have never known any professional thief to reform—which is another way of saying that he changes culture completely and permanently. He may *pack the racket in* because things get too *hot*, or because with advancing age he fears imprisonment more than he once did and at the same time has to depend on diminishing reactions in the practice of a highly skilled manual craft. "Then we could work until it got too hot and by 'too hot' I mean there'd be too many beefs coming in. So then you'd have to pack it in." "Joe Goss knows about my last fall, but no previous episodes. I handle over ten grand a season but do not carry a key to the money boxes. Don't believe I'd be tempted anyway, for at 59 there is a real fear of consequences" (letter from a professional who has *packed it in*). He may *square up* permanently or temporarily because there is a life sentence hanging over him as an habitual criminal. "But I said, 'I'm gonna square up. I'm gonna do the right thing.'" "Society don't give a guy a decent chance to square up. In a hell of a lot of cases they make it so goddamned hard." But he only conforms to the dominant culture superficially. Basically his motives, his attitudes, and his values remain unchanged. He has simply been forced to stop doing what he had been doing to make a living. Often he substitutes something less likely to *put him away*, such as dealing in a gambling joint, or touting at a racetrack, or working at some very minor *racket* like *pimping*.

But we have gone far ahead of the child in the subculture. There are no organized schools or systems of education within the subculture; it has been said that there are "schools" for pickpockets in large cities, run by professional *fagins* who turn youngsters into expert pickpockets; it has been said that they go so far as to set up dummies, fully dressed, which have bells attached to their pockets; the children are then taught to pick the dummy's pockets without ringing any of the bells. This suggests a touching scene, with all the little scholars chanting *left britch, right britch, prat kick, raust,* under the baton of a slyly beaming old Fagin. It smacks more of Dickens and sentimental journalism than anything taking place in the modern pickpocket's subculture. While it may have been a fact somewhere and at some time in the past, I can find no evidence that it has been practiced recently in the United States. Says an experienced *road man* with a wide knowledge of the criminal subculture: "I never had no such training. I never heard tell of a school for the whiz, and I never in all my life heard any cannon mention such a thing. One thief turns out another. That is, he teaches him. I was taught to reef a britch from the bottom so a tweezer poke would wind up in the palm of my hand. Back in them days there was nothing but tweezer pokes out in the corn belt."

What is the child-thief to be taught? Most of his early education is very informal. He absorbs a knowledge of the *racket* from those about him even before he is old enough to think of himself as a participant. Perhaps the most important factor is his early realization that it is possible to commit theft from the person; this has the same sort of impact that learning that it is possible to drive an automobile has on a young child. Very shortly he likes to be up behind the wheel, driving like a fireball, though actually the car is not in motion. When it is in motion, he identifies with the driver, and long before he is old enough to drive, he knows exactly how it is done; had he never seen anyone drive a car, he would never think of it in motion, and would have to make an entirely new set of adjustments to accept it as a vehicle. And so with the child in the house. Once he realizes that theft from the person is possible without *rumbling* the victim, whole new horizons have opened.

Anyone who has raised children knows that stealing comes to them as naturally as breathing. The attitudes of the parents and especially the other siblings toward this tendency are all-important in determining the attitudes of the child. After much careful and patient teaching, he may eventually learn that stealing is not acceptable behavior in the dominant culture; he learns something of property rights, and develops feelings of guilt when he violates them. But the thief-child has exactly the opposite experience. He knows not only about stealing, but about theft. He learns, no one knows how early, that his parents or his older brothers and sisters not only approve it, but are adept at it. The other children he is likely to play with have similar knowledge, or participate in a culture where this behavior is accepted, at least by the males. The aura of secrecy surrounding it, the taboo nature of the craft, the knowing looks, the brief, cryptic discussions of it in undertones, serve to emphasize its importance. Very early he is pretty thoroughly indoctrinated with the idea not only that it is all right to steal, but that it is a fine and admirable thing, and carries status.

About this time, he learns one very important thing. He is taught that it is laudable indeed to steal from a *sucker*, but that stealing from his own family or, later, his own friends, is a low and reprehensible thing; sometimes the emphasis falls so heavily upon the former principle, and so lightly upon the latter one, that he never fully grasps the idea that one must not steal from his own kind. This boy will never make a *class cannon*, though he may become a thief.

Thus he learns to recognize and identify the subculture as contrasted to the dominant culture, and soon collects a set of appropriate symbols for each. Not only does he learn to respect the craft of thievery, but he learns all the other standards and values of the subculture, and embraces them. Throughout boyhood and adolescence he has these reënforced by experience and precept, and by the time he is fourteen or fifteen years old, he is ready to support himself by thievery, though by this age he is seldom anything like an accomplished pickpocket. He probably simply steals anything he can and sells it wherever he can, his pickings being limited by the range of technology which his older friends and associates have at their disposal. He knows the general argot of the subculture, but as yet not the specialized aspects of it. He is just a growing hoodlum, and may never get any specialized training whatever.

The first word of the whiz lingo I can remember hearing was "poke," but I can't be sure that was actually the first one. This is just the first one

I remember. All the lingo of the whiz was foreign to me then. That was when I was turning out. Then I learned some more. After I got around with other cannons, I heard some more and picked it up. By the time I was twenty, I could spin the lingo like an old-timer, or at least I thought I could.

His development has not, however, gone unnoticed by his elders and others who could use him in the subculture. He must be known to have *grift sense*, *grift know*, or *larceny sense* before anyone will further his education in any way.

Yeah, that takes a lot of grift sense. There's a thousand different ways you have to maneuver, in other words the whiz is a lot of psychology. You've got to maneuver a man, particularly if you are by yourself. You got to think twice as fast as him and faster than all the coppers that are looking for you, so you got to do some thinking. So wherever the spot might be, you got to take the whole thing into consideration. Suppose you had been going up in an elevator, it would have been an entirely different thing. Well what would I have done then? Going up in an elevator, I might have burned him in the neck with a cigarette or pulled his hat down over his ears or something. I had to make him take his hand off, I had to make him let go of that money. I couldn't take it out of his hand. I had to make him take his hand off it. You have to make the situation. . . . You got to make the break yourself. You understand what I mean? The play is there, the dough is there, the man's got money in his pocket. You've got to have grift sense to take it away from him.

Also, he must know someone who can use a boy with light fingers, a good personality, and strong affiliations with the subculture. This last is very important, for it determines whether he will be loyal to his associates and his work, or whether he will yield to the first police pressures, or sell out at the first opportunity. In other words, he must also have *grift guts*. Without a doubt, he already has some sort of police record, even though it may be happily concealed behind the well-meaning anonymity of juvenile court.

Let us say that there is a professional *whiz* who has noted him around the hangouts and has taken a liking to him. The boy responds. The first stages of this relationship remind one of a dog finding a new master. The boy runs errands for the thief. He does his bidding in every way. He curries favor by catering to every whim of the professional. He takes messages to his lady-loves, "That's one of the first jobs I ever had—reading his mail. I used to have to read it for him. A lot of notes from broads that was carrying the torch for him. He'd say, 'You are just a punk kid, but you are OK. You come up to the hotel with me, because I want you to read my mail.' That made me feel like somebody. And why not? He was the best guy in the world, a prince among men.''

He finds *connections* where he can buy narcotics for his hero; he probably begins to *chippy around* himself, despite the warnings which the professional is likely to give him. This friendly relationship goes on for some time, off and on, as the thief is in town or in the neighborhood. By the time he is eighteen or so, he is ready to be *brought out* or *turned out*. He is also probably a full-fledged heroin addict, having learned how to use the needle and to take *main line shots* from other youngsters, if indeed not from the hero himself.

Already the professional has come to like the boy, and has made up his mind that perhaps he could be taught. The thief likes to have the boy build up his ego with loyalty, with praises behind his back, and by defending him against all critics. The boy may already know a good deal about the thief; he may even have asked him to teach him to be a pickpocket too. Also, the boy is already *grifting* in a crude way, cheating at cards or dice, and selling *hot* merchandise, and always has some cash in reserve. The pickpocket cannot be free on the streets, and successful, without a certain streak of cynicism; he reasons that if the boy is going to be a thief, he might as well be a good one; he remembers his own youth, when someone *turned him out.* "Old John Snarley turned me out." "I was turned out by Windy Dick Preston." "Well, I turned out in the Village before the hangout was Hinky Dink's scatter." And so, when there is a convention in town, he may take the boy along as a stall.

After some rather solemn instructions and admonitions, they go to work in the crowd. The boy must know who is boss. He instructs the boy to watch him for an *office* indicating which victim to take, then *put his hump up* as he has been shown. The tool picks *easy scores* and *kick outs*, letting the tough ones go. The boy isn't much help, but he is in there trying. They take two or three *pokes* during the evening. He gives the new man his share, and says maybe he'll use him again sometime. There is also a conference afterward in which the tool criticizes every move the boy made, and analyzes every mistake he made. If the boy can take this kind of "chewing out," it is one sign that he may make a good stall. If he blows up, or loses his head, or becomes defensive, he will never make a pickpocket. At least, he can hardly work with a good mob.

This venture may be repeated from time to time; the thief is in town without his stall; the boy knows the city and likes the work. They make several such tentative forays, with no *falls*. Then the tool takes his new stall to a state fair in another city for a day or two; the boy is learning fast and responds to teaching. Some day he may make a *bang up stall*. But he is still working on a very tentative basis with the tool, who has his own stall who travels on the road with him, or works regularly in some other big city. Suppose this steady stall "goes sour," or has some woman trouble, or *takes a fall* which looks as if it is easy to *fix*, but is not a *turn out* after all, and he has to go away for two years. The tool, who can *muzzle around* a bit *single o*, but who isn't by any means a *single handed gun*, comes back for the boy and makes a proposition to *fill him in*. The boy has saved up some money, and has $300 which he will put up for *fall dough*, which is welcome, for the tool has just *dropped a man* and that is always expensive. "We dropped a man before we hardly made a score."

The boy has *busted out*. He has been *joined out*. He is part of a mob. He has *mobbed it up*, though he might be stretching this phrase a bit to apply it to a boy making his debut in a two-handed *outfit*. He is a *cannon* now, and *on the whiz*. He is subject to all the trials, troubles, and pleasures which have long been the lot of the second oldest profession. And lest his *joining out* go to his head and he become a *sensational punk*, his mentor continues his instruction indefinitely. In fact, he rides the boy unmercifully.

Many a night in a hotel room they *punch gun* or *punch whiz* and the whole lore of the subculture is gradually made familiar to him. "Guns like to punch whiz when they get together and they tell funny things about eggs they have pushed around. Peter men don't punch much guff as a rule, but sometimes the scat will loosen them up for some good yarns. But guns learn that way, from the mistakes other fellows made." Every mistake he makes is called to his attention, and ways are suggested to overcome that one next time. He learns to take more and more of the responsibility of a stall, and may become quite proficient. This is mechanical proficiency. However, most of what he has to learn goes beyond the rather elementary physical act of theft; he goes out "big-timing it" and meets other *guns*; he has to learn about people, about the psychology of the mark, about ways and means to handle a *fall*, about the police and their ways, about travel and hangouts and *fixers* and bondsmen and various jails and prisons and a thousand other things which an effective *gun* needs to know.

He discovers how important a *good front* is; consequently he buys expensive clothes and keeps them *sharp*; sooner or later he sees sad examples of how disastrous it can be to *look bad*. He hears about the *seams* and learns to use them. He learns about *plants* of all kinds, ranging from a secret hiding place for drugs in the flush-box of a toilet in his hotel room to a *heel plant* for money or drugs in the hollowed heels of his shoes. "A fellow also plants for a heel touch, but this isn't a heel plant, unless the guy is a heel" (humor). In various *cans* and *joints* he learns about the more intimate *kiester plant*, and volumes more to make him prison-wise.

More than that, he begins to meet other *cannons* of all levels and kinds. They begin to know him, and he may get a *monicker* or underworld name, which means that he is known and accepted. He learns more and more about protecting himself and the tool too. He learns how to *bring a mark out* or *take a mark out* of a bank or station or other place where he has acquired or *flashed* a fat wallet. He learns how to *case* a mark after the *touch* has come off, following him to his train or bus and being sure that he didn't *blow* before he was safely away. He learns how to *shade the duke* and how to *cop the score* from the tool. He learns all the tool can teach him, and from then on he will be self-taught, because no pickpocket knows all the answers, and every *touch* presents variables which may be disastrous if not understood or controlled. Eventually he will learn from other *cannons* he meets or works with, including those he meets in jails and prisons.

He meets some *cannon broads*, who can be shapely girls indeed, and who may interest him if heroin is not already his only mistress; he has the experience of getting *nailed*, *snatched in the neck*, *clawed down* and *guzzled*, not once, but many times. He learns how to differentiate between a *shakedown* and a *bad fall*, and how to deal with each. He may get *lagged* and do some time in prison; in fact, it will be surprising if he does not. He will learn when to *lay dead* and when to *go out*, and if he gets *raw* or out of practice, he will find how to *sharp up*, and after a year or so in *stir*, he may find that he has lost some of his confidence. "When I got off the road, I would lay dead for a few weeks." Little by little he accumulates the spoken wisdom of the *grift*, which is passed from mouth to mouth when the boys are *punching the guff* or *chopping up old touches* or *cutting them up* or *punching gun*. He learns the code of the subculture as he has never known it before, and understands how important it is that he observe it. He now knows the specialized argot, or at least much of it. If he is going to stay *with it*—and he is now *hooked* beyond redemption—he will need every bit of wisdom and philosophy he can get, and if one cannot be a philosopher of sorts, he can never be happy on the *whiz*.

If he is unusually ambitious, he may try his hand at becoming a tool also, and he may prosper; he may fall back on card-sharping, and become a dealer or stick-man in some gambling joint in order to earn *side money*. He learns how to always keep *fresh money* coming in so that he does not have to bite into his savings except in great emergencies. "One of the best angles is that it's fresh money every day." His income may be good, as incomes for pickpockets go, and he may cultivate cultural pursuits like improving the breed in bookie-joints, or playing at craps for large stakes, or fancying women. However, the chances are that he will stay with his first love, the needle, and that the habit will lose the glorious drive and tingle that it had at first, and become the *chinaman on his back* who drives him like a slave to get more money to buy more *junk*. "And when I did take junk, I'll say this, when I did take junk, although it drove me like a mule, the only satisfaction I ever found in life I found in junk. They could take me out there and behead me in the morning. . . . That wouldn't mean anything, but I'd use junk tonight if I could get it."

His attitudes became case-hardened. He finds that, as a young man with plenty of money, he is very popular amongst his kind; he can *fix a beef*, and have some illusions of his own importance; however, he has to learn that when he is broke, his friends will *chill* on him quickly, that people are not so anxious to lend him money as they were to borrow it, and that the *fix* is a relentless animal which eats lettuce steadily, and in large quantities; other- wise he goes to *stir*. He finds his only security, however, in the subculture; the dominant culture has turned against him com- pletely, and he has rejected most of its values. He knows that all *suckers* are against him, and he is against them. He is a professional thief. And once he has become a specialized thief like a pickpocket, he will probably continue in that activity all his life. The chances are that he will never go back into the dominant culture, and they are equally good that he will not climb out of his pedestrian craft in this subculture to bigger *rackets*. It has been tried—and in some cases it has been accomplished—but the average pickpocket does not change.

But usually if a guy's a pickpocket, he knows what the score is as far as he's concerned. He knows that he's got a living there. So he goes out and if he only gets ten pokes a day, he's got grocery money, anyway. But if he goes out on one of them other capers, he don't know what he's got, because you have to specialize. If you're going to specialize in a certain subject, you have to concentrate on that. A man's capabilities is only going to carry him so far, and he can't do it. I have never knew—I have never known—I have never known a pickpocket to be successful at another racket.

In fact, the mere framework of specialization seems to keep a pickpocket where he is, to "freeze" him in his occupation. He has no need to learn anything else to practice his *racket*. The very practice of it precludes his learning anything else; while he may be highly skilled at removing a wallet, there his abilities, legitimate and illegitimate, usually end.

No, that wouldn't change your way of thinking. The moral of what he just said a minute ago is this: ninety-nine and ninety-nine one-hundredths percent of organized society as we know it today are not going to give a thief with a record . . . they're not going to give him a chance. Our chances of squaring up . . . well, we've got two. A bum chance and no chance at all. If you've gone this far down the river, there's no way back. Just like he said. . . .

Well, he might have a chance. But he's a heavy. In between his criminal activities and a prison sentence here and there, he's become an expert welder. And an iron-worker. He can do a lot of different jobs. And this boy [a short-change artist] has a lot of qualifications. He has a good education, he can read and write very well, and there is a lot of things he can do that he has picked up in the world.

Now you take a guy like me. . . . I don't know anything. I've centered everything I know on how to make an illegitimate dollar. I don't think about trying to make money any other way. Every time I've had a legitimate job, always one of those tornados strikes, or a windstorm comes up, and first thing you know I find myself out in the cold again. So I center all my alleged brain, my thinking power, whatever it may be, on trying to make an illegitimate dollar . . . which of course big business is trying to do the same. They're trying to phenagle us all out of a dollar.

And so the pickpocket, however expert he may be in his *racket*, is limited to that craft. Nothing he learns in the subculture can be applied in the dominant culture; his very professional skill inhibits him psychologically from learning anything he can use while he is in prison, where educational facilities are available. And he sees no way of learning anything in the dominant culture which might be applied in the subculture. Consequently he remains a pickpocket, usually on whatever level he was *turned out* originally.

On the other hand, if he does not make the grade as a good pickpocket, he may develop talents for lesser things. There are several *rackets* which are commonly associated with the *whiz* in the minds of the public and the police, but which are not to be confused with pickpockets strictly speaking. These operators working on related *rackets* recognize this to be a fact, and it is confirmed by professional *cannons*, who generally know about these *rackets*, but differentiate them from the *whiz*. In most cases, *cannons* feel that their way is somewhat superior to these other ways of making a living, though this is not always true. Certainly *class cannons* excel any or all of them in technology, in organization, and in personal attributes.

These *rackets* and the *whiz* have this in common: they are all part of the *grift*. They all take money from the person of the victim, who does not know that he is being robbed; also, they differ from certain *heavy* operations in that on the *heavy* (stick-up mobs, etc.) the victim is very well aware that he is being robbed, but cannot help himself because of the threat of force, or the actual use thereof. In a broad sense, they are all *sneak jobs*, though one or two of them come very close to the borderline of the *heavy*.

Normally, as we have said, a thief is *turned out* by an older and more experienced man. Within the fraternity this is generally thought to be the only way an individual can become a professional thief. At the same time, *thieves' blood* is regarded as hereditary, and a man or woman whose parents or immediate relatives are thieves is thought to have a better chance of *turning out* (with the tutelage of an experienced professional) than some unfortunate renegade from the dominant culture who wants to associate with the criminal subculture. Following is an account of a young woman from the dominant culture who taught herself to become a thief and developed into what might possibly be called a professional, even though her techniques were completely unorthodox. An arrest and conviction (perhaps unlikely in view of her appearance and lack of association with the criminal subculture) would probably put her in touch immediately with professionals who might *wise her up* and absorb her into the subculture. She is, in effect, a kind of *lone wolf* thief, though not of the intellect and skill which seem to characterize successful thieves of this type.

Well, the croaker says, "Just let him rest," so I did, and left him up in the kip [the stall had ptomaine poisoning] and I went out on the street to muzzle around single handed for a while.

In a few minutes one of them Union Square shorts pulls up and stops at that School Street intersection and there's a hell of a tip there. So I jump out of the tip and beat a mark. One of them big pancake pokes. I don't know if you ever seen one of them tweezer pokes that looks like a pancake. So I pitty-patted off the stand and started walking down the street. And I hear somebody coming tap, tap, tap. And I say, "Heels, huh?"

So I stopped and looked in a window, looked around to see who was coming. It was a good-looking gal. I'm telling you twenty-one or twenty-two years old—I know she wasn't twenty-five. So I walked again, and when I stopped to look in a window, she stopped. I go on down the street and tap, tap, I hear them high heels coming again. So I stop in the next window. I'm going on down Medford Avenue. So I get down to the next corner. I turned on the next corner and said, "I'm going to stop this crap. I'm going to see what's going to happen." So I turned the corner and just stood there. She turned the corner right behind me and I said, "Hey, what do you want?" And snatched a hold of her like this. "What are you following me for?"

She said, "I just wanted to see what that pocketbook had in it." She said, "I've got one here, and I'm going to see what it's got in it, too." She didn't know no lingo. A funny thing about this. She didn't know nothing. She didn't know nothing about turning over a poke, or nothing like that. She said, "I'm going to see what this one's got in it myself. I want to know what yours has got in it."

So I said, "What interest is that of yours?" So I said, "Let's take a walk on up here across the bridge to the park. I want to talk to you." Man, I'm telling you she was pretty. We go over and sit on a bench in the park. I turned mine over—had $68 or $70. I don't know what it had. A pretty fair score, a decent score. She turned hers over and she had $100 or something in hers. I never seen her working at all. I never noticed her in the tip. So young and innocent and everything. I never paid no attention to her, so she starts tailing me, you know, following me. Finally I said, "How did you make me?"

She said, 'How did I do what?' So I explained it to her. She said, "I seen you down there with that other fellow."

I said, "You did?"

She said, "Yeah, who is that man?"

I said, "What, do you turn out to be a policeman? What do you want to know who he is for?

"Well," she says, "I seen you two down at the boats this morning."

I said, "You did?"

She said, "Yeah, I seen you down there. I seen that grey-haired fellow and that little good-looking black-haired man, too."

I said, "You seen them down there too? How in the hell do you get around and I don't know you?"

She said, "There ain't nobody that knows me."

I said, "They don't?"

"No, nobody knows me."

I said, "How about putting up all this money together and then dividing it up?" I said, "Since you seen me and I seen you and we're all here together."

She says, "OK."

I think it was $168 or $170. We put it together and chopped it up. I said, "What are we going to do with these pokes?"

She said, "I'm going to do what I always do."

I said, "What do you always do?"

She said, "I always put them in the sewer."

I said, "That's a good place for them; they ain't going to harm anybody down there."

She said, "Well, you give them to me." She went in her pocketbook and she had a piece of newspaper folded up. A piece of newspaper, you know, just the right size. So I set on the bench and she walked down the street and put them in the sewer. She come back and set down on the bench. She called off and described every cannon that is working Boston at that time. She described every one of them. She didn't know their names, but she described them. So we sat on the bench.

Finally I said to her, "How about you?"

She said, "Well, there ain't nobody that knows me."

"Yeah," I said, "I know you . . . and I'm going to tell everybody about you. If you don't tell me about yourself. I'm just going to tell everybody."

"Oh, please don't do that," she said. So I finally got the story out of her. She's married to an automobile mechanic and she wanted pretty things. Pretty clothes, dresses, one thing and another. And couldn't . . . they didn't have no kids. But he couldn't provide them. And so she told me, she said, "I've got a bank account. All by myself. He don't know nothing about it."

"You don't know it, sister," I thought to myself, "but you've got fall dough and all, and you'll need it some day."

So I said, "What is the first time you ever seen me?"

"The first time I ever seen you was in the Shubert Theater and you got a pocketbook coming out." She didn't say "beat a mark," she said, "You got a pocketbook coming out of the Shubert Theater."

I said, "How long ago has that been?"

She said, "That's been about a month." And she sat there and told me about every cannon that was hustling that town.

I said, "Well, let's see what you can do." She had little tiny hands and little tiny fingers. And you know how she got pokes? She put her whole hand in. Her whole hand. . . . She didn't know how to reef or anything. She didn't know nothing like that. So I said to her, "You think you can steal?"

She says, "Yeah. You know what I done? I got this pocketbook two or three minutes before you got yours. I went back up on the curb and waited for you to get yours." She didn't say "score," she said, "I waited for you to get your pocketbook." She didn't know no lingo or nothing, you know what I mean?

So I said, "Well, you want to take a ride with me? You want to take a ride out the Avenue? After all it's Saturday afternoon."

She says, "How about that other man?"

"Well," I said, "how about *your* old man? He'll be there when I get back, you don't have to worry about it. Let's take a ride."

We took a short and she took five scores. She don't know what the block is or the frame, or nothing. She didn't know how to use me, but I'm helping her. I just wanted to see her put her duke down. She took that tiny hand, and put it all the way down in the guy's britch and come out with it. She'd raise that man's tog and put her duke down there just like it was legit. I'm telling you she would come out with that dough and that guy would pay no more attention to her than nothing. Now if it had been me, and I had put my hand in there like that, I would have got my head knocked off. We go out and she gets five scores going out and coming back. And we knocked up, I think, about $200.

We got off at Union Square. When we come back, we cut up that dough and she said, "I got to go home now," and she hopped in a cab and took off. And I never seen her to this day. It's the damnest experience I ever had in my life—strictly a self-taught thief.

Several related occupations have already been mentioned. The *center britch worker*, for instance, usually is or has been a pickpocket, but he has fallen on evil days. Perhaps too many *falls* have caused him to *blow his moxie*. He gets himself a girl who has probably been a prostitute before she accepted his bed and board, and when he has a period when he cannot work, or does not want to work, or is afraid to work, she readily returns to her own profession; he promptly takes her earnings and thus technically at least becomes a pimp; he does not solicit for her as a rule, nor does he do anything else for her except serve as her lover, if she is not so addicted to drugs that she has no interest in sex for herself. As the reader may guess, he is not a highly cultured type, and he generally loses caste—if he had any—when he *joins out the odds*. Other pickpockets now say that he makes his living from the pocket which lies directly between the *left britch* and the *right britch*, that is, the *center britch*. Sometimes he continues as a part-time pickpocket, but more often he gets one girl after another and eventually steals less and less from the *suckers* and takes more and more of his living from the *center britch* or the *middle britch*. And thus he establishes himself in the least admirable vocation a man can have, though it is indeed an old one. "A cannon turning pimp is a middle britch hustler."

Also, the *moll buzzer* (male or female) is not strictly speaking a pickpocket, though the *racket* is closely related. It is a highly sensitive *sneak job* in which some of the techniques used by pickpockets are also used. But the thief takes money from the purses or handbags (*hangers*) carried by women, and does not take it from the person, except rarely when a woman's pockets are actually picked (*patch pocket worker*). Sometimes pickpockets also double as *moll buzzers* at certain times, though a professional *cannon* usually balks at this even if he can perform the theft better than a full-time *moll buzzer*. "There's a season for moll buzzing, around the different holidays." A purse-snatcher is a very crude amateur-type thief who robs women also, but is not in a class with the *moll buzzers*.

Then there are the *mary ellen hustlers* or *mary ellen workers*. These thieves have gone away beyond any tactics that the *clout and lam* or *rip and tear mobs* ever contemplated. They prey upon victims who may or may not have had a few drinks; they like to find a man walking alone in or near the red-light district, and they approach him three or four *strong*, pretending to have had a few drinks themselves, laughing loudly, and talking about a girl named *mary ellen* whom they have just seen.

Yeah, and Mary Ellen workers. They'll grab a guy and pull his shirt tail out and say, "We was just over at a whorehouse and a girl pulled her dress up to here," and fan him across the britch, and they'll say, "She had a big fat rump," and they'll reach around and fan his prat. And they'll say, "She had the biggest tits ever," and grab him up there. And that kind of thing. That's against my bringing-up.

They swarm all over the victim as they pass him on the street, playfully pulling his coat up over his head to show how far up her dress was, and sometimes pulling his pants "down to here" to show how far this lecherous lass had exposed herself. All this happens very swiftly in a hail of boisterous horseplay, and they pass on, leaving the victim to put himself back together again, after which he may discover that his wallet and any other cash reserves he may have had are mysteriously missing. Of course the name "Mary Ellen" or the initials M. E. are not always used, but the racket takes its name from the fact that the original feminine inspiration for this *racket* seems to have had that fetching name.

Mary ellen workers operate everywhere, but Montreal is reputed to have more of them than any other city of comparable size.

Mary Ellen hustlers are not looked down on by other pickpockets. It's a racket in itself. It's not done any more in big cities. The reason is that it's a bad racket. It gives the place a bad name. When the hustlers get through with the mark, he's got both his hands up over his head, his shirt tail out, his hat over his eyes, and he's stripped clean."

Donicker workers or *donicker hustlers*, also known as *crapper hustlers* and *coin throwers*, usually work *two handed*. They follow a *fat mark* who is about to enter a public toilet. When he selects a stall (this *racket* is often worked in pay-toilets in hotels or railway stations) one man moves into the cubicle on either side of him, and all three are ensconced on the throne, apparently happily engaged. Then one of the operators drops a heavy coin, such as a half dollar, and rolls it across the stall occupied by the victim toward the stall being ostensibly used by the confederate. This distracts the mark, and this distraction may be increased by some *cross fire* or prepared dialogue between the two operators. Under the smoke screen of mild confusion, one of the operators, by way of retrieving the coin, or returning it, frisks the trousers of the mark underneath the partition, since they are already conveniently draped near the floor. The one with the wallet hurriedly departs, leaving the mark in no condition to follow immediately, while the partner remains behind to *case* him if he *blows*.

Lush busters, *lush hunters*, or *lush workers* go on the prowl for drunks, or men sufficiently *juiced up* to be robbed without much interference. They are one or two degrees in status below the *flop workers* described previously, and have little acceptance by professional *cannons*, who have no use for a victim who is not up on his feet and going somewhere. In a similar class are those very reprehensible thieves who *operate* or *perform an operation* with a razor blade or other small sharp instrument in order to remove wallets in a crowd. This is indeed an ancient art (cutpurses operated in medieval Europe), but held in low repute by modern quality thieves.

Ball busters, *ballocks workers*, or *bollix workers* are thieves who usually work in pairs. One approaches a man in a tavern or on the street and *cuts into him* on the subject of sex; some mobs solicit the man for relations with a woman, some prefer the homosexual approach (as being less likely to carry a *beef*) and during the brief description of the delights which await him, the mark's testicles are grabbed by one member who might by courtesy be called a stall. As the mark winces in pain, the stall increases the pressure until he is sure that his partner (who might also be called a tool, if we do not care how we define a tool) has secured the victim's wallet. They then *blow him off* and disappear, leaving him somewhat the worse for wear. This, of course, borders on the *heavy rackets* because of the force used, as well as the lack of a *sneak* approach.

The next step is direct violence, though the victim may be so surprised that he does not recognize the assault as an attempt to steal his wallet. This is called *the arm*, and is operated by one or two thieves who have no objections if the victim is somewhat intoxicated. A strangle hold is applied by one and (if there are two) the other takes the wallet. This hold is called a *gilligan hitch* on the West Coast, a *mug* on the East Coast. In New York City, such an operator is called a *boffman* or *mugger*. He is also generally known as a *muscle man*.

Thieves who specialize (either via pocket-picking skill, the *lush roller* approach, or the *gilligan hitch* route) on lumberjacks or other seasonal workers who get paid off in a lump sum at the end of the season are called *jack rollers*, *jack sneaks*, *jack gaggers*, or *jack hustlers*. Some of them are simply pickpockets who specialize in this work. These operators go after the entire pay of the worker, which may be a considerable sum. Because such workers are more common in the West and on the West Coast, the *racket* is more prevalent there and is little known in the East.

It should be repeated that none of these specialties is accepted by the *whiz* as belonging strictly to that profession and some of them are looked down on to a degree by capable *class cannons*. All of these related *rackets* employ certain less technical skills and training also, but they cannot be described here. Most of the operators who practice them, however, simply lack the natural skill, the training, the character—or all three of these attributes— to be competent pickpockets.

It becomes increasingly obvious that youngsters are not *turning out* on the *whiz* the way they once did, with the result that the sub-culture is diminishing in size as the old-timers die or *pack it in*. It has been estimated by reliable informants that there are, as of 1955, about a thousand *class cannons* operating in the United States. Ten years ago there were probably five or six thousand, suggesting a very rapid decline in numbers. Furthermore, most *class cannons* now operating are around fifty years of age, or older. The *locals*, as of 1955, probably number around twenty-five hundred (if we exclude the riffraff of Harlem), which figure also represents a large decrease in recent years.

While the pickpocket will never become extinct in our society, he will probably be so reduced in numbers within the next generation that he will no longer be a very significant factor in the criminal subculture. On the other hand, a change in our economy or in our social structure could possibly revive the *racket* and populate it with competent youngsters. This, however, is an outside chance. The odds are that this subculture—once one of the most populous and lucrative in this country—will atrophy and survive only in a small core of diehards who will be looked upon as criminal curiosities.

CHAPTER XI

PLACES TO WORK

The pickpocket's workshop is the city street. In fact, a *local cannon* reminds one of a small haberdasher or petit-bourgeois merchant whose entire life is spent in his business. (This is, to some extent, true of *road mobs* too, though their days and hours are less regular.) He sallies forth at regular hours—often early—and works systematically and diligently. He puts in a full day. By this, he means at least eight hours. If there are *doings* or a *come off* attracting out-of-town crowds, he may work overtime and be on his regular *beat* in the morning. There is a certain smugness about him and more than a touch of babbittry, especially if he is a *home-guard* or *local*. He has a certain proprietorship in his district or street; there is even a sense of pride about it. He may tell you frankly that he *owns* it.

Perhaps no other type of criminal is so sensitive to crowds, so readily responsive to the movements of people on the street, so automatically and reliably alert to the swirls and eddies of humanity on the pavement. His rapport with these crowds, in their many different moods and in their very different tempos, amounts to almost a sixth sense. He reaches out the antennae of his *grift know* into the street, samples the tenor of the crowd, and reacts with great sureness and complete self-confidence. Whatever the time of day or night, whatever the occasion, the season of the year, the weather, the temper of the people who throng the streets, it comes through to him and he responds like a bird dog to the scent of quail. His very close rapport enables him to melt into the crowd without becoming in any way conspicuous; his scent of marks to be *taken* alerts him and arouses all his predatory instincts. He moves effortlessly with the crowds, smelling them with his finger tips. There is about him something of the cat, as well as something of the mouse, and something of the fox, as well as something of the still hunter. And a touch of the poet, though he never gets his song into words.

Perhaps the most striking element in his professional make-up is his feeling of superiority to the people he is going to rob, or those whom he is robbing, or has robbed. If they work for a living, they are *slaves*. When they appear in throngs on the streets at the same time, they become *slave grift*. They are soulless robots who make the dominant culture hum; they have no freedom, no glorious insecurity, no need to live by their wits. They live humdrum lives in humdrum homes, where they spend the very dull hours until they will return again to their very humdrum jobs. The only interesting thing about them is that they carry wallets. And so the pickpocket coldly and surely and with the objectivity of a surgeon removes the wallets, while his contempt for the persons on whom he is operating knows no bounds. They are *slaves* and he is in business for himself.

He is equally alert to the streets when they are sparsely populated, or when people move in ones and twos. He does not have to have a large or heavy crowd to work in. Because the public has been impressed with the fact that pickpockets work in crowds, there is a widespread belief that they cannot work anywhere else. This is not true. As a matter of fact, many inferior pickpockets can *work* dense crowds and get away with rough, slipshod work, but some of the smoothest *sneak jobs* one can imagine are done by first-rate *cannons* in a very sparse crowd, or in no crowd at all. For instance, a *two handed jug mob* is *planted* outside a *jug* or bank waiting for a man who is known to be going there to withdraw $2500 in cash. The stall may *tail* him in just to be sure he makes the withdrawal, and then *bring him out*. When he leaves the bank in mid-morning, there are no crowds on the street. There are just a few people walking here and there. Yet that man will be robbed right in broad daylight and within sight of everyone on the street. And he will not know it until he returns to his office and *blows*.

A crowd is, to a pickpocket, a *tip*, a *press*, a *crush*, or a *push*. "The guns were so thick in St. Paul during the State Fair that you could hardly get out of a gun tip. And we got into a tip that was so good even I, as bad as I am, got a few of them, you know." "Three troupes is up against this push already." It may also be just *grift*, especially if it is *work* in a certain type of crowd which is more or less standardized. Thus *hoosier grift* is the crowd at a country fair or a small-town street fair. *Push grift* is a dense, excited crowd where the technical niceties may be dispensed with. "It's really more of an areaway than anything else, the way I see it, and man, it's push grift. So I'm going right and left, you know, and every time a sucker steps up, why, boom, it's gone, and I pass the poke." A *murderer's push grift* is even more of a set-up for the

rough tool or even the *root and toot, rip and tear, clout and lam* boys.
An example of this would be a football crowd entering or leaving
a large stadium. "Nothing can beat a football crush . . . it's
murderer's push grift." A cheap crowd, one hardly worth working
is a *pea soup tip*, especially among *shots*. *Penitentiary grift* is a crowd
which is dense and cannot move, such as a large crowd waiting to
enter a train gate or to come off a ferry. The pickpockets do not
like to *work* until the crowd is in motion, and they will wait as long
as necessary before beginning operations.

Large, excited crowds, however, are the exception, and most
cannons operate consistently *on the drag* in whatever kind of
crowds happen to be there. Some favor the *chutes* or subway
system; others *hustle* the *spots* which are bus stops (*get ons*), transfer points, stations, or other places where people congregate briefly.
Others like to *load them on*, or work through the crowds boarding
cars, robbing one or two as they get on, then at another stop, to
unload them, and rob one or two getting off. "They think there's
got to be a terrible big tip. And I've took my partner many a
time and loaded one sucker on a streetcar or getting on a train or
bus. You only need one man, that's all." If a particular *spot* is protected by *whiz coppers* who take, it is a *right spot*; if it is not, or is
particularly dangerous to work, it is a *hot spot*. A locality or even a
town which is well protected (with *wrong coppers*) and very dangerous is *on fire*. "Well, you know, you can set Chicago on fire in three
days, if you really get in there and work." "The town's on fire, I
tell you."

If an area or a community has been worked so heavily that it is
now impossible to work there at all, it is *burned up*. Sometimes a
street or a district is called a *line*, and then the *line* can be *burned
up*. Some pickpockets work the *traps*, or types of transportation in
which one enters a turnstile and must ride on through to another
station; thus a thief cannot *load them on* and leave the station,
as he might at a bus stop; however, good *cannons* are careful about
backing out of any *tip* where people are boarding cars or buses in
numbers, for *whiz dicks* are on the lookout for that kind of move to
rank a pickpocket. A thief's comment on the preceding statement:
"I don't think this is right. It's incomplete. It's from the point of
view of the mob—you say, 'He ranked that sucker,' it's one of
the mob that ranks him. 'We framed for the sucker and I was
about to beat him for his poke and some broad ranked the sucker.' "

Some mobs *work the rattlers*, or trains, especially interurban trains, the old-fashioned *railroad grift* in which mobs rode the trains everywhere, *unloading them* and then *loading them on* at every station. "Some gun mobs don't do anything but play the rattlers, and it is called railroad grift." Exceptions are excursion trains, convention trains, and political campaign trains, which run irregularly and which stop at small, unprotected stations. When the train is likely to carry *fuzz*, some mobs drive in a car from stop to stop, *hustle* the crowds at each stop, and drive on to meet the next crowd at the next stop. When a train stops at a station, it becomes a *rat stop*. When thieves ride the trains over the country, usually working crowds at various cities away from the railroad stations, they are *hopscotching*.

Some *cannon mobs* travel consistently, or *hopscotch* until they find a *right spot* and *grift* it for a few days or even longer. They try to avoid the *gag towns* or places which are especially tough on pickpockets—or at least on out-of-town pickpockets. "New York is a gag town. Also Philly. Most of the top coppers in Philly started on the whiz detail." *Gag towns* are also known as *smart towns*, and unless a mob wants to chance it working *on the sneak*, or unless it has an *in* with some individual detectives by which a day or two of *hustling with a shade* or *hustling with pro* can be had, it had better give this type of town a *pass up*, or *buy through* it. "There is no such a thing as working right in New York any more." The *steer* or *folderman* for the mob is supposed to find out these things in advance; in fact, without a vast fund of such knowledge about all towns, a *road mob* is severely handicapped.

Like all pickpockets, *road mobs* do not like to buy anything unnecessarily. This includes transportation. The old-timers are expert at *beating the donicker*, or using the toilet as a hideout to avoid paying fare; they also know how to manipulate *hat duckets* or steal them in order to appear to have paid their fare. If they can find a *thieving con* or a *kinky kayducer* who will *cop the short*, it reduces the *working nut* considerably. "Railroad kayducers that will pass you up when you tell them you'll see them later—they'll cop the short fare." That is, they do not buy tickets, but make arrangements with the conductor to pay a considerably reduced fare in cash, no questions asked. The more economies that can be effected in this way, the less the mob is *on the nut*, and therefore the less has to come *off the top* or *off the head* or *off the cap*, which is the total *knock up*. This means more profit all the way round. *Class mobs*, however, do not favor *burning* the railroads, for it may cause them trouble later on.

Most pickpockets like to have one or more *lay off spots* or *hideaways* where they can live quietly without working, and be seen in public without police interference. "No sooner he'd get a couple of G's than he'd head for a lay off spot and he wouldn't come out till he didn't have a nickel." This retreat from the hurly-burly of the profession is thought to have a wholesome effect on the nerves and most thieves avail themselves of such relaxation at intervals calculated to preserve them intact well into old age; often relaxation at such sanctuaries is improved and assisted by an attractive female companion who may not know that her escort is *on the rackets*.

Since pickpockets are often competent at stealing all sorts of merchandise (though the *boost* is not properly a part of their *racket*) they commonly provide the necessities of life by theft. This may even include groceries. Generally, however, pickpockets steal clothing ("Wearing a boosted tie each day helps break the monotony") ("With Christmas near, I always dread the annual clouted ties"), jewelry, tobacco and smoking equipment, fountain pens and pencils, etc. When pickpockets maintain a home or apartment, they steal as much of their supplies and equipment as possible. This may be *clouted* from local department stores, or may be shipped home by a thief on the road. "All cannons like to trim hotels for linen and blankets and silverware and send it home." "If you are going to put the bee on a hotel, don't ever hang around the office, and you'll never be made. If you are short on sheets or blankets or tablecloths or napkins or any of them things, just buy a boarding-house deceiver. Then find the linen closet on your floor and help yourself. Stash it in the kiester and express it home. It is a good thing to have plenty of good linen on hand at all times."

Some mobs pay their hotel bills as a matter of public relations— *class mobs* mostly—and others make it a policy to avoid paying when they leave. "The best way to trim a hotel is to register with the night clerk and go out when the day clerk is on." "This is the carry-out. You register in one hotel and your partner in another. You each stay six days in your hotel and leave before you get your tab. The night before you leave, you register at your partner's hotel without your kiester, but with his screw. He does the same at your hotel. The next morning you both carry the other fellow's baggage out and pay for one night. So what."

Certain cities are known as *right spots* where thieves can *cool out,* that is, live for a while without police interference. These cities vary from time to time, according to the political complexion of the administration and the strength of the underworld organization. A town which is *right* today may be *wrong* tomorrow, so thieves distribute their patronage according to the local temperature. Says an old-timer: "One night I counted 143 cannons in a scatter in the Village. That big Exposition was on. Dayton Sam was working with pro at the front gate. Chicago Ed played the spindle inside the grounds. Jerry Daly played the dinks in the grounds. Inspector Hunt was the right fuzz, and was the man fitted for all grift. He was at the Harrison Street Police Station." Toledo was once noted for its hospitality to thieves, and especially to pickpockets, as was also St. Paul. This *cannon* is a "booster" for St. Paul: "Guns held a national convention at St. Paul annually. Toledo had it only once. That was when Brand Whitlock was mayor." "At one time in Toledo, Ohio, the cannons had a baseball team just among themselves, and large sums of jack was bet." Says another: "At one time in St. Paul, Minnesota, the cannons grifted Minneapolis, but didn't turn a trick in the Sainty City. Big John was the man to see." The same thing holds for certain neighborhoods in certain cities at certain times, and thieves soon get the word. "At one time around Forty-Second Street in New York City, if you howled, 'Stop, thief,' everybody took it on the lam." Likewise, some towns also get the reputation for being *wrong.* "Milwaukee is noted for being the toughest city in the Midwest to grift in or to lay dead in. So don't go there, as you'll last longer on the outside than on the inside."

It appears, then, that modern pickpockets do not enjoy the combination of hospitality and immunity that they did a generation ago. Even in cities which shelter other forms of crime, the pickpocket is not always welcome, largely because of the "heat" he may generate (if he works there) and because he does not rate in the big-time *rackets*.

All mobs have regular places for *meets*, and prearranged places to reassemble if they become separated in the crowd while working. "In case of a split out we always made a meet at the shed." *Local mobs* have their own arrangements based on local conditions; *road mobs* make frequent use of the O.B. (post office) and the *shed* (railroad station) for meeting places where out-of-town people are often seen and will cause no comment. "Richards around the shed is very easily made as they plant around the ducket window and if you are Joseph, you'll make any fuzz that might be flying around." "Richard Dick was made punching gun with a strange cannon in the shed this morning where old man Gar blowed his okus." Also, these buildings are often either located in or near the districts where pickpockets would be *hustling*. Furthermore, when pickpockets communicate, it is generally through General Delivery; when they send money to their families or to repay a loan or to replenish their *fall dough*, it is often done by Postal Money Order; and even if there is no pressing business which takes them to the O.B., it is always a good idea to leaf through the "wanted" posters generally displayed in post offices just to keep track of who is wanted and for what, even unto one's self.

Both *locals* and *road mobs* also have certain *hangouts* where they congregate. These are usually *scatters* or saloons with good political connections, or *goulash joints* (restaurant-cafés) where they can eat and drink and meet their friends. Sometimes these *hangouts* are bookie-joints, barber-shops, news-stands, etc., which *front* for book-makers; in the old days many of them were brothels where pick-pockets were welcome and protected and where they spent considerable time and money. "Give a cannon plenty of cush in a notchery, and boy, does he lay it on the line." Here in the hangouts they not only *keep meets* safely and inconspicuously, but *chop up old touches*, or *cut up old ones*, or *punch gun*, which consists of talking shop and rehashing old times; there is always someone with *one for the end book*, or a story that is hard to believe. Also these *spots* are relay centers for the *grapevine* by which news is transmitted rapidly and accurately.

Good *cannons* have a knowledge of all local holidays and other festivities, and try to *work* them whenever possible. Some of these holidays are best in the morning, some in the afternoon, and some at night. For instance, in Salt Lake City, the Fourth of July is generally considered a *morning day*. The times of specific holidays in certain localities are designated as *days*, and both *locals* who may get together a *knockabout mob* and *road mobs* are interested in attending. "August 14 is Litvak-Day in Mahoning City." "By accident we run into a Dago Day upstate, and we make a big day of it." "It was some big Church Day. Bishop Pendergast was laying a cornerstone." Likewise, large picnics, lodge conventions, labor-union activities, etc., attract pickpockets, who have little interest in what goes on, but turn out in force and *rung up* so as not to attract attention as outsiders; that is, they dress like the people there even unto overalls or working clothes, and, if it is a convention, they may register and get badges, streamers, novelty hats, and any other paraphernalia to make them look like delegates.

There is among modern pickpockets a tradition that certain mobs have exclusive rights in certain areas, although all pickpockets do not observe these rights, and some perhaps do not even know about them. This tradition is reflected in arrangements with the police which give certain mobs or certain individuals the exclusive right to work in these districts at certain times. Thus a certain mob may say that they *own* this street or that district, and others, generally speaking, will respect this right. "The Big Mob owned the ferry, but we had a shade at the amusement park." Pickpockets may refuse to work in an area because it is known that another mob has the *X* on that *spot*; this probably indicates the survival of the very ancient custom of marking or inscribing walls or pavements in areas sacred to one group; there are still old-time tramps who make actual chalk marks as communications to others who may also work these areas; the marks used by tramps go well beyond the simple *X* of ownership and constitute a fairly comprehensible code. *Road mobs* often disregard these local proprietorships, if they know about them, or hustle in areas where they do not exist; this fact may partly motivate an enmity between *locals* and *road mobs* in certain cities, with the *locals* acting as watchdogs for the police in reporting any *whiz* in an area which *belongs* to the *locals*.

CHAPTER XII

ETHICS AND MORALS

The subculture of thieves has a rather full set of mores which govern—or are supposed to govern—their behavior. In some cases —kindness to children or animals, for instance—these mores may be identical, or nearly so, with those of the dominant culture. In others—the belief, for example, that a man who does not protect his money from theft has no right to it—there is a considerable distance between the subculture and the dominant culture. Here we can touch upon only those phases of ethical and moral beliefs which go with making a living, and hence are related to the technology either directly or indirectly.

Probably the heart of the ethics of pickpockets involves the relationship between partners, or among members of a mob. This has evolved throughout the ages, and manifests itself in our own times in the form of different ethics for different levels. Since it is obviously impossible to cover all levels and gradations—and generalizations made along such fine lines of division would not be sound anyway—it might be best to look at two extremes, the top and the lower levels near the bottom.

First, among *class cannons*, each pickpocket owes complete loyalty to the mob. If he is not prepared to support them, he has no business *hustling* with them. This support is moral, personal, and— with some limitations— financial. His financial obligations go only as far as his *fall dough* would indicate; that is, if he has put up an equal share of $4500 *fall dough* with two other *guns*, he is obligated to the extent of $1500 if any of the three—including himself—has a *fall*. When that amount of money is spent, he is free of financial obligation, though of course he still owes his moral support. Even though he is known to have more cash in reserve, or with him, he has no obligation to spend that money to fight the case of another member of the mob. However, he might decide to advance additional cash if he knew his partners well and rated their credit highly, or he and the other free partner might go to work diligently to *knock up* a fund to add to the *fall dough* already in the hands of the *fixer* or lawyer.

This was over on the East Coast. In the spring of the year. If I'd had a hundred dollars more, I'd've had fifteen grand fall dough, for the mob, I mean. Well, we had some people in the can. We had two guys and a gal in the bucket and we had to raise some money and we had to raise it quick. I musta stole . . . I don't know how many pokes I stole in one day. I think the best I did was twenty-two. Twenty-two pokes in one day and we didn't have enough to pay room rent. Just blind steers. So my partner, he said, "Let's do something. We got to get these people out." We'd already spent what we had. Like I was telling you, if I'd have had a hundred dollars more I'd have had fifteen grand, and we'd put all this money up, and there's three people still in the bucket. We can't get them loose, and my partner said, "Let's do something."

Likewise, if a *pick up* is *filling in* with a *class mob* temporarily, he may put up only a limited amount of *fall dough*, say $300. In this case, the other two members (who might have up $2000 *fall dough* between them) have an understanding with the *pick up* that they will be responsible to him, in the event of a *fall*, for only $300 each, which matches the amount he has in the kitty. When they have spent their $600 (plus his $300, if he had that much) on any *sucker trouble* which the *pick up* may have, they have fulfilled their obligation. Of course, if he is well liked, or there are other unusual circumstances, they might agree to go a little higher, especially if it looked as it they could *beat the rap*. However, they can, when $900 has been spent, walk out of the picture and leave him to fight his own case without money, or go to prison, and their reputations are clear. Even the man they walked out on would not consider himself *dumped*; he would realize that he had had all the insurance he had paid for.

If a *class mob* agrees to *fill in* a third (or fourth) member, not because he is needed, but because he has just had some bad luck and needs help, each would specify in advance how much *fall dough* he is willing to risk on this *pick up* who will, presumably, be filled in without *fall dough* of his own. Some mobs might refuse to put up any *fall dough* for him, but this is not likely among *class cannons*. They would calculate the risks and estimate what a *fall* might cost. Then they would agree to *go for* him up to a certain conservative limit thought to be sufficient to cover him in any ordinary difficulty. If he should *take a fall*, however, and the fall dough was inadequate, he would have no additional claim against the other members; in fact, he would have received a gift from heaven. If he *beat the rap*, he would recognize an obligation to pay back the *fall dough* put up for him—when he was able to do so; he would owe this money to the mob and would repay it to the men who put it up, or *stood for* it. Even if he got *settled*, he would still have this obligation after he got out of *stir*. While debts of this kind are not always paid, the obligations are there; a *class cannon* recognizes them and pays them; if he does not, his reputation suffers; if he ignores enough of them, he loses his standing as a *class cannon*.

If you're with a class mob, it's a different thing. Here's another thing. For instance, you pick a guy up. Here's a guy that just got out of stir and you say, "Well, I'll give you a couple days' work." You're already three-handed, and you fill him in and so you're four-handed. Maybe this mob has got six thousand dollars fall dough, two grand apiece. Now this guy you fill in, this fourth man, he fills in and you fill him in with an understanding to this extent. We'll say, "We're pretty fat, doing all right. We'll give you a couple days' work and we'll fill you in to this extent, we'll go for you as far as $500 apiece. Now you ain't put up your two grand fall dough, you understand." The guy's just got out of stir and just got home. He needs a suit of clothes; he needs this and that. Now you make an arrangement with that man that if you have any trouble, you're going to go as far as $500 apiece to help him. At the end of the five hundred, that's all she wrote."

It should be noted here that the informant has used the verb *fill in* to cover the work of a temporary *pick up*. While this is not strictly accurate, it was the most convenient way to describe this theoretical situation. *Class mobs* usually regard a man who is *filled in* (or a *fill in*) as a permanent addition to the mob or a permanent substitution for a member *dropped*. On the other hand, a *pick up* is understood to be only temporarily working with the mob. The mob agrees to give him a *day's work*, which may mean from several days to several weeks. Sometimes a *fill in* may be accepted without *fall dough* with the understanding that he will build it up as rapidly as possible, the other members meanwhile *going for* him to the extent of a prearranged amount.

Class mobs are almost legalistic in their insistence that all arrangements be understood in advance. Some mobs have a permanent, standing arrangement which all members know and respect. Others vary this arrangement from day to day or even from *score* to *score*. However, the variation must be stated and understood in order to avoid trouble. For instance, some mobs operate permanently under this succinct contract: *in with the grief, in with the gravy*, which means that anyone with *fall dough* up is entitled to his share of all *touches*—even though he may have been delayed, or sick, or otherwise unable to participate in the *action* of the mob. These maxims are also used in the negative.

Others use the formula *in with the pinches, in with the pokes*, which comes out to about the same thing; any member who risks his *fall dough* for the other members of the mob is entitled to his share of the daily *knock up*, whether or not he actually participates in the theft.

If they're in with the grief, then they got to be in with the gravy. And vice versa, if they got fall dough up. Say, for instance, it's a three-handed mob and you got three grand fall dough up. Now because a guy is five minutes late, he might have gotten held up in traffic, he might have gotten stalled, anything might have happened. If he's got his fall dough, there ain't no way you can cut him out of that money. Because if you got pinched, you're going to use his money to get out of jail with. So if he ain't there, and you play for a mark, and he only has six bucks, that's two bucks apiece. If he's got a thousand dollars up and you step up and beat the mark with only six bucks and you get snatched in the neck and it costs you twelve hundred to spring, he loses four bills. You can talk on that all day. With class mobs, it never varies. With pick ups, yes. They'll use a thousand different angles to cut a guy out of a nickel that he's got coming to him. If he's not in with the pinches, he's not in with the pokes. If he's in with the pokes, then he's in with the pinches. But remember that's in mobs with fall dough up."

Some mobs vary their arrangements to suit circumstances, but these variations must be stated verbally whenever one member wishes to invoke them, and the mob must understand what this variation is. For instance, let us assume that two good professionals are *hustling* together; one ordinarily is the *wire* or *hook*, while the other is a stall. This arrangement holds *while they are working together*, but may be varied in this way: the partner who is the *hook* when they work together is obviously the better *hook* of the two, or he would not be playing that role; however, the other partner, who stalls when they work together, is also capable of working by himself under certain circumstances; he is not good enough to be a real *single o cannon*, but he can take *easy scores* when he is working by himself. These two men have up between them $2000 *fall dough*. Now it is fundamental that each is responsible for the other *while they are working together*.

But what about those times when they are working on their own, *single o*? Those occasions are taken care of by an advance arrangement. One says to the other, "I'm going out for breakfast; want to go along?" "Yes," says his partner, and they go together, knowing that anything they *take off* is to be split equally. But if the partner says, "No," that leaves a problem. Is he *in with the pokes and in with the pinches?* He hasn't said. So the first pickpocket will ask "Well, are you in?" "Yes," he answers, "I'm in." That means that he can lie in bed and sleep while his partner goes down the street to breakfast; if the pickpocket going to breakfast makes a *single o score* on the way, he must give his partner half of it. If, on the other hand, he *rumbles* a mark who *beefs gun* and has him arrested, the pickpocket lying upstairs in bed is responsible for his entire share of the *fall dough* if it is needed to *spring* his partner.

But if the partner lying luxuriously abed had said, in answer to the question, "Are you in?" "No, I'm out," then anything the other partner did on the way to breakfast would be his own business; if he took off a $600 *touch* he could keep all of it; if the *fuzz* lit on him and he couldn't brush it off, he might become involved in a very expensive legal action; he might even go to prison. His somnolent partner could rest easy, for he would have no obligations whatsoever. "You're either 'in' or 'out'. That's the way it works, and you got to declare yourself in advance."

Likewise, certain members of any *class mob* may *declare themselves out* on any type of touch which they do not like, or which in their judgment may lead to disaster. A Jewish pickpocket may *declare himself out* while a rabbi is being robbed; he does not collect any share of the proceeds, neither does he risk his *fall dough* if the *fur* should pounce just as the *touch comes off*. A Roman Catholic can do the same when a *buck*, or Catholic priest, is robbed. He avers that he is *not in with the pinches and not in with the pokes*. This ability to *declare* oneself *in* or *out* at will extends throughout the fraternity on a *class* basis, and such *declarations* are respected as binding contracts. However, it should be understood that these clear-cut arrangements do not extend throughout all levels of pickpockets.

This type of declaration—*in* or *out*—has all sorts of applications. It is one of the focal points of ethics amongst the *whiz*. Arrangements may even occasionally be made to cover certain objects or articles stolen, in contrast to others; that is, one member of a mob may *declare himself out with* jewelry, but at the same time be *in with* any money or wallets. Sometimes, for reasons of personal pride, preference, lack of knowledge of certain types of theft, superstitions, or unfavorable conditioning by the *law* or others, certain operators avoid certain types of theft.

We go in this joint four-handed. And it is winter time and there is a whole bunch of overcoats on a rack. And this one tool, he is just out of stir, and he ain't got no overcoat of any kind. And it's cold outside. So I say, "Otto, pick yourself out a nice coat. Here's a chance for you to get a nice coat. I'm going to get myself three or four."
And he says, "Jack, I come into here to steal pocketbooks."
So my brother—he's sort of like I am—he says, "I'm with you."
I says, "All right, you guys ain't in."
They says, "No, we ain't in."
"All right," I says, "you're out."
Now they was in with the dough, but they wasn't in with them coats. And do you think we give them any of the ones we got? "You guys can go buy yourself an overcoat."

This avoidance is respected by the rest of the mob, who will, if possible, nevertheless execute the theft by themselves if they can. If the tool *declares himself out* on a priest, for instance, but his two Jewish partners decide to *take* him, one of the stalls who has had a little experience *hooking* will play the part of the *wire*, and the other stall will *put his hump up*, thus making a *team* out of what had been a *troupe*. These two will be particularly careful, however, for they realize that the *wire* is not a real expert and that any *fall* resulting will have to be handled by them, without financial aid from the tool. On the other hand, they will *split* any *score* they take evenly between them.

Class mobs normally work very closely together and are as conscientious and regular about their work and working hours as any legitimate business man.

What I mean, work is really spending eight hours. Spend eight hours hustling. You spend eight hours hustling, you'll get twenty-five scores, if you're gonna work, I mean, blind. You're not working jugs, you're just going out and doing the best you can. You gotta get off the nut first, you gotta get $300 for them coppers. That's the first thing to get. I mean you gotta take them as they come. You haven't got the time then, even if it's a class mob, you haven't got the time to waste waiting at the jug for them put ups. For big touches. You gotta take ten twenty-dollar pokes, you know, in preference to waiting for one two-hundred dollar poke."

This means that they have prearranged times to start work and established hours to *break*.

These hours will vary from mob to mob and from city to city according to circumstances. Often there is no straight eight-hour period, but rather two, three, or more periods the length of which may be determined by the time of the *show ups* at police headquarters.

Whiz mobs all try to get up before the coppers get up and close up before they come out of the show ups. Now you gotta find out them things before. . . . Now take Detroit, for instance, you can go to work at 5 o'clock and knock off at 8:30 A.M. You got three hours and a half. Or you can go to work at 6 o'clock in Chicago and knock off at 9, because the show up's at 9 o'clock."

If there is a large *slave grift* going to work on the early buses or trains, a certain *local* mob may work these crowds on regularly selected days and at precise periods—preferably while the pickpocket detail is known to be elsewhere. Each day the mob works, therefore, they *keep the meet* at a prearranged place and time. This is essential, for once the mob starts working, it is difficult to stop and rehash plans which have all previously been agreed upon. Each man is expected to *keep the meet*, and tries to do so if he is a *good man*. One who habitually *misses meets*, expecially *morning meets* or *going out meets*, soon faces criticism and may have to take down his *fall dough* and look for another mob to work with. Excuses for *missing meets* are sometimes delicately referred to as the *three esses: shit, shave, and shine*.

Normally, however, the rapport between members is good, though pickpockets are somewhat temperamental and clashes of temperament among *whiz* working together are common. "You won't find many whiz mobs who can get along for even twenty-four hours. They are just like old women. It's difficult to get a mob that will stick together for any length of time," says a *class cannon* who has had his personal problems. Nevertheless, personal conflicts aside, *class mobs* have very strong loyalties to each other; their assistance to each other in times of trouble usually exceeds the amount demanded by the code rather than otherwise. Some pickpocket partners have *grifted* together for many years despite minor disagreements.

At this point, it might be well to say something about the place of women on the *whiz*. Among *class mobs*, women are usually accepted as equal to men in every way professionally. They are dealt with on the same basis, have the same responsibilities regarding *fall dough* and assisting other partners in trouble, etc. This applies to a *whiz moll* working with a mob or a partner. The *broad* is paid her share of the *knock up* just like any male member, and she is expected to produce; however, a male member cannot take his girl friend on as a stall and put her in *center field* (let her go through the motions, but not actually work like the others) in order that the two of them can get two shares of the *knock up*. Usually, however, the *whiz molls* who work with a mob are not related to the male members. When the woman is married to or living with one of the men, she may be dominated by him, and may have to give him most of her *end*. But that is an arrangement between them; the mob pays her off in full. Some *whiz* are very generous with their women; others take a dim view of what a woman deserves.

There is a decided survival of the double standard among the *whiz*, and any *cannon moll* who wants emancipation and independence should work *single o* or find herself a girl partner. She can then keep her love life separate from her work, and spend her money as she pleases. Some of the best ones do just this. Among the lower brackets of pickpockets, women may have a rather bad time of it—and after one knows these women, the rough tactics of the male become more understandable.

Women who are not working with a mob may sometimes travel with them, each girl joining her man after the day's work. (Pickpockets who work together often do not live together, nor do they associate after working hours, except in the case of a man and woman working and living together). However, this is not common; if a male pickpocket has a nonworking wife, or children, he leaves them somewhere in a house or apartment when he travels out from that center. In the case of *locals*, a house or apartment is maintained more or less permanently in that city. Male pickpockets of the better class—like thieves in general—are very possessive about their women and insist on monogamy—on the woman's part.

But chastity is a condition which they cannot always be assured exists, especially if they are not together all the time. The men, however, tend to be promiscuous when the opportunity arises, though a little fun on the side is not regarded as detrimental to a good solid relationship with their wives. "The fixer of Omaha had a habit of getting himself a young broad and dressing her up with mink coats and loading her with ice that he had stood for. Then some cannon would come along and nail her. And he didn't crave it. He must have lost about a dozen babies that way. He sure had the needle out for guns."

As a matter of fact, pickpockets do not have quite the same sex problems as other people because the rate of drug addiction is so high among them. Once they start using an opiate—and a very few still try to smoke opium if they can get it or if they can afford it—their interest in sex diminishes with the degree of addiction. While it is not universally true, as is believed in medical circles, that opiates remove the sex urge and sexual potence entirely, it is true that, in many cases, normal sex drives are substantially reduced. Some pickpockets who are addicted appear to carry on a regular sex life without much reduction in libido. Nevertheless, even when sex is not the main attraction, a thief likes to have his woman (who may be also addicted) and he usually has some sort of permanent or semipermanent feminine tie.

Once a woman is recognized as belonging to a certain pickpocket, this relationship is respected by others (excepting those Lotharios who would like to steal her) and if her man *falls* and goes to prison, or cannot work during a considerable period of trial or probation, his partners feel a certain sense of responsibility for supporting her. If the man is broke, his partners or his friends may *pass the sheet* for him. This means that someone circulates through the hangouts and solicits money; sometimes there is an actual *sheet* of paper on which names and amounts are recorded; again, the solicitors simply remember who contributes and tell the man how much was taken and who contributed it.

Among better-class thieves, these *sheets* are considered loans and are repaid if the thief wants to maintain his standing. Among low-class thieves, a *sheet* may be unheard of. Of course there is no legals means of collecting the debt, nor is there any desire to do so, but "bad news travels fast" as the saying goes, and, if a man does not pay back such loans when he is able, they will not be forthcoming again. This is true likewise of money loaned outright from one thief to another, or to a thief by a *fixer* or professional gambler or any other person. To a thief, then, credit is more important than it is to the legitimate citizen, and he tries to keep it in good repair; thieves who do not cannot raise any money when it is needed.

A *sheet* is sometimes passed for a man without dependents if he takes a *wrong rap* (is convicted for a theft he did not perform) or a particularly *rough one* (one carrying an unusually stiff penalty, or giving him an undue amount of trouble and expense). Also, several mobs may *throw a night* for some unfortunate thief, which consists of a beer party or raffle to raise funds. This money may make things easier for him in prison, or it may be used to help defray heavy *fixing* expenses or legal costs. Recipients of such largesse must be duly observant of the code of the *grift*, however, or they lose standing. For instance, a woman or woman with children will be supported if her man is a *class cannon* and goes to prison. This support may come to her from one of several different sources at irregular intervals, usually in the form of money orders or cash. It will continue as long as she does not have anything to do with men; as soon as she "steps out" and the fact becomes known, her support stops, and if her new-found friend does not take over her support, she may have a hard time of it. Fortunately for marital felicity, prison terms for pickpockets are not often long.

Here is an example of how a formerly famous thief lost standing by his behavior following a *sheet passing* which might have been repeated now and then; he is getting old and arthritis has crippled his fingers.

I don't suppose you have heard of him. He was hanging around and they took up a collection every time he come around. All the guns that were there would throw in a sawbuck or a fin, and he'd say, "My bloody bloomin' fingers is stiff and I can't do no good." And he says, "I'd do the same for you." He'd been all over the world. So he come down there one night, and son, here's what cooked his goose. And so one gun started off with a quip. He says, "Aw, let's put the ding on him." So they passed the hat around and the guy must have gotten three or four G's. Tens and twenties in the pot. And so they took it and gave it to him. And he goes down on Charity Street or one of those zigaboo neighborhoods. And some gal clipped him for the dough. So what do you think happened? He fingered her and goes to court and testifies against her. And he come down there, and he must have come down there a thousand times after that and he didn't get a dime. Not a dime."

These obligations on the part of professionals are not charity; they are part of the mores of the subculture. Charity is taught toward people in distress (members of the dominant culture included), and thieves feel strong obligation to help crippled persons, blind persons, or others who have had disasters which handicap them in the making of a living. No pickpocket with any principle whatever would rob a cripple or a blind man. One informant told me that he had once inadvertently robbed a blind man. It was in a heavy crowd and he had already *taken off the score* and passed the man when he caught a *flash* of the man's white cane. By the time he found him again, it was impossible to return the wallet without being seen, so he went his way much disturbed. This incident continued to bother him for some years afterward. This attitude toward cripples and other handicapped people is strongly reenforced by superstition, so that the motivation for showing them consideration is not so thoroughly altruistic as it might seem at first glance.

Charitable feelings are also sometimes extended to other members of the dominant culture, although I can only conclude from the evidence which has come to me that a member of the dominant culture must be in a rather advanced state of physical dilapidation before a thief allows his condition to interfere with the natural act of theft. For instance, one informant lifted a wallet containing $880. Naturally, this seemed good. But the following morning a newspaper sob story appeared which revealed that the victim had just withdrawn the $880 to pay for surgery and medical treatment for his ailing wife. The mob read this story with considerable distress. They decided to investigate the truth of the story by telephone. (Marks are known to lie about these matters, even unto claiming that wallets contained more than they actually did.) They got the writer of the story as well as the doctor in the case on the telephone and verified the circumstances. They decided that this was the time to perform a magnanimous act. So they put $440—*half* the *touch*—in a plain envelope and mailed it to the victim.

This act, it should be noted, is very unusual. The subculture teaches all members to prey upon members of the dominant culture; part of this antipathy is undoubtedly a result of the accumulation of centuries of conflicts between the two cultural levels; part of it is based on the warfare with the law, which is supposed to represent the dominant culture but which is sometimes vulnerable to bribery, therefore meriting the distrust and fear of the subculture, since it seems to operate upon no principle whatever— except the size and nature of the bribe. Part of it may be an attempt to rationalize the act of theft from persons who are unsuspecting and whom the thief has never seen, and whom he has no logical reason to harm; this line of thinking is projected further into the conclusion that all members of the dominant culture get their money by dishonest means anyhow, and therefore the thief may serve as a sort of handy instrument of poetic justice. The general philosophy is "Never give a sucker an even break," and this philosophy is usually followed to the letter.

In line with this philosophy, the thief is taught both by precept and example never to *throw his mob*, that is, to betray any of his confederates to the police, or to leave mob members in the hands of the *law* without giving them assistance. There is a strong sentiment against *tipping off* any *touch*, even though it might have been *taken off* by one's enemies, to the *fuzz*. In fact, a thief learns that it is frowned upon to *cop a plea* (plead guilty in return for a light or suspended sentence). Likewise, one should never *tip off the racket*, or tell anyone, especially a member of the dominant culture, how pickpockets operate. "Never wise up a sucker," is the way it is put, and this aphorism is repeated over and over again. It is a cardinal sin to be a *fink* (stool pigeon). "Harry hustled for a month with us before we tumbled he was a fink for the feds." If you are going to buy anything, buy something *hot*; it shows solidarity against the dominant culture and, at the same time, helps some struggling thief to stay in business for himself; besides, it is much cheaper, as many a member of the dominant culture has discovered. Some pickpockets "carry brief cases" into which they put stolen goods for sale or for their own use. Never *knock* anyone else on the *racket*, even though you don't like him personally.

Always give the *office* if the *fuzz* comes around. Always be alert for a *plant*, or frame-up. "As soon as I took a gander at that rig-out, I figured it for a plant." Always *split out* your tool before you think of your own safety. Always *skin* any nonthief if you have the opportunity. If necessary, be willing to *stand for* a partner if he is having hard luck and *takes a fall*. "I'll stand for the pinch," he says, "but let the Kid go. His wife is in the hospital." Always assume that an officer of the law will *take*. "He'd take a red-hot stove." "I always found that a Chicago policeman would take *something*." Never trust anyone you've heard is *wrong*. Don't talk to *dicks* or persons said to be stool pigeons; if you must talk to them, don't be seen doing it. Don't mix up with *suckers* personally or socially. Be careful who knows your address and telephone number. Never *round on an office*; it might be *fur*. And so on.

Burning or *sinking* your partner or a member of your mob is most reprehensible. This consists of purloining from him a portion of his *cut* or his *bit*. It may be done either by holding out some of the total *knock up*, or by *weeding the pokes* while they are in the one's hand; it may be done by either the tool or the *duke man* while he has the wallet in his possession; some unscrupulous thieves have raised the art of *weeding* either a wallet or a *bundle of scratch* to a high degree of perfection. As it passes through their hands, it loses a bill or two; this is called *burning* a *touch*, and is done as often as possible by a certain class of pickpockets. These are known as *burners* and are avoided by smart *cannons*. The act is also sometimes called *paying (someone) off in the dark*. These things are not supposed to be done; those who insist on doing them suffer ostracism from the company of *class cannons*, at least so far as working is concerned, although all pickpockets must stick together in other matters affecting the general security.

While the act of *burning* is often referred to, there is strong reason to believe that among the better class of pickpockets it is rare, but becomes increasingly common as one goes down the scale. When I asked one *class cannon*, for instance, how many times he thought he had been *burned* in more than thirty years of *grifting*, he thought back carefully and said that he did not think he had ever been cheated of his share of the *knock up* by a regular partner, although he was not so sure about several *pick ups* he could remember. He agreed that it was common among *pick up mobs* and very common among *jig mobs*. "Weeding would be taking out money that I didn't want anybody to know about. If it was part of the knock up, that would be cleaning the *poke*." Of course, it is impossible, when interviewing representative pickpockets from these levels, to get them to admit that it happens in *their* mobs; it is always the other fellow who does things like that.

However, the practices of *cutting up the scores* among various groups may be revealing. The *class mobs* work from the *going out meet* until a *break* is arranged; if they are all *schmeckers*, or narcotic addicts, they have a prearranged time to *fix* or *take a bang*; they stop and take the necessary time to do this, often in a rest room, sometimes in a hotel room. First, they usually *turn over the leathers*, or wallets which one or both stalls are carrying; it is customary for more than one pickpocket to be present when this is done, although sometimes the number of wallets encountered or unexpected hazards may force the stall who is carrying them to hastily *turn them over* and *ding the dead ones*. This is not generally done, however. The stall carrying the *pokes* feels a strong responsibility for them and is held accountable for them whenever the mob is ready to *turn them over*.

> There was a fellow who worked with me once; he weighed 350 pounds and he had a large mustache. He looked like a typical mark. And one season we were in Savannah, Georgia in back of Ringling's. Well, I was four-handed and I was handing them to Big Bill. And one time we got into a tip there and one of them jig mobs nailed him. He had the pokes in his coat tail, you know. So we're going out to turn them over, and when we hit the spot where we should turn them over, why of course there was nothing to turn over. He was very, very conscientious. He was apologizing this way and that way and saying he'd make them good. Well, how are you going to make them good when you don't know what was in them? "It's not your fault," I said; "you can't make them good anyway." Well, we got back in another tip and it was the same thing. And did he get sore. They were after him. I suppose some of them knew him, for he was an old-timer."

Incidentally, it is not uncommon for lower-class pickpockets or *jig mobs* to rob other mobs, especially strange mobs.

Sometimes a mob might *grift* all day without *turning them over*, but this is unlikely except in the case of a *jug mob* which takes a limited number of *pokes*. Any pickpocket who has on his person more than one wallet is something of a hazard both to himself and to the mob, for each wallet can count as a separate offense if he should be caught. Therefore, it is safer to have cash only. *Class mobs* usually count the money each time they *skin the pokes*, one stall commonly is responsible for all of it, and an accounting in full is made at the end of the day. When there is a woman with the mob, she usually carries the *knock up*. The day's *take* is the *knock up*, and the mob usually pools expenses for the day (the *nut* or the *working nut*) and this amount is taken off the *top* (the total *take*) after which the remaining profit is divided equally. If any *fix* has been paid by any member, for instance, that is considered expenses of the mob, and is taken off. Travel expenses, meals eaten together, etc., are all pooled; hotel bills may be paid (if they are paid at all) by individuals if they are living in separate hotels. Any deficiencies in *fall dough* are made up, or, if the *fall dough* is not deemed sufficient, a certain portion of the *knock up* may be set aside *in the seams*. After all these items are taken care of, the remainder is divided equally and each man gets his *bit* to spend as he pleases. Some *class mobs* keep records daily, but settle up every week, especially when these mobs are prosperous and when they buy their narcotics together, with one member handling the considerable amount of this purchase made on a weekly basis. *Single handed cannons* work to suit themselves. The cautious ones *turn over* each *poke* soon after they take it and get rid of the evidence; inasmuch as they have no stalls to *split them out* and to carry the *leathers*, they must be very careful about having a stolen wallet in their possession long. "In Ohio, every leather can mean five years, if you're convicted."

The pickpocket's dealings with the law have been recorded earlier. His attitude toward law made by the dominant culture is largely cynical. He has learned by experience that the law does not apply alike to all people; that the custodians of the law can often be bought; that if one has no money, his "record" is likely to go heavily against him; that certain lawyers are adept at using technicalities of the law to *beat a right rap* (a theft actually committed); that, on the other hand, a *wrong rap*, or a charge based on a theft which the thief did not commit, is very difficult to *beat*, even with a good lawyer. He thinks of himself as being *home free* on all thefts for which he has not been arrested, and it does not seem unfair to him that he gets by with hundreds of thefts for every one involving arrest. He has served time in prison; perhaps he has made some professional contacts there; but he has not noticed that it has rehabilitated him in any way; in fact, he feels that imprisonment not only undermines his character, but robs him of incentive, allows his techniques to get *raw*, and makes him unduly dependent on a totally undesirable institution set up by the dominant culture.

When you go in, now your trial is over, you got your time and everything and now you head for the joint. They furnish your clothing, your toothbrush, your toothpaste; they give you a package of tobacco, they put you in a cell and you got a bed, and you got clean blankets. They wake you up in the morning to get breakfast. In other words, everything is furnished. Now you stay in there two years, five years, ten years, whatever you stay in there, what difference does it make? After a year or so you've been . . . after six months, you've become accustomed to the general routine. Everything is furnished. If you get a toothache, you go to the dentist; if you get a stomach ache, you go to the doctor; if you can't see out of your cheaters, you go to the optician. It don't cost you nothing.

If you're sweeping the floor and that is your job, sweeping the corridor, you get just the same as I do if I am the dietician's secretary and have to work twelve hours a day at the typewriter and on a set of books. And look, they don't differentiate between people, you know what I mean, or initiative, or a guy who tries to better himself a little bit. So you mop the floors, and I am a clerk. I sit at a typewriter. I try to better my education, I attend the library. If there is any educational facilities there, I take advantage of them.

All right, we do our bit and we hit the gate. You got $25 and I got $25. You get a suit of clothes; I get a suit of clothes. Now when we step outside that penitentiary, I don't care if it is Walla Walla, Atlanta, Ohio, Michigan City, or where it is. When we step outside that penitentiary, we step into a different world. There is no resemblance, there is no comparison, to what you go through in the penitentiary, because you're free. All right, you're free and you've got $25. Before that runs out, you have to rob somebody. So do I. And we'll both be raw and out of practice.

Don't you think that somebody, somewhere, could revise this thing so that a guy lives in some similarity? . . . Of course, they can't put a big blue-eyed blonde in bed with you at night and let you go to night clubs and the picture shows. I don't mean that, but I mean that . . . but I mean make the inside life a certain semblance of what it is outside."

The pickpocket realizes that the laws were made to protect the dominant culture; nevertheless he feels satisfaction if sometimes he can pervert them to benefit the subculture. We might say that he holds that the laws were written to protect the rights of professional criminals as well as professional *suckers*, and he is entitled to all the protection he can get. To a certain extent, he is right in this assumption, for the Constitution is very broad in the coverage it gives to the right of the individual; it was framed by men who had only too recently been familiar with the evils of government which made no provision for the rights of the individual regardless of his calling. I have heard conscientious law-enforcement officers complain that the law seems to give the criminal more protection than it does the noncriminal and the officer; they find it hard to realize that the Constitution was written not to help policemen catch criminals but to protect the rights of man. Because of the long tradition of prosecution inherent in the thief's subculture, the thief is very much aware of any protection given him by the law, and is more than happy to use it whenever he can.

As a matter of fact, most thieves, especially those in the United States, have much to be thankful for. They *grift* during an entire lifetime and may serve two, three, or even four short prison sentences. Some may get longer sentences, but these are innovations. Some have never been in *stir*, though all of them sooner or later are arrested, *shaken down*, and perhaps given a *bit* in a jail or house of correction. The price they pay for an entirely parasitic existence at the expense of the dominant culture would seem to be not exorbitant, though what the dominant culture expects to get from this price it levies is obscure. Aside from the slight protection society gets while the thief is confined at public expense, no basic changes are made in the thief's attitudes, mores, or behavior patterns. In fact, incarceration can be guaranteed to case-harden his attitudes, improve his technology, teach him new ways to evade the law in the future, and give him some valuable contacts in his own subculture which he might not have made outside prison walls.

Therefore, we would say that the thief's attitude toward the law is also philosophical; he reasons that sometime the piper must be paid, and he cannot be unaware that the price is very cheap, everything considered. In fact, his respect for the dominant culture probably suffers because the dominant culture so consistently seems to tolerate him and his brethren with so little serious interference. Actually, the dominant culture is a place to work and make a living—and a good one. The admission fee to this preserve where well-heeled marks can be *taken* is, in terms of penalties, ridiculously low for those who know their way about. However, for the less skilled and the less knowing, the way of the transgressor can be hard.

In the preceding paragraphs we have been talking about *class cannons* or pickpockets in the upper brackets so far as techniques and connections are concerned. As we go down the scale in professional standing, we find these ethical concepts degenerating until in the lower areas of the profession many of them would not be recognizable. By way of contrast, we might summarize the salient points of differentiation between *class cannons* and the riffraff and rabble who call themselves pickpockets, in order to show that the ethical and moral standards outlined in detail above are not universally observed in the subculture. It is impossible to separate these concepts level by level, largely because of the irregularity of the pattern in which they occur and because of the fact that many groups pay lip-service to certain ethical concepts, but honor them largely in the breach thereof.

If we examined some of the less prosperous Negro or Puerto Rican mobs, we would find, first of all, that their concepts of ethics and morals were very vague compared to *class cannons*. We could just as well include lower-class white mobs also, for these levels are social rather than racial. There would be great argument over what is expected of a pickpocket in a given situation. There would be little loyalty to the mob; if a tool gets *batted out* or *nailed* in the act, he is in jail; the rest of the mob goes on its way and finds another tool. There is no *fall dough*, in the sense of resources for the mob to use as needed. There might be small amounts of cash owned individually, but these would not be shared. There would not be orderly arrangements about working agreements, but confusion, arguments, and occasionally knife battles or fisticuffs. Each member would be trying to get the best of his partners in any way he could. For instance, if one stall was not present when a *touch* came off, he simply would not get any money; he might never know of the *touch*. Mob members may participate irregularly or sporadically; their division of labor is not so specialized and each one works for himself as much as he can.

There is no such thing as daily or weekly tallies, with everyone settling up. Each time a *score comes off*, the entire mob runs behind a billboard or other protective cover and *turns over* the *score* together, each one carefully watching the others. There is a saying among this class of pickpockets that "the first count is the best," meaning that the contents of a wallet dwindle as different people handle it. Women may work with these mobs, but usually without the status women have on upper levels; they belong exclusively to the man who uses them. When a lower-class pickpocket *joins out the odds* he may mean that he has a *broad stalling* for him; he is just as likely to mean that he has her *on the blocks* or *on the turf*; she is street-walking, with the proceeds going to her man, who is more of a pimp than a pickpocket. Such a man is referred to by other pickpockets as a *center britch tool* or *middle britch worker*, which is a humorous play upon the various specializations, real or imaginary, which pickpockets develop.

Some dips make good center britch tools. You know who I mean. He advanced from box-car tool to center-britch tool and was noted for being the biggest shiny rat that ever came out of Canada, and boy believe me, you'd have to be a big rat. He had a broad that hustled for him for years, and when he got kissed in with a mob in the Village, he blowed her off for some other twist."

On these levels there is little if any sense of responsibility for the woman; in fact, she is expected to provide for the man much of the time. Women do not commonly work alone as pickpockets in this area, but many of them are *boosters* or shoplifters on a part-time and semiprofessional basis.

Neither men nor women on these lower levels commonly become *road workers* unless they happen to be *carnival lice* and travel off and on with these organizations; even so, they are rare outside the big cities, where they live and work on a very thin margin of security. They have little if any sense of obligation to anyone financially; their policy is to borrow from anyone foolish enough to lend them money, but never to repay a debt if possible. They do little to help each other when in trouble. They do not accumulate any reserves. Anything they make goes for drink, gambling, or narcotics. In the event of a *fall*—which is an ever-present hazard, considering their techniques and their organization—they usually *take the rap*. One type, for instance, is a *floater*; he never makes any permanent contacts anywhere, he owns nothing—not even luggage—and he lives from day to day on whatever he can steal.

They hate the law and fight the law rather than dealing with it, and their hostility toward the dominant culture is also more marked. However, many on this level are willing to act as stool pigeons if they have the opportunity. While they have the youth to *make the center britch* they may get by with a girl, but most of them head early for Skid Row or the penitentiary, or both.

Nevertheless, they are recognized as thieves by *class cannons* (who will look down on them) and all the gradations in between, for every pickpocket is aware that he might well end up on Skid Row or in *stir* if he gets enough bad breaks. Although the better operators do not want to associate with these less successful ones, and cannot afford to work with them under any circumstances, there is a common sense among them that they all belong to the same profession. This consciousness of a common way of life among thieves is very, very old.

A WORD-FINDER LIST FOR WHIZ MOB

DAVID W. MAURER, *University of Louisville*

THIS *Word-Finder List* is intended to facilitate the use of the linguistic and lexicographical elements in *Whiz Mob: A Correlation of the Technical Argot of Pickpockets with Their Behavior Pattern*, *PADS*, No. 24 (November 1955).

Each entry in the *List* represents a lexical element in the text of *Whiz Mob*, together with the pages on which it occurs. These argot elements are listed exactly as they occur in the text, regardless of variants in form such as singulars and plurals, tense-differences, or parts of speech. It has seemed impractical to consolidate elements under any system of main-entries, largely because separate meanings and usages often differ too widely to permit consolidation. However, each form in the *List* will direct the reader to all examples of that form, and a perusal of the text will show how that form is used in any particular situation within the running text. Only italicized or quoted forms are catalogued, and from these references, together with the sentence or statement in which the term or idiom appears, the reader can easily make his own structural analysis. Several argot terms which appear with great frequency, such as *mob*, *tool*, *stall*, etc., are not generally italicized in the text and are not included in the *List* except in those special cases where they are italicized or occur in direct quotations.

Since the main purpose of *Whiz Mob* was to place linguistic elements and special aspects of human behavior in juxtaposition, it is suggested that the reader take into consideration this relationship, which we might call socio-linguistic, when making structural observations. The illustrations which are quoted, usually following italicized words or idioms, are taken directly, without editing, from the speech of professional criminals recorded on sound-tape during interviews, and are intended to clarify both the social and the linguistic situation automatically. It should be noted that this is by no means a complete listing of all the argot used by pickpockets.

THE WORD-FINDER LIST

a mile away 96
accordion poke 114

aces 116
action 64, 72, 73, 74, 80, 184

got my mitt down 66
goulash joints 179
grabbed me by the throat 109
grabbed right 146
grafter 98
grapevine 26, 154, 179
grease 148
greaser 107
greasing 148
greasy 133
grift 19, 21, 25, 30, 32, 34, 35, 41, 49,
    54, 59, 60, 71, 98, 115, 116, 144, 163,
    165, 174, 176, 178, 190, 194, 196
grift guts 159
grift know 25, 75, 101, 159, 173
grift right 146
grift sense 25, 40, 41, 71, 75, 159
grift with the pro 146
grifted 144, 187
grifter 33, 98
grifters 25, 26, 35, 43
grifting 96, 160, 193
grifting right 146
grifting with a shade on your tail
    144
grifting with a squealer 89
grifts 75
grinding it up 116
grinding up nickels and dimes 116,
    152
gun 89, 95, 99, 144, 162
gun mobs 176
gun moll 103
gun molls 99
gun pit 125
gun tip 174
gun turn 36
guns 43, 69, 72, 99, 138, 140, 141, 161,
    174, 178, 181, 189, 190
guzzled 162

hack 155
had me by the throat 109
had the needle out 189
half a c 116
half-assed pickpocket 101
hall of fame 147
handle 156

handled 80
handling 109
hanger 76, 104, 115
hanger bingers 103, 105
hangers 169
hangout 160
hangouts 23, 24, 179
harness bull 106
harness bulls 139
harness coppers 139
harness cops 139
harvested 51
has them right 146
hat duckets 176
heat 137, 145
heavy 130, 134, 164, 165
heavy gees 18
heavy man 48, 50
heavy one 120
heavy operators 50
heavy rackets 30, 34, 38, 48, 54, 59,
    92, 171
heavy worker 99
heel 87
heel plant 162
heist mob 92
hide 77, 114
hideaways 177
high jackers 98
hijackers 93, 98
hip 109
hit and run 68, 72, 93, 95
hit the gate 196
hocus 114
hocus pocus 114
holler copper 108
home free 195
home guard 98, 173
home guards 98
hook 58, 60, 62, 69, 120, 155, 184
hooked 163
hooking 62, 186
hooks 100
hoosier 106
hoosier grift 174
hoosiers 36, 77
hopscotch 151, 176
hot 55, 137, 152, 156, 160, 192